THE THERAPEUTIC COMMUNITY

*A Successful Approach
for Treating
Substance Abusers*

Lewis Yablonsky, Ph.D.

GARDNER PRESS, INC.   New York • London

Gardner Press Distribution
c/o M.&B. Fulfillment Service
540 Barnum Avenue
Bridgeport, CT 06608
(203) 366-1900

Foreign orders except Canada, South America, Australia, and New Zealand to:
Afterhurst Limited
27 Palmeira Mansions
Church Road, Hove,
East Sussex BN3 2FA
England

Orders for Australia and New Zealand to:
Astam Books
27B, Llewellyn Street
Balmain, N.S.W., Australia

Library of Congress Cataloging-in-Publication Data

Yablonsky, Lewis.
  The therapeutic community.

  Includes index.
  1. Substance abuse—Treatment.   2. Therapeutic
community.   I. Title. [DNLM: 1. Substance Dependence—
rehabilitation.   2. Therapeutic Community.
WM 270 Y11tb]
RC564.Y33   1989   362.2′938   87-19625
ISBN 0-89876-145-X

Printed in the United States of America

Design by Publishers Creative Services

Contents

Preface and
Acknowledgments

This book on therapeutic communities is for substance abusers, and their families and friends. And since almost everyone has a friend or family member whose life has been crippled by substance abuse, this book is for you.

If you are hooked, you will find in these pages case studies of people who were in your shoes, entered a therapeutic community, and have come back to live a life free from alcohol and drugs. The process for this life-giving treatment that thousands of former substance abusers around the world have utilized is presented in a clear and precise way so that you can determine whether you want to continue your downspin to oblivion or return to the human race.

For those of you who have a relationship with a person who has this disease, after learning about the problem, you can offer that person some hope by recommending that he or she enter a therapeutic community (TC). Beyond this simple but significant opportunity to help a friend or relative, you may find out by reading this book that unknowingly you are part of the problem, and that by changing your relationship, you can help your friend or family member make a comeback to a healthier, happier way of life.

My research and professional experience in the substance abuse field go back to 1950, when I became a graduate student in sociology and psychology at New York University. My early experience with the drug problem emerged when I began working with violent gangs in New York in the early 1950s. (See my book *The Violent Gang*, Macmillan, 1962.)

In 1953 I became the director of a Crime Prevention Program on the Upper West Side of Manhattan for a community-based organization sponsored by Columbia University and 13 other institutions and agencies located in that part of New York City. As part of the program, I developed a variety of traditional counseling group projects for drug-addicted gang members, and learned a great deal about the complex substance-abuse problem that persists in urban areas.

Around this time, when I was completing my Ph.D. degree in sociology at NYU, I became a student of psychiatrist Dr. J. L. Moreno, founder of psychodrama and group psychotherapy, who at that time was a professor there. I worked with him at his Beacon (N.Y.) Psychiatric Hospital—and directed psychodrama and group therapy sessions with hospitalized addicts and alcoholics. Part of my work also involved doing psychodrama and group therapy with adolescent drug addicts at New York City's Riverside Hospital.

Dr. Moreno was a pioneer in the TC movement, not only because of his invention of psychodrama, but because he was the first psychological theorist and practitioner to comprehend the important and valuable role patients can play in their own therapy. He was the first therapist to consciously utilize patients as cotherapists in the "therapeutic community" that he developed and directed with his wife, Zerka Moreno, a brilliant psychodramatist in her own right, at the Beacon institute. Through his theories on sociometry, he was also one of the first theorists and practitioners to see the vital necessity of treating not only the identified patient, the addict, but also the family as a sociometric total unit. Dr. Moreno's concepts of sociometry, psychodrama, and group therapy set the stage for the development of the TC movement. My 25 years of work with him in New York, at various hospitals and in the community, provided a valuable perspective for understanding basic concepts of the therapeutic community and facilitated my later research into the TC movement. (See my book *Psychodrama: Resolving Emotional Problems Through Role-Playing*, Gardner Press, 1980.)

I heard about Synanon, the first TC devoted to addicts and alcoholics, in 1960, when I was invited to present a paper on my work with gangs at a United Nations Congress on Crime and Delinquency in London. At the congress a sociologist from the University of California at Los Angeles (UCLA), Donald Cressey, who had been studying Synanon, told me about the organization's anti-drug program.

Given my peculiar professional background and interests, when I moved to California to teach at UCLA in 1961, on my second day in Los Angeles I visited Synanon. It was clear to me that the organization was a model for treating addicts that brought together many of the elements of psychodrama, group therapy, and Alcoholics Anonymous (AA) into a unique residential therapeutic community.

At Synanon I met, and became a friend and colleague of Charles E. (Chuck) Dederich, its founder. Dederich, an ex-alcoholic who had become drug-free through AA, was a creative genius at developing innovative therapeutic group methods that worked effectively for treating addicts and alcoholics. His charismatic leadership was vital to the development of Synanon and the overall world TC movement.

Over a six-year period (1961–1967), I immersed myself on almost a daily basis in working with Dederich in Synanon's development, and as a participant-observer carried out my research into this godfather of TCs. My intense personal and professional involvement in every aspect of Synanon's organization and development resulted in my book *Synanon: The Tunnel Back* (Macmillan, 1965).

Over the years I followed the evolution of the TC movement in the United States, and worldwide, with great interest. The full force of the growth of the TC movement for treating addicts was revealed to me most dramatically at the eighth and ninth World Conferences on Therapeutic Communities. The eighth conference was held in Rome (1984) and the ninth in San Francisco (1985). I gave papers at both conferences. At these fascinating meetings, I had an opportunity to communicate with therapeutic community leaders from almost every country. Different aspects of TC therapy developed in Synanon in its early days—including the "encounter group," the ex-addict as therapist, and various dimensions of the TC social structure—were all subjects of heated discussion and analysis at both conferences.

I was impressed with the fact that the original Synanon in California, of which I was a part in the early 1960s, had become a replicated and integral part of treatment in all other therapeutic communities. There were now hundreds of Synanon-like TCs in operation around the world. Beyond the various communities themselves, TC concepts and methods have been incorporated into many traditional hospital settings. Notable in this development was a TC patient ward developed by Dr. Michael Solomon at Metropolitan State Hospital in Norwalk, Calif. and a program called "The Family" at Mendocino (Calif.) State Hospital.

At the conference in Rome, I became especially intrigued with the enormous TC developments in Italy. The Italian organization, Centro Italiano di Solidarieta or as they are known worldwide "Ce.I.S." (pronounced "chase"), was responsible for the management of over 20 TCs throughout Italy. In addition to its TCs that worked directly with addicts, Ce.I.S. had developed a significant educational center that trained not only Italian TC leaders but professional and ex-addict counselors who were TC leaders from other countries.

In many respects the Italian TC movement, founded by Father Mario Picci with the support of Pope John Paul II and sparked by the leadership of Juan Corelli and Tony Gelormino, has become a prototype, and now serves as the innovative cutting edge of the worldwide TC movement. Building on the inherent cultural strength of the Italian family, Ce.I.S developed new significant approaches for the addict that incorporate the addict's family into the TC process in a unique way, which is delineated in this book. Their Educational Training Center at the Castel Gandolfo Institute Rome, has become a most valuable and important core educational system for the burgeoning world movement.

Since September 1984 I have taught over five week long training workshops at the Ce.I.S. school on the "social structure of TCs," psychodrama, and group therapy for TC leaders and mental health professionals from Europe and elsewhere. Given the axiom that the best teaching engenders the most learning, my work at Castel Gandolfo and several Ce.I.S. TCs produced considerable new research findings and energized my long-standing interest in the structure and process of the TC.

In addition to these noted contributions to this book, I would gratefully acknowledge my appreciation to Bette Fleishman, Naya Arbiter, Rod Mullen, and a number of other members of the Amity TC in Tucson, Ariz. The Amity group facilitated my research by providing data on many innovations that have been woven into their TC. Based on my on-site visits to Amity and lectures by Amity members on the social structure and methods of Amity, I learned a great deal about significant new trends in the TC field that were valuable in the completion of this book.

Another significant professional experience that has produced vital research knowledge and has helped to shape my perspective on the therapeutic community is my work at the Van Nuys Psychiatric Hospital and the Coldwater Canyon Psychiatric Hospital in Los Angeles since 1983. In these innovative mental health facilities, I have directed group therapy, psychodrama, and drug groups with hundreds of adolescent substance abusers. The hospital administrations provided the freedom for me to integrate various unique therapeutic community concepts into the programs. The staffs of these hospitals—especially, Bill Boyd, Steve Wilson, Virginia Classick, Lee Bloom, Richard Hartley, Richard Sherman, and the several hundred adolescents who participated in the program—provided me with support and many new ideas on how to integrate the system and techniques of the TC into a traditional hospital setting.

The experimental program with adolescents in the hospital involved a number of older ex-addicts who participated in the encounter groups in the hospital. These ex-addict counselors from the Delancey Street TC in Santa Monica helped to demonstrate how ex-addict professionals can work effectively with university-trained professionals in a traditional therapeutic hospital program.

In addition to the acknowledgments noted, there have been many other innovative methodological developments and a large number of significant research projects regarding TCs in the past ten years. I wish to acknowledge, with gratitude, the enormous contribution made to this book by all of these practitioners and researchers. Notable in this group of TC pioneers are some other people who deserve my special respect and gratitude. These include Alfonso Alcampara, Lars Bremberg, George DeLeon, David Deitch, Sherry Holland, Wolfgang Hechman, Norman Herman, Jack Hurst, Maxwell Jones, Martin Kooyman, Ben Krentzman, William O'Brien, Don Ottenberg, John Ridley, Jim Reed, Ottavio Rosati, Mitchell Rosenthal, David Smith, and Chester Stern. I want to especially acknowledge my gratitude to Julie Gury, who assisted me with the final draft of the book. I am also enormously grateful to my superb publisher Gardner Spungin who provided valuable support and direction in editing and publishing the book.

In summary, this book incorporates the contributions of many people in the TC field. It is, however, primarily based on my professional group therapy work and psychodrama with drug addicts and alcoholics since 1950, with special emphasis on my recent work with adolescent substance abusers and my extensive "participant-observer" research into American and European therapeutic communities.

The Therapeutic Community contains information that should be of value to every person concerned with the problems of alcoholism and addiction. This includes not only people who manifest the problem, but their friends and families as well. It should also be of value in preventing people from using these poisons and falling into the pit of addiction. So-called "recreational drug and alcohol users" should learn from this book whether they are really practicing denial and stand on the precipice of alcoholism and addiction.

In addition to this audience, the book should be of special interest to professionals and paraprofessional ex-addicts working in the treatment of addicts and alcoholics. I have here defined concepts and methodological practices used in TCs that can serve as a blueprint for constructing a model program for controlling drug addiction with different age groups in any type of community or culture.

The book traces the history and development of TCs and delineates the concepts and methods that make therapeutic communities work for people of all ages, from all walks of life, in varied cultures. It describes in the context of varied case histories how substance abusers can make a significant change in their lives and become sober, happier, and more productive people. In this respect it parallels the *Alcoholics Anonymous* and *Twelve Steps and Twelve Traditions* books published by AA. My perception of TCs is that they are the residential treatment counterpart of Alcoholics Anonymous.

The data contained in the book should also be of value to the average citizen—since everyone is potentially vulnerable to, or affected by, the monstrous substance-abuse problem. The book is, however, mainly dedicated to those people, and their families, who are in the throes of a drug–alcohol problem and are seeking a way out of their self-destructive deadly dilemma.

Lewis Yablonsky, Ph.D.
DEPARTMENT OF SOCIOLOGY
CALIFORNIA STATE UNIVERSITY
NORTHRIDGE, CALIFORNIA

THE
THERAPEUTIC
COMMUNITY

1

The Contemporary Substance-Abuse Problem and Its Effective Treatment

The drug problem that the therapeutic community attempts to combat has reached awesome proportions on an international level. The deleterious impact of the problem not only affects the self-destructive abuser and family but it has also insidiously intruded into the political relationships of nations. From the countries that supply the drugs (and have their own share of addicts) to the major nations that illegally import the various poisons, the problem is increasingly part of everyone's life. As major political powers agonize and attempt to develop flimsy blockades to prevent the flow of drugs into their societies, too often they lose sight of the simple fact that if there were no addicted consumers in the world, there would be no problem.

Despite the variety of efforts to combat the problem on a worldwide basis, the number of addicts has proliferated. And not only has the number of addicts increased, but the problem has become more "democratic" and widespread. Formerly, severe addiction was primarily restricted to the lower socioeconomic segments of society. Today the problem is found among people in all walks of life. People of all ages—in high schools, universities, sports, publishing, entertainment, corporations, and industry—have become addicted to drugs and alcohol, and the problem has infected those of both high and low status in these various fields.

1

There is also increasing evidence that the problem now tends to begin at an earlier age. Although young addicts are found in the elementary schools; in high schools around the country it is estimated that over 80 percent of the students have tried some illegal substance; and that many youths are addicts and alcoholics.

In the early 40s, less than 3 percent of the high-school population experimented with drugs. Today the statistics are almost reversed. The fact that more than eight out of ten adolescents have used some kind of drug during their teenage years sets up a pattern of substance abuse that too often continues into adult life.

The abuse of drugs in high school is often referred to by teenage users as "recreational drug use." In my view the popular phrase is a misnomer that attempts to deny and obfuscate the seriousness of the addiction problem. This casual attitude about the substance-abuse problem, carried by adolescents into their adult life, exacerbates the overall problem of our society.

Another factor related to the general substance-abuse problem in the United States is the proliferation of a *variety* of drugs in the illicit marketplace. The former staples of substance abuse, such as alcohol, marijuana, and heroin, have been joined by PCP, "ecstacy," "designer" drugs, cocaine (in various forms, including "crack"), and an increasingly larger selection of addictive pills. Most contemporary substance abusers do not restrict their use to one drug, but use the variety of available substances.

Also, certain drugs that were formerly perceived as fun and games by many people have turned out to have long-term and even lethal effects on the users' personalities and lives. Notable in this context are marijuana and, especially, cocaine.

Individuals who began smoking marijuana several years ago for "fun" discover too late that they have become amotivational, "vegged out," and strongly psychologically dependent on the drug. Cocaine, formerly a rich person's party drug, in a more marketable form known as crack has penetrated into all segments of society — and has had a destructive impact on many users' lives. In particular, a number of well-known athletes, men in perfect physical condition, died from heart failure shortly after using cocaine. On the contemporary substance-abuse scene, adolescents are heavily into the use of crack cocaine, and are susceptible to its short- and long-term lethal consequences.

Another cataclysmic problem related to substance abuse is seen in the dark clouds forming around the complex relationship that exists between the intravenous use of drugs, sex, and AIDS. In one recent research report from New York that I heard when attending a drug conference in Amsterdam, it was determined that 50 percent of the intravenous drug users in New York City had the AIDS virus HTLV-III/LAV.* The drug problem increasingly exacerbates the AIDS problem as intravenous substance abusers, especially prostitutes, have sexual relationships with members of the general population.

Many people relate sexually and through intravenous drug use, in this contemporary complex world of crime. The therapeutic community (TC) movement has a vital future, albeit an as-yet-undefined role, in ameliorating this burgeoning problem that is entwined with substance abuse.

WHO IS AN ADDICT?

The melange of widespread drug abuse in all segments of the society, and the variety and combinations of drugs used, has somewhat clouded the definition of who is an addict. However, definition is important in determining who requires treatment and what form of treatment should be given. The form-of-treatment issue further boils down to whether the person can be effectively treated in the open community or requires an inpatient program. Another related issue is how much time is required for the addict to resolve his or her problem successfully in a program.

The question of when a person is truly addicted and the form of help needed is a very complex issue. In most cases, when the user's family and friends perceive the person as addicted to a drug or alcohol, the addict denies the addiction. Because of this denial, the addicted person refuses to take the basic first step in treatment: admitting to being an addict or an alcoholic.**

*From Don C. Des Jarlais and Samuel R. Friedman, "A.I.D.S. and Intravenous Drug Use," a paper presented at the 15th Institute on Drug Abuse in Amsterdam, the Netherlands, April 1986.

**Throughout this book the generic terms "*addict-alcoholic*" and "*substance abuser*" refer to people whose lives are dominated by a drug or drugs, whether heroin, marijuana, cocaine, alcohol, or psychoactive pills. The terms, therefore, also refer to the alcoholic. Whatever the drug, the substance abusers involved require some therapeutic intervention in their lives to free them from their self-destructive enslaved existence.

Based on my research and observations of the drug-abuse problem over the past 30 years, I would delineate the following elements as present in identifying the *drug addict-alcoholic*, or substance abuser.

Overwhelming Need

Substance abusers have an intense conscious desire for their drug of choice — or a variety of drugs. They have a mental set where acquiring and using drugs becomes the paramount fixation or concern in their lives.

Self-Deception and Denial

Almost all substance abusers in the early phase of the addictive process, when confronted about their addiction deny they are addicted. This takes the form of lying to others and deceiving themselves about the amount of drugs they use, the degree to which they are dominated by their drug habit, and the fact that the drug has become an integral part of their day-to-day behavior and that their use of drugs has negatively affected their personal relationships. Their favorite defensive platitude, in one form or another, is: "You're crazy. I can quit anytime I want to." Somehow they never want to — unless some outside pressure is brought to bear, or their life becomes intolerable.

Periodic Abstinance

Most addicts occasionally become drug-free for a period of time when their habit becomes too onerous or to prove to themselves that their self-delusive platitude, "I can quit anytime I want," is true. The period of abstinance is usually a very short one, before they return to their addicted way of life.

The Addict's Self-Image

After a period of time as a user, the addict's drug abuse becomes a central focus of the person's behavior — and in many cases represents his or her identity. The addict no longer denies being an addict, after having tried to quit a number of times and failed. The true addict now begins to feel most at ease with "friends" and cohorts who have the same drug problem; and these friends more and more constitute the addict's primary group. Addicts increasingly become alienated from people, friends, and family members who are not drug abusers. They become identified by others, even if they do not accept the label, as being, for example, a "pill head," an alcoholic, a "junkie," a "coke head," or a "pot head." The perceptions and responses of others have a mirror effect that begins to sink into the addict's self-concept, and this perception by others reinforces the addict's self-image and identity as a drug abuser. The user now has developed a firm self-concept of being an addict or an alcoholic.

TREATMENT ISSUES

The treatment process and the length of time required to complete it are often determined by the social-occupational background and status of the addict. It is apparent that a corporate executive or a talented professional in his or her occupation presents a different type of social-personal background as related to the addiction problem than an unskilled, street criminal, heroin addict, or an adolescent addict. This is not to say that some people who have high socioeconomic and educational status do not have as insidious an addiction problem as the street addict. However, in terms of a person becoming reconnected to a nonaddictive lifestyle, there are more or less positive social elements in each addict's background.

A high achiever who becomes addicted may have more positive elements in his or her life that can aid in treatment than does an alienated adolescent or criminal addict. It is, however, often these very elements of power and status that can insulate these high-status addicts from effective help. Their money and power can render them untouchable in terms of treatment because it takes a long time before they hit the wall of failure and self-destruction that will propel them into treatment. For example, the treatment received by former first lady Betty Ford became a cause célèbre because few people of her status publicly reveal that they have a problem, and then in fact do something about it.

AA, based on its lengthy experience, postulates that alcoholics or addicts often must hit "bottom" before they decide to quit their addiction. A substance abuser's "bottom," or what I would call "hitting the wall of failure," is different for different people, depending on their power and status.

The manner in which a powerful person can avert the treatment he or she desperately needs is revealed in the classic case of Earl Long (Huey Long's brother), when he was governor of Louisiana. Governor Earl Long had severe personal problems complicated by alcoholism and manifested disturbed behavior. His wife had him committed to the Louisiana State Mental Hospital. Long, using his power as governor, fired the head of the hospital, took over the hospital, and ordered his own release.

On an ultimately more deadly level, John Belushi presented another prototypical case of the use of power to promote one's demise. Belushi was a successful entertainer despite the fact that he was obviously a drug addict. It was almost impossible for his friends or relatives to intervene in his downward spiral toward self-destruction because he was able to maintain his successful position as a performer—and at the same time had the power and money to continue his addiction. His money and status kept him from hitting "the bottom," which might have propelled him into treatment and saved his life. In contrast to a Belushi or a Governor Long, the average substance abuser who is not insulated by prestige is more likely to confront the full force of hitting the wall of failure.

Age is another significant factor in confronting one's addiction or alcoholism. In particular, adolescents and dependent children ("children" who are sometimes in their 20s) who become addicts are often shielded from confronting their wall of failure by their parents and family. In my many years of experience working with adolescent substance abusers, I have found that most of them are either shielded or rescued from hitting bottom by their parents; and this rescue and denial process prolongs and makes their addiction problem more severe. Since most adolescents are dependent on and supported and rescued by their parents, they do not usually hit the "painful wall" or bottom that would motivate them to seek the help they need. Their families become "enablers" or coaddicts, and the adolescents seldom fully experience the ultimate pain of their addictive behavior. Because of this they are resistant to accepting help or treatment.

Another factor that complicates the treatment needed by adolescents and dependent children (of all ages) is the protection they receive from their enabler. Because of the enabler's help, they are still enjoying some of the good feelings of drug use—without its painful down side. As a consequence individuals in this category have not yet felt the painful consequences of their substance abuse. This debilitating process can go on for many years when a substance abuser has a "protector" and "rescuer." When the enabler quits, in effect, "helping" or rescuing the substance abuser with the problem, the substance abuser may then seek the help needed.

Most research validates the fact that the majority of young substance abusers are likely to come from families where one or both parents and a sibling are also substance abusers. In this type of situation, in addition to the factors cited, the use of drugs or alcohol is more likely to be an ingrained part of the "normal" social background; and it becomes more difficult to help such an addict to become drug-free than the addict who comes from a relatively "clean" family background.

Part of the insidious problem with these adolescents that blockades treatment is the hypocrisy of their substance abuser parents. Such parents have little impact when they tell their children not to use drugs. Their hypocrisy often facilitates the adolescent's addiction.

It is apparent from this discussion of treatment issues that drug-–alcohol addiction is often difficult to precisely diagnose. This is increasingly due in part to the proliferation and variety of drug-use patterns. Another difficulty is that the victims of the disease, the substance abusers, too often deny or practice self-deceit about the existence of any pathology. Moreover the fact that family and friends, are often enablers, and thus are part of the problem, tends to complicate the issue further by their response to the addict's behavior. All of these complex factors necessarily affect the kind of treatment program that needs to be prescribed for the addicted person.

The medical–psychological model is the approach that has historically dominated the treatment of addicts and alcoholics. This treatment approach, simply stated, involves professionally trained psychotherapists who operate on the assumption that addicts have a basic emotional problem that propels them into the abuse of drugs. The basic assumption is that if the psychotherapist can help the drug–alcohol victim identify and resolve this underlying psychological problem, he or she will stop using drugs.

The medical model approach (whether the therapist is a psychiatrist, psychologist, social worker, or counselor) implies that the therapist has the knowledge and techniques for helping the addict rid himself or herself of a drug habit if the addict cooperates with the therapist.

This approach is often attempted in the open community in a clinic or office setting. The odds that an addict will kick a habit through the medical model in the open community are greater with a person who is well motivated, has high social status and a reasonably good family situation, and is solidly established in an occupation. The method is apt to be unsuccessful with the typical alienated addict-alcoholic who has family problems, is not firmly established in an occupation, and has crippling emotional problems. Most people who are hooked fit into the latter category and require a therapeutic community setting to effectively treat them.

Another problem with the traditional professional approach is related to the fact that the addict has greater access to drugs in the open community. The addiction compulsion is usually much stronger than the positive therapist and therapeutic process. Consequently very often the client attends therapy sessions in an intoxicated state. This factor sabotages the therapeutic process, since dealing with an intoxicated person in the open community is extremely difficult.

In brief, because of these intervening factors, it is difficult to reach most addicts in the open community. I am not being critical of the basic assumption of the medical–psychological model that helping the addict comprehend his or her underlying psychological problems is vital to recovery. Of course, developing some level of self-awareness about the compulsion to use drugs is a necessary part of the treatment approach, however, it is first necessary for the addict to become drug-free before he or she can deal with resolving emotional problems.

In this regard there has emerged in the burgeoning drug-addict treatment industry an approach that often produces a limited "cure." In recent years there has been a proliferation of widely advertised programs that detoxify the addict or alcoholic, without significantly treating or affecting the addict's underlying emotional problems that inspire the drug abuse. In these "detoxification programs," the addict seldom stays in long enough in a sober condition to work out the compulsion to use drugs—or the underlying psychological conditions. About all that most 60–90-day short-term cures do is detoxify the addict for a brief period—without significantly affecting the basic drug-abusing life-style. Although this type of quick-cure program may be helpful to some addicts, for the most part, it involves a brief placebo effect that seldom lasts.

My research reveals that effective treatment for most addicts requires ample time both to detoxify the addict with the aid of a support group, and to explore and resolve the basic social-psychological factors that propelled the addict into the addictive behavior. These ingredients are the basic elements of a true therapeutic community.

DEFINING THE THERAPEUTIC COMMUNITY

A true TC approach for treating the abuser incorporates the basic AA approach of using recovering addicts as cotherapists in a supportive group environment, and the medical–psychological assumption of the vital need of the addict to understand his or her social–psychological problems in a drug-free community for a reasonable period of time.

Based on my extensive research into TCs over the past 25 years, I have concluded that there are several basic factors that must exist in order for an organization to be defined as a true TC: (1) voluntary entrance; (2) the use of various group methods, especially the encounter group process; (3) the proper use of addicts as cotherapists in the program; and (4) an open-ended social structure that allows the entering addict to move up the status ladder of the organization into an increasingly responsible therapeutic position in the TC.

Voluntary Entrance

By "voluntary entrance" I mean there is some level of motivation on the part of addicts to participate in the TC program, and that they are not being "sentenced" to a program against their will. There has to be some commitment to become drug-free, even though their motivation may be fueled by other considerations. Some of the other factors that influence an addict's "commitment" to a TC program on entrance may include a sense of helplessness about life as an addict; on the verge of becoming totally alienated from family and real friends; on the verge of losing a job because he or she has lost the ability to maintain a cherished occupation; or the addict may choose a commitment to a TC instead of being involuntarily confined to prison as the result of a court decision.

Thus voluntary entrance means that there is some level of participatory motivation on the part of the addict to enter the program. Even though that motivation may be low in the beginning, the addict has made a decision to become drug-free since in a TC—unlike a prison or closed hospital ward—he or she can leave at will. From this weak beginning, the embers of commitment must be fanned by TC compatriots into a glowing fire of motivation to become and remain drug-free.

Group Processes

The encounter group in a TC is a basic vehicle through which the recovering addict explores personal problems and the commitment to become drug-free. In addition various supportive, educational, and psychodramatic groups are of great value in the recovery process. All bonafide TCs utilize some form of encounter group at the core of their treatment program. One reason for doing so is that *all* addicts practice some pattern of self-deception about their lives. To combat the addict's self-delusions that keep him or her a self-destructive addict, a small group situation is required in which the addict can be confronted by group members who will help the addict better understand the realities of his or her life situation.

A basic subject discussed in a TC group for a recovering addict revolves around the general AA first step of *accepting the fact that you are an addict; your life has become unmanageable; you have no control over your addictive behavior; and you cannot use any addicting chemical substances ever again.* Most addict-alcoholics will overtly agree to the statement that they are addicted, but on some inner emotional level they do not believe it or refuse to accept the reality that they are substance abusers. The encounter group helps them deal with these and other self-delusionary issues in the TC.

The encounter group also enables a substance abuser to become a cotherapist to his or her peers. When the "doctor" substance abuser is combatively yelling at a target, "You are an addict and you can never use any kind of drug ever again" in an encounter group, the recipient of the verbal attack may hear and accept this truth—but of equal importance is the fact that the person making the statement may hear it for himself or herself.

The group process in a TC, especially the encounter group, does not only deal with the self-delusion of the recovering substance abuser, it is a situation where each resident's progress is evaluated; work and organizational problems in the TC are resolved; each person's responsibility for his or her own recovery is discussed; and personal family problems are analyzed and treated. The group process in a TC therefore, does not always involve harsh verbal battles—participants are often supportive of each other and rationally analyze the variety of problems that recovering addicts encounter in their movement toward personal growth and becoming drug-free.

Most TCs have varied forms of groups. Some involve long-term group sessions, which last two to three days and are often called "trips" or "marathons." "Group probes" on significant problems are a form of intellectual investigation into relevant issues. Many TCs in their group process utilize a form of psychodrama on a regular basis and when the need arises. The essence of these varied groups is that substance abusers become cotherapists to each other in a TC for personal and social growth.

Ex-Addicts as Cotherapists

An important element in a TC is the fact that shortly after entrance and detoxification, the substance abuser assumes considerable responsibility for his or her own treatment. They are forced to confront the realities of their life situation by others who have made the trip from feeling abject helplessness to a point where they have taken considerable control over their own lives.

The ex-substance abuser is equipped to be an effective peer therapist for a number of important reasons: First, ex-addicts in a TC have been through the throes and conflicts of their original problem. They know all of the "dope-fiend" rationalizations and self-deceptions that keep a substance abuser on drugs. They know the brief "pleasure," and also the enormous pain, of using drugs or alcohol. They comprehend on a deep emotional level from their own experience what it is like to live behind the smokescreen of drugs.

Second, they have gone through the complex process of personal change in a TC program. They know the early painful traumas of confronting their own lives more directly. They have experienced the various phases of reorganizing their relationships with their family and friends. They have developed coping mechanisms for dealing with the temptations of sliding back into their former state of existence.

Third, because of these two sets of experiences—a life as an addict and first-hand knowledge about the recovery process—the ex-addicts in a TC have developed some special insights and skills. They are not easily outmaneuvered or conned by recovering addicts. They quickly acquire the respect of the "copatients," because they can see through the rationalizations and ploys that they once used themselves. The result is a communication that has more therapeutic power than that usually achieved in more traditional professional therapy. These paraprofessionals also know from their day-by-day experiences the self-discipline required to continue to stay clean.

The fact of the significant value of ex-addicts as cotherapists in a TC does not exclude the university-trained psychiatrist, psychologist, social worker, or counselor. In the TC movement, there was, in the early days, an effort to exclude professional therapists because, as one TC leader commented, "They never helped us get off drugs because they don't really understand us."

In recent years this attitude has changed dramatically, and professionals have become a significant part of the TC movement. This is due to a better understanding by professionals of the psychodynamics of addiction and its treatment that has been revealed by 50 years of AA and 25 years of TC experience.

Today the management and leadership of many TCs are shared by ex-addict professionals and professional professionals. The TC system has, therefore, become a more cooperative venture; and this is revealed by an analysis of the social structure of contemporary TCs.

The Social Structure of TCs

One of the most important contributions of the TC to the treatment of addicts is found in the TC's social structure. It has a distinctly different organizational form than is found in other, more traditional therapeutic institutions.

Most traditional therapeutic structures have a two-tier *caste system* of organization. There are the "doctors" and the "patients," the "correctional officers" and the "prisoners," the "healers" and the "sick." This castelike division is based on the premise that if patients follow their doctor-therapists' instructions, they will get well. Most correctional organizations reflect this type of medical model.

A true TC does not have a "we–they" caste system. It provides an open-ended stratification situation. Upward mobility is distinctly possible in the organization, and, in fact, upward movement in the system is encouraged, and is perceived as a positive factor in self-growth and becoming drug-free. As one TC leader told a newcomer during an indoctrination session: "In a couple of years... you just might be a big shot around here and have my job." Not only is upward social mobility possible in a TC, but healthy status seeking is encouraged. This type of upward mobility is not possible in a traditional institution since the professional therapist has a lock on his or her power-status position, and "patients" remain in their clear-cut role.

A TC organization assumes, with some supportive evidence, that a person's position in its hierarchy is a correlate of social maturity, "mental health," increased work ability, and a clear understanding of the organization. Another assumption is that the social skills learned in a TC structure are useful within the larger society. The "we–they" problem does not exist in a true TC structure since the administration and the "patients" are one and the same, and upward mobility is encouraged in this open-ended stratification system.

In a TC addicts find *a new society*. They receive support, understanding, and affection from people who have had life experiences similar to their own. They find a community with which they can identify, people toward whom they can express their best human emotions, rather than their worst. They find special friends who will assist them when they begin to deviate or fall short of what they have set out to do—to develop personal growth and remain drug-free. In the new society of the TC, they develop the ability to express their best human qualities and potentialities; and these personal-growth factors are transferable to living a happier, more productive, drug-free life in the larger society.

2

Historical Origins and Developments

Ex-Criminals Help to Reform Felons

"Criminal therapy," the use of ex-criminals to treat criminals, is a major break-through in criminology, according to Dr. Lewis Yablonsky, University of California at Los Angeles criminologist.

In an article in the September issue of "Federal Probation," a leading criminology publication of the Federal Government, Dr. Yablonsky described the important new treatment for criminals.

The technique originated, he pointed out, at Synanon House in Santa Monica, Calif., a unique self-help community for rehabilitation of drug addicts. Over the past year several "graduates" of Synanon have effectively introduced "criminal therapy" at the Federal Terminal Island Prison near Long Beach, Calif.

Dr. Yablonsky, who is also Synanon research director, said, "We have found that former addicts with long criminal backgrounds and prison experience often make the most effective therapists for younger addicts and delinquents who have embarked on similar criminal careers.

The ex-criminal therapist has "made the scene" himself. He cannot be "conned" or outmaneuvered by his "patient." He quickly gains the grudging respect of his "patient" and there is rapport. The result is a communication that penologists and others in authority find difficult to establish with others who by their criminal background, are defiant of authority.

In this new approach "being clean" (of crime, drugs, and violence) becomes the status symbol. A reverse of the criminal code occurs and any slip back into criminality means great loss of face in the group.

The New York Times Sept. 30, 1962

The concept of utilizing ex-offenders or ex-patients for the purpose of treating people with a problem has a long history. In this century several contributions to this model are notable. Psychiatrist J. L. Moreno, who invented psychodrama and many dimensions of group therapy around 1910, early on perceived the value of people being cotherapists in a small group therapy process. He wrote extensively about the concept of the professional group therapist's and psychodramatist's major role of getting people in group therapy to help each other to resolve their problems. The effective professional's role was, according to Moreno's basic viewpoint, mainly as a catalyst and coordinator of the group's therapeutic energy.

Maxwell Jones, in the 1940s, utilized patient-power principles in setting up a form of therapeutic community in mental hospitals in England. He attempted to have the mental patients in his groups work with each other toward strengthening their ability to function in the outside social system.

A major breakthrough in paraprofessional therapy, related to the TC movement, was the creation and development of Alcoholics Anonymous (AA). A.A. began in 1935 when a stockbroker and a medical doctor, both alcoholics, pooled their knowledge about the ravages of alcoholism. They spent over three years, on a trial-and-error basis, in developing the basic tenets of AA that were utilized in their own recovery. In AA the sharing of the pain of alcoholism—reports of success stories, support group meetings, the utilization of recovering alcoholics as sponsors, and a 12-step method that an alcoholic can work through— has had a profound impact on reducing the problem of alcoholism on a worldwide basis.

In my own work with violent gangs in New York City in the 1950s, I hired ex-gang members to work with gangs. (See Lewis Yablonsky, *The Violent Gang*, Macmillan, 1962.) These paraprofessionals knew the turf—and intuitively understood the problems that violent gang youths were struggling with since they had "been there" themselves. This enabled them to help many youths extricate themselves from the gang warfare, drug abuse, and crime that were rampant in their neighborhood. I also utilized the treatment energy of ex-criminal parolees who were leading successful lives to communicate with neighborhood delinquents in small groups.

They were effective in communicating the benefits of a crime-free life-style to budding delinquents in small group situations that I constructed as part of my overall crime-prevention program.

THE SYNANON APPROACH

The first TC devoted to the treatment of substance abusers was founded by Charles E. Dederich, an A.A. graduate, in 1958 in Ocean Park, California. I first learned about Synanon at a United Nations Conference on Crime and Delinquency in London in the summer of 1960. One evening, at an informal gathering, this experiment for treating addicts was described to me by the noted criminologist, Dr. Donald Cressey.

According to Dr. Cressey, Synanon involved a small group of addicts and alcoholics living together in an old beach house now located in Santa Monica, California. The name was born when a recovering alcoholic, who was trying to say "seminar" and "symposium" at the same time, slurred the words into "Synanon." When Charles E. Dederich, a former alcoholic himself who recovered through AA, the founder of the group, heard the word, he immediately seized upon it as an appropriate name for the new organization.

In Synanon, recovering addicts and alcoholics regularly participated in seminar discussions and a form of group psychotherapy that involved encountering each other's behavior in small group sessions. Dr. Cressey sketched a vivid picture of the group: loudly arguing philosophical concepts and amateur psychology into all hours of the night while a hi-fi blared jazz music in the background. I especially remember his description of an addict going through drug-withdrawal pains on a living-room couch in the center of this bizarre scene. The human situation he described seemed strange, but it did make some sense to me that it would probably take a radical set of circumstances to get addicts off drugs since, from my viewpoint at that time, most other methods had failed. I was intrigued with the approach. Consequently, about a year later, in 1961, when I received an appointment as a professor at the University of California at Los Angeles, I seized the opportunity to research Synanon. I will here describe the development and characteristics of Synanon in detail because it is the prototype of many TCs I have visited and researched over the past 25 years.

My first visit to Synanon in 1961 surprised me. The immense five-story red-brick armory was nothing like the beatnik beach house I had visualized. There was a large, respectable black-and-yellow "Synanon House" sign on the front of the building. Somehow I had expected Synanon to turn a more clandestine face to the world.

The large front door to the building opened into an impressive waiting room. On a bulletin board near the door, I noticed pictures of many celebrities with Synanon members. One picture showed Chuck Dederich and several other Synanon members talking to several visiting movie stars. Also in the foyer was a counter with a variety of Synanon literature. There were reprints of articles on Synanon from *Time, Down Beat, The Nation,* and other publications.

Several feet from the entrance, a young man seated at a desk greeted me in a businesslike manner. He asked me to state my business and then sign a guest register. I noticed that he had the healed scars of an ex-addict on the inside crook of his arms. This "administrative approach" coming from a former addict was a startling experience.

I told him who I was and that I had made an appointment to visit the place with a man named Charley Hamer. He called my name into an intercom that connected with the coordinator's office. I was now apparently properly checked into the building, and the squawk box answered back, "Send him on up."

It became increasingly difficult to believe that the place was entirely managed by ex-addicts. Everywhere I looked, I saw signs of efficient organization. On my way to the second floor, I passed a sign stating "Business Office." The large room had rows of typewriters, with people banging away on them, files, and the other accoutrements of an office. On my right was a small theater marked "Stage One." The hall was carpeted with a variety of obviously donated assorted rugs which were well worn but neat and clean.

On the second floor, I saw men and women bustling around in different directions. They all seemed to be on important errands. With the exception of the sight of several jail-scarred faces and a young man going through drug-withdrawal pains in the center of the living room, I found it difficult to believe this was a "drug-addict rehabilitation center."

Charley introduced himself, welcomed me, and introduced me to another member, Jack Hurst. Jack was a thin young man, about

32 years old. (I later found out that he had been an addict for nine years prior to coming to Synanon.) Charley was about 60. He was ruddy-faced and very talkative, with a Southwestern twang to his voice. His opening remarks lauding Synanon were very much in the style of many intelligent tough "cons" I had met in my past prison work and research. Most of these old-timers had their theories on treatment. There was one major difference between Charley's monologue and what I had heard in the past. He was not talking from the position of the locked-up failed criminal who now saw the "light" sitting in a cell. He was talking from the unusual position of a living embodiment of his rap, and this encouraged me to listen to his story more attentively.

I later found out that Charley was probably one of the oldest ex-addicts in the country. The first drug he used was opium, which was given to him by a Chinese family in Oklahoma in 1922. This had launched him into over 40 years of leading a life of crime and addiction.

Before Charley and I could get any serious conversation under way, I observed that most of the people in the house had gathered in the front room. I was informed that the encounter groups were about to take place and that we could talk further "after they were kicked off." According to Charley: "The game is our form of what you probably call group psychotherapy in your business. People here go to these sessions three evenings a week. In the game, people can dump their emotional garbage, have their self-deceptions exposed, and learn about themselves. It's kind of pressure-cooker group for working out your problems."

At this point a young man, Bill Crawford, walked to the front of a large fireplace in the middle of the living room. He took charge of the 35 to 40 people sitting around the room. Almost all of them seemed to be nervously smoking and drinking coffee at the same time. He spoke casually from notes he had on a clipboard: "Laundry goes out tomorrow. We're down to rock bottom on food money and yet some of you keep leaving half cups of coffee all over the place. Knock it off!... Let's welcome a new member who came in today, Joe Sommers."

The group of ex-addicts vigorously applauded as they looked toward a slim youth of about 22 years old. He was huddled under a blanket on a couch in the middle of the living room, apparently going through withdrawal pains from his drug habit.

After the applause for the newcomer stopped, Crawford announced groupings for the evening: "Tootsie, Donna, Jimmy,

Henry, Betty, Harry, Janis, and Candy will meet in the business office." Eight people got up—some of when went to the restaurant-type coffee urn in the dining room and got coffee—and then went down the stairs. Crawford continued: "Bill, Reid..." With each reading of names, another group moved out, assigned to another location in the building.

Charley Hamer showed me one of the rooms set up for the groups. Chairs were placed in a circle, so that everyone faced everyone else. The room began to fill up with the assigned people. Soon loud curses and shouts were coming from the various rooms. I was somewhat disturbed by the violent voice pitch. I knew, from my past institutional experience, that the type of shouting I was hearing was often a prelude to, or accompanied, physical violence. Hurst sensed my reaction and told me about Synanon's cardinal rules, "Two capital offenses in Synanon are physical assault and using drugs or alcohol. One thing we encourage in our groups is that people speak their true feelings. What you are hearing is a lot of angry people speaking their truth."

Charley suggested that we go to the coordinator's office, where it was quieter. I was informed that the coordinator's office was the "nerve center" of the building and that it "coordinated" internal and outside activities. The office contained intercoms, telephones, card files, maps, printed directives (for example: "All trips to the dentist are to be cleared through Bill..."; "Meeting of department heads Tuesday at noon in the business office..."). The room contained a variety of furniture. I later learned that "everything, including the clothes we're wearing, is donated."

In the office an attractive young woman, about 21 years old, was on hand to answer phone calls during the group meetings. Charley Hamer introduced Monica to me and invited her to join our discussion of the organization.

The group sessions continued to rock the building with noise. I asked whether this was usual. Hurst described a variety of groups. The ones going on that night were the standard floor games and were mainly encounter catharsis-type sessions. They help people to get a lot of emotion out of their system. Participants argue and fight over what happens to be bugging them at the time—they think they have a rotten job; someone has an attitude problem; someone can't take orders; self-image problems; someone never talks at all or talks too much.

Hurst continued: "We try to get to the person here. Probably the reason group therapy and jail or psychiatry never helped me is because most of the therapy dealt only with the symptom of drug addiction.

"This is one of the problems with many professionals. You are all involved with drug addiction. You want to know how an addict uses, how much, and all that crap. Around here we are interested in helping ex-dope fiends grow up by talking about living clean."

The terms "dope fiend" and Jack's edge of hostility began to get to me. I said, "Why do you say 'dope fiend' rather than 'drug addict'? Isn't that what you were, an addict?"

"I call myself an ex-dope fiend, and the noise 'dope fiend' best describes my past behavior. During one of my 'periods' as an addict, I careened around highways on a motorcycle with long hair and a leather jacket—the whole bit. You know, the 'Wild One.' I went through other scenes too. I was even married for a while as a dope fiend.

"Let me give you a real example of my dope-fiend behavior. I don't think I told you this ridiculous story before, Charley. It really describes this dope-fiend thing.

"First get the background. I'm living in northern California. I went there on one of my runaway geographic cures. You know, I was trying to clean up by getting out of Los Angeles and away from the scene. Of course, it wasn't working. I would charge into San Francisco on weekends to get my dope.

"Anyway, here I am with my wife in this small town. I'm trying to work as a carpenter on a construction gang. My pregnant wife is with me in this burg. It's a city of about 10,000, with one doctor.

"In the middle of the night, my wife begins to have labor pains. We get into the car, and I take her to this dinky little hospital. The only one there is a nurse, who won't call the doctor until she's sure my wife is going to give birth.

"I hold my wife's hand and reassure her that all will be well. This goes on for about an hour. Meanwhile the nurse is preparing my wife, anesthetic and all that. She finally calls the doctor, and he is on his way.

"Now in the middle of this 'beautiful-young-couple-having-a-baby, waiting-for-the-doctor scene,' in the back of my head I'm trying to figure out how I can get at some of the dope the nurse pumped into my wife's arm! There's the bottle of Demerol sitting on the medicine table.

"My wife's pains are getting closer together, and the doctor still hasn't arrived. All of a sudden, the nurse let out a gasp. There is the baby's head. The nurse says, 'Let's get her into the delivery room.

You're going to have to help. The doctor ought to be here in about 15 minutes. Put these on.' Then she gives me a doctor's smock and rubber gloves, ties the mask around my face, and says, 'We got to deliver the child!'

"This catches me off base. Here I am trying to be lovingly concerned for my wife's welfare, help with the delivery, and at the same time get the dope. My wife is screaming her head off. I hold her hand and keep inching my way closer to the anesthetic tray where the bottle of dope I want so badly is sitting. I finally snatch the bottle of Demerol and tuck it safely away in my pocket under the smock. Now I feel comfortable, and I'm ready to help deliver my child.

"At this point the doctor arrives, and I become a bystander. From about seven feet away, I watch the doctor deliver the kid, cut the cord, take the crap out of the kid's mouth, give him a smack—and nothing happens. He gives the kid mouth-to-mouth resuscitation, and still nothing happens. He dumps him in hot and cold water and all that. Finally the kid, who had started to turn blue, lets out a bellow, and then he is okay.

"But what I vividly remember about the episode is that I couldn't really get concerned about my wife and the kid until I had stolen the dope and had it securely stashed away. Now you know why I call people who use drugs 'dope fiends.' They will do anything for drugs. Rich or poor they'll use their family or anyone close to them, because drugs dominate their life. They are literally dope fiends."

Monica, who had been listening, shyly interrupted: "Maybe a little story about one of my experiences with drug addiction using cocaine and heroin will explain why the term 'dope fiend' seems pretty accurate to me for describing our past behavior.

"If I remember this incident correctly, some guy, a trick [a prostitute's customer] claimed he wanted to marry me. I had a very bad habit going at the time, and it's all very vague. I remember this trick had a lot of money. He said he loved me and wanted to help me kick my habit. I thought I wanted to clean up, or at least this was one of my attempts. Anyway, I went to his apartment. He hid my clothes, my shoes, blouse, and purse—almost everything—so I couldn't leave. All I had left on was a pair of jeans.

"Naturally, when I started getting a yen after a few hours of kicking, I asked him for the rest of my clothes so I could go score some drugs. He flatly refused to give them to me, and we had a big hassle.

"His apartment was near one of the main boulevards in Hollywood, and I remember running out the door, with him after me, down Sunset Boulevard. I was wearing nothing but my jeans. Anyway, there I was racing down the street, with him trying to catch me. Some guy on a motorcycle was going by. He spotted me and screeched to a stop. You know the type—black leather jacket, a Hell's Angel. He pulled alongside me (remember, I was topless) and he 'whoom-whoomed' his motorcycle motor, in a weird wolf call.

"I jumped on the back of the cycle and told him someone was after me, and if we didn't move out fast, we's both be in trouble. So we went speeding down Sunset Boulevard and lost the guy following us. I then had the motorcycle cat drop me off at my dealer's house, and I scored some drugs."

As we continued to talk, I became increasingly impressed with the stark honesty and candor of the people. Never in my professional experience, and certainly not in various prisons in my research with street gangs, had I encountered more direct and honest responses to any questions I chose to ask. I said, "You know, I've done a fair amount of research on crime, and in particular with violent gangs in New York. I've never had the experience of such frank responses to my questions. After all, none of you know me that well."

Jack picked up this point: "Around here, we operate on what we laughingly call the truth principle. If you want to look at it that way, part of our therapy is truth and honesty. We have nothing to hide or creep around about. We aren't proud of our past behavior, but at the same time we can't go around paralyzed with guilt. It would just incapacitate us."

I was also impressed with their articulate responses to my questions and commented on this point. Hurst replied, "This is not by chance. Obviously I am no grammarian. I only had a ninth-grade education. But we do work on communication here. That's part of our business. Each noon we have a seminar where we place some concept on the blackboard, and then everyone discusses it. For example, the one we had this noon was, 'We attack in others the evil we dimly perceive in ourselves.' We analyze this kind of concept and argue about it. This helps our verbal ability. Although I may not be too sharp now, when I first came in here I talked out of the side of my head. You know—everyone was 'man.' We do have some middle-class alcoholics, addicts, and some college graduates; however, many of our people were into hard crime. Some of the guys, when they come in here, know one word, 'stickemup.' After awhile, as a result of groups and seminars, they develop their verbal skills. Part of our program involves going on speaking engagements to different community and educational organizations."

Monica showed me what they called a "concept box." It was a standard six-by-six green office card box. On file in it were about 300 concepts. Emerson, Freud, Thoreau, Nietzsche, Lao-tse, and Betrand Russell were some of the names I noticed. These philosphers and their ideas were discussed at the noon seminars.

Two hours later the groups were breaking up and people were streaming to the coffee urn and a sandwich table. Everyone seemed lively, hungry, and bright-eyed. I was amazed. There appeared to be no animosity at all among individuals who, minutes before, had been screaming at each other. In group psychotherapy sessions that I had run in prisons and hospitals, post group hard feelings would often persist for days among group members.

I later learned that the rules of the encounter-group interaction were to express your innermost harshest feelings. Of course, upon leaving the group session and reentering the day-to-day world, civility and good manners were demanded. Many people have difficulty understanding this simple distinction between encounter-group rules and the expectations of normal behavior outside of the group. The allowance of freedom of expression in the groups is a valuable therapeutic tool; however, life would be difficult if people were constantly to express their deeper raw feelings in regular societal situations.

I was highly impressed with my first encounter with Synanon—and learned a great deal about the organization from these first impressions. The experience motivated me to plunge into an intensive six-year period of research and personal experience to learn more about the organization. In the process I became a good friend and colleague of Chuck Dederich—and an active participant in the development of the TC movement in its formative years.

Charles (Chuck) Dederich, as the founder of Synanon, was the central figure in the invention of the contemporary TC movement. His story and the history of the growth of Synanon in the first few years (1958–1961) were revealed to me over the ten years I spent researching the organization (1961–1971), and writing my book on the organization, *The Tunnel Back: Synanon* (Macmillan 1965).

Chuck was able to plunge into the development of a new approach to life as completely as he did because of his lack of commitment to any specific system of ideas, but a limited belief in many. His involvements with philosophy had included the study of Freud, Thoreau, Lao-tse, Buddha, Saint Thomas, Catholicism, Plato, and Emerson. At the time that Synanon was founded, Chuck was a man with no firm position, searching for meaning to his own alienated life.

He had been a roaring alcoholic on and off for 20 years and had been through a variety of jobs and wives. Alcoholics Anonymous had accomplished its mission of symptom removal; however, Chuck's restless urge continued. His life lacked completion and was generally self-defeating. When he felt that he could win or succeed, he would smash the track he was on and begin anew. This happened to him when he quit college as a sophomore at Notre Dame, as a junior executive in the Gulf Oil Company, and later as an employee of Douglas Aircraft in California.

Shortly before founding Synanon, Chuck had been a devotee of AA, but although it helped him quit drinking, he found it limiting because he felt the problem of alcoholism and addiction required a live-in residential treatment center. In retrospect, also, it seems that any approach not completely developed by Chuck himself was too binding for his roaring ego. The development of Synanon confirms this speculation. Chuck appears to need an "empire" based on his own ideas. Synanon, therefore, became the first TC and the residential live-in counterpart of AA.

Chuck's financial situation when he began what became Synanon was rock bottom: "I had no job, a few bucks in my pocket, and was living off unemployment benefits, in a small apartment near the beach in Ocean Park, Calif. With some friends from AA, I had set up a Wednesday night 'free-association' discussion group in my little pad. I had a foldaway closet bed, or the room would be full.

"Most of the people had some psychoanalytic orientation, and the early sessions were focused around sexual problems. Some of the group had had analytic couch work. Our language was pseudopsychology.

"The group was set up to explore 'a line of no line.' The meetings were loud and boisterous. Verbal attacks on one another were a keynote of the sessions. I could detect considerable lying and self-deception in the group. I began to attack verbally and viciously — partly out of my own irritation and at times to defend myself. The group would join in, and we would attack and caricature people's self-deception, pompously inflated egos, and general bullshit, including my own. The sessions intrigued all of us and soon became the high point in everybody's week."

At first the group meeting had a rotating moderator, but Chuck's bellow and his apparent analytic ability projected him, after several meetings, into the permanent-leader role. The group sensed that he could verbally attack and defend better than anyone in the group. This constituted the early development of the TC encounter group concept. The group process seemed to carve the attacked person down to a sense of reality, and this proved to be therapeutically beneficial.

Chuck noted some positive changes in people in the group. It seemed to him that these resulted more from the intense verbal attacks than from the analytic approach or the supportive problem solving. "As a result of these vicious 'haircuts,' people seemed to grow before my eyes." The people involved at that time were mainly alcoholics.

The meetings were held once a week. The disaffiliated group of about seven men and six women increasingly looked to Chuck for leadership. With their growth, he grew. His attacks were at first disorganized and "almost exclusively from the gut." He began increasingly to measure them for positive therapeutic effect. With his own growth and greater feeling of personal security, Chuck felt that he was developing a new method of therapy. He became further involved in building an organization or structure for administering this new therapy. The organization produced several more clean alcoholics, and this further reinforced Chuck's belief in the verbal-attack method.

Around this time there were about 20 people living in various apartments close to the hub of Chuck's personality and apartment clubhouse. Some worked at outside jobs, but most were jobless, alienated people. Chuck became crystalized in the thoughts of most of them as a wise father figure. His developing inner strength appeared to be the cohesive force that held the cluster of general misfits and alientated men and women together. At that time the direction of the "movement" was not clear, not even to Chuck. He was, however, very conscious of "more addicts moving in who had cut down on drugs, and some who were making noises in that direction."

A store-front building was rented, and this was used as a larger clubhouse. Chuck still lived in his small apartment, but went to work at the "club" each day. It became his job. The group of "ex-addicts and ex-alcoholics" met regularly in the clubhouse. Most of them were ex-alcoholics, however, there was a growing number of ex-addicts from all walks of life.

Among this early group was the man I met on my first visit, Charley Hamer. I felt Charley was an especially "hard case" recalcitrant drug addict, and I was most impressed with the fact that Chuck and Synanon had managed to help him kick his habit for, at that time, a period of over a year.

I was motivated to get Charley's story because it reflected the dynamics of Synanon's early days told through the voice of one of their notable successes at that time. I spent a number of lengthy nights taking notes on Charley's long voyage into addiction, and the Synanon process that had rendered him drug-free. (Charley had entered Synanon in 1962, where he became drug-free and worked as a "TC professional" helping others up to his death of natural causes in 1982.)

"I was born May 1, 1903, in Henryetta, Okla. My first encounter with narcotics was at the age of 19 (1922), from association with a local Chinese family. I was introduced to opium and smoked it for three years. My first hypodermic injection happened in 1925, with the residue from an opium pipe (*yen-shee*). About one year later, I began using morphine intravenously. This drug, in the pure form, was obtained from unethical doctors, pharmaceutical houses, and dealers. I built up a large tolerance and used 15 to 25 grains per day. I obtained money for my drugs by theft, robbery, confidence games, etc. Narcotics were cheap in those days, selling at from $35 to $75 per ounce. I used morphine and cocaine until 1933, and was then introduced to heroin. I came to California in 1937, and remained free from drugs until 1943, using alcohol to excess during this period. I again started using opium by injection and orally. I shipped out with the Merchant Marine from 1943 to 1945, and used many drugs—cocaine, hashish, morphine, heroin—around the world. In 1946 I again started using heroin, and used it constantly, except for the times I spent in prison, until coming to Synanon in 1959.

"That summer I was walking down by Ocean Park, when I ran into Johnny B., an old dope-fiend buddy of mine. He started telling me he was a director or something of a place for cleaning up junkies and alcoholics. I naturally thought he was crazy. But I thought I'd look into it, because I had a hell of a habit and wanted to clean up. Nothing permanent, mind you, but just to reduce this bitch of a habit I had going.

"He took me down the street to an old store-front building. He told me he was going to take me through the house and over to where a couple-or-three directors (whatever that was) were going to interview me. I was completely confused, dirty, ragged, and had about $2.50 in my pocket. As I was going through this room, I saw a guy I'd known for years, Billy G., peeling potatoes. I had been in jails and a couple of penitentiaries with Bill. I went on out the back door on the way to this pad, and there was Harry C. sweeping up. He was an old friend I used to shoot dope with, and I felt, 'Well, Jesus Christ, as soon as I get back from this interview, I can probably score from one of these guys.'

"I went into this interview, and there sat Jesse Pratt, a junkie I'd known for 20 years. With him was this woman and Chuck Dederich, who I later found out was the founder and king freak of the outfit.

"Jesse didn't know me. That's the kind of condition I was in. I was strung out [heavily addicted], and Jesse couldn't actually believe it was me. So he jumped up and said, 'Well, it's Charley. He's an old, old friend of mine and I have to agree it's him after looking a little closer.'

"I weighed about 118 pounds. It's pretty hard to visualize me at 118 pounds, since I now weigh 170. I looked like I was dead. I get awfully skinny when I get strung out. I had a 28-inch waist—Jesus, a man of my age.

"Then Chuck gave me a little talk and said, 'Take him back over there and let him lie down and we'll see what happens.' I lay there a couple of days. Next night they were having meetings all over the area. When they called their groups, they said, 'Come on, Charley, let's go,' and I said, ''Oh, no, not me—I ain't going nowhere.' I wouldn't go to a group or anything for a week.

"When I was laying there, I was mainly thinking of getting up and splitting. I was trying to get two or three guys to score for me, like, 'Go get me a bottle of terpin hydrate' [a narcotic cough medicine]. But no one would get me anything. I was going through terrible withdrawal pains. These two broads there—Helen and Rosie—took a personal interest in me. Those girls actually saved my life. Rose stayed up with me three days and nights. Gave me bed baths and wiped my puke up. I had a bad habit and just couldn't get up off the couch. I was sick as a dog.

"Each night Chuck would come and shake hands with me. Every night, and he'd say, 'I'll say good-bye tonight, because you won't be here in the morning.' And in the morning, he would say,

'Well, goddamn—are you still here?' This presented some sort of a challenge, and I believe now it kept me there. Nothing else might have worked at that time.

"This big, hairy, uncouth-looking individual Chuck was the main thing that kept me there. Him and the two girls babying me those three days or so. They stayed up with me and never let me alone for a moment. That combination did the impossible. Another thing that hit me was the sight of these long-time addicts, Harry, Johnny, and Jesse, clean. This I refused to believe.

"Harry had a strange approach. I asked him repeatedly, 'What are you taking?' He'd say, 'Nothing, man, nothing. Absolutely nothing,' I'd say, 'Oh don't bullshit me; I know you're taking something,' 'No, no,' he'd say, 'nothing's happening.'

"Harry told me, even when I was laying there kicking, 'Charley, I'm going to be real frank with you. This is the only place for a dope fiend. Believe me, I've been around here for almost five months, and I know it will work, I don't think it'll work for me, but I'd like for you to stick around, because Synanon needs people with a little age on them; guys like you with a long history of addiction.

"I couldn't imagine at that time that Synanon would ever get anyplace. They were trying to move us out of that old dump at Ocean Park every other day. They would come down one day and cut the electricity off for an hour, then the gas. Christ, they would of cut off the air if they could.

"I got up off that couch and got my first gig [job] about a week later. I had kicked a real boss habit. I was still alive and still there. Phil was the breakfast cook, and he had to go to the hospital for an operation. Phil told someone, 'Charley here will be the new breakfast cook.' When I heard about this, I said, 'No, man, I ain't going to be no breakfast cook. Don't know anything about being a cook and ain't got no eyes for learning how to be one—or anything else for that matter.' But anyhow, Phil said, 'Yeah, I know you can do it.' So he got me over to this old stove we had and showed me how to put hash brown potatoes on. Incidentally, I was a pretty good cook, but I was denying it. He showed me the little routines he had, and I got up and tried it the next morning. I did all right for awhile.

"I began to notice in those days that some people were secretly chippying [using a little dope]. Nothing important—some terps, pills, a joint [marijuana] once in a while. But for some reason, I stayed clear of it. When I use dope, I can't use a little.

"My dope habit would go like this. When I get in a position

where there's a whole lot of dope and no hassle, here's what happens to me: I become completely demoralized—demoralized in this particular way. When I've got no worry about hustling dope, I get to looking at myself. There's a fear in me that maybe I'm going to sit right there and destroy myself. Nobody loves me. I have nothing to do with anybody. I'm completely alientated from my family. And here I am sitting in a pad with a whole lot of dope. Then I get frightened. It's not the fear of running out of dope, 'cause it looks like there isn't going to be any end to the dope. The only word I can use is 'demoralized.' I'm the kind of guy that does not want just one fix. If I use, I need a lot of dope. If I was in the penitentiary and the guys in the cell next door had a fix and I'd be invited, I might refuse...I'm not saying I didn't take a fix occasionally in prison, but I wouldn't give up five packs of cigarettes. Five packs of cigarettes are more important to me in the penitentiary than one fix. I don't like just a little dope, because afterwards I feel bad for days.

"So in Synanon I stayed away from these few little chippying cliques. But don't get me wrong—I hadn't bought Synanon at that time. I figured I'm there for 30 days to kick my habit. I wanted to get my physical health back and be clean enough so that my habit wouldn't cost half as much money when I got back to the streets. I had no thoughts of really sticking it out for more than 30 days.

"The next big thing that happened to me was enormous to my way of thinking. At the time there was very little money in the organization. Chuck came around and gave me the job of shopping. He gave me what little money they had to go shop for food! He asked me to go down and get $5 or $10 worth of groceries and get a meal together. He gave me their whole bankroll. He also gave me the key to the old icebox we used to have, where we kept the keys to the cigarettes (and the little coffee that was stored there). I couldn't accept it at first.

"Then I took this job where I have to go right past a drugstore. I got this $10 in my pocket that nobody will miss a buck from. Believe me, this was a goddam challenge for me to get by that drugstore. I didn't have a yen after those 90 days. I wouldn't call it guilt that stopped me. I wanted to go in there and get a bottle of terps. I don't think I understood the meaning of the word 'guilt' at the time. But somehow, I got by and I got those groceries and I got back and we got a meal together.

"I don't know why Chuck trusted me. Maybe he did this to test me. Maybe he looked at it like, 'Here's a real old-timer who finally got on his feet and looks halfway human.' Chuck worked in strange ways. I never asked him about this. Maybe he did say to himself, 'Here's a guy that might have a little moral fiber, but in order to find out, I'm going to give him this $10—all we got—and see if he comes back with it.' That could have been it; I'm not sure. But whatever the reason, to me it was an important milestone. I gave it a lot of thought. Why did the man trust me?

"After that I drifted along pretty good. I performed the kitchen job fairly well and I was more or less completely honest. I didn't take anything, outside of a couple of candy bars and a package of cigarettes. These things would make me feel guilty now, but didn't bother me then. Those were about the only infractions that I committed.

"About that time, something important happened in the club that affected us all. I was known as the big cop-out [revealing the truth].

"It kicked off like this. A junkie by the name of Kenny, who was a close friend of mine on the outside, was batting around the club and getting loaded. He took a little here and there. He disappeared one night, and Reid, an ex-addict who was then the leader next to Chuck in the club, nailed him when he came in. He was definitely loaded. This was around midnight. We asked him where he'd been and said, 'Kenny, you're loaded.' He denied this. He wouldn't listen to reason and was going to split. He was in the midst of packing his clothes, and Reid and I were standing up there giving him a haircut [telling him off]. He was packing his clothes and saying, 'I don't have to put up with this shit.' Now Kenny and Reid were real tight [good friends], so Reid said, 'Well, you crazy son of a bitch, if you're going, I'm going with you!' And Kenny said, 'Well, you don't have to.' We just couldn't get him to cop [admit the truth]. If he'd just cop, well, everything would have been all right, but he wouldn't cop. 'If he cops, we save his life,' was the way we were thinking.

'Christ—admit you're loaded and unpack your clothes and don't split!' 'No,' he said, 'I'm not loaded.' Again Reid started to go with him. Then Reid and I threatened to fight him. By that time there were seven or eight people gathered around us, and somebody, I don't remember who, said, 'Well, Kenny, there's nothing wrong with admitting you're loaded. I got loaded the other day. I admit it.'

'That kicked off something. Now Reid and I weren't copping to nothing yet. Then another guy said, 'Hell, yes, Kenny. I got loaded today.' Chuck wasn't there at this time, and Reid and I were standing there, hanging tough. Finally we got to the point where we said to Kenny, 'Well, yes, you dirty bastard, we're loaded half the time. Kenny, tell us you're loaded and forget about the whole thing.' He wouldn't do it. Kenny said, 'You can snitch on yourselves if you want to.' Then, finally, Reid said, 'You can call me a snitch if you want to, but dammit, I got loaded with you two days ago, and I'm going to tell it!' Then Kenny flipped and said, 'Boy, you dirty fink bastard...' Then every goddam person there admitted to something to get Kenny to cop. And he still wouldn't do it.

"Finally someone woke Chuck up, and we got all the broads down from their rooms across the street. It turned out that everyone who'd come in that room had got loaded since they'd been there. About half had some kind of a beef, and everybody copped out to their slip with drugs.

"Chuck wondered what was going on in the middle of the night. We explained it to him. 'We're all copping to our sins. We're trying to save Kenny's life here, and he's still packing his clothes.' So then Chuck said, 'Everybody that's gotten loaded since they've been here tell about it,' and everyone opened up—everyone except Richie and his wife Portie. Finally Richie copped. And Portie was still hanging tough. 'Not me,' she said. 'Well,' we said, 'you're going with Richie. You ain't going to deny you got loaded with him?' She was the last one to cop.

"Something strange happened from that time on. No one, except in a few rare incidents, used any more dope in Synanon. Something happened to me that night. After the cop-out, I went to Chuck with the keys and money. I told him, 'Here's the money and here's the keys.' And he said, 'What's that for?' I said, 'I resign.' He said, 'Why?' 'Well, man, I can't be trusted with money. You just heard me cop out.' 'Well,' he said, 'what's that got to do with anything? Stick those keys back in your pocket, and the money too.' That son-of-a-bitch Chuck just wouldn't give me the chance I wanted to split."

The cop-out phenomenon appears to be something that happens in all TCs at some point. At first there is an illusion of everyone being drug-free. When people begin to admit their abuse, it produces a core of totally drug-free members. From that point on, the TC functions, for the most part, as a drug-free community. There are always a few deviants in every group.

The next significant phase in Charley's evolution was his appointment as a director in Synanon after he had been there for a year.

"When Chuck made me a director, it frightened me. 'Jesus,' I said to myself, 'am I capable of being a director?' I think I verbalized this to them. Chuck said, 'Well, you've been acting like a director, so now you're officially a director.' This did something to me.

"After I was made a director, I still had one foot out the door. But I remember, after everyone had congratulated me and called a general meeting to announce it, I really started thinking. I thought about it for two days and two nights. I even thought of splitting. I was so scared. I really hadn't planned to stay this long. I thought six months, at the most and here it was getting on to nine months.

"Nothing too much came out of this self-examination. Later, something happened that may sound trivial, but was a very important factor in my decision to stay. Here I am, I told myself, a director, and I'm pretty undecided. Well, goddam, I am a director! I've either got to go tell these people I want to resign or I've got to make up my mind to act like a director and do something about it.

"This is the incident. Four or five days after I was made a director, I was walking down the hallway on the second floor, on my way to the toilet, and I saw this cigarette butt on the floor. I reached down, picked up the butt, and put it in a trash can.

"I began to think, 'Here I am picking up butts off the floor! Maybe I finally joined the program. This must be some indication, because I never did anything like that before in my life for any organization.' Damn if this thought didn't hang me up for over an hour. I went out on the balcony and stood there and thought about it. From that moment on, so to speak, I was with the program. It meant to me, 'I'm going to stay here now. I'm not going to split.' I stayed awake all that night thinking it over. I guess I'm hooked on this organization."

Charley did stay clean in the program for over 20 years—and became an effective director, drug counselor, and role model for many younger people who went through Synanon.

The dynamics of Synanon and some of its basic methodology at that time were delineated in a public presentation Chuck Dederich made in 1958 at a Southern California Parole Officers' Association Conference. Dederich's description of his pioneering TC was as follows:

"The Synanon Foundation is a nonprofit corporation which has emerged as part of an overall phenomenon which is taking place on the beach at Ocean Park, Calif. At this time it appears that an environment has been created that seems to have a beneficial effect on some alcoholic and addicts.

"We have here a climate consisting of a family structure similar in some areas to a primitive tribal structure, which seems to affect individuals on a subconscious level. The structure also contains overtones of a 19th century family setup of the type which produced inner-directed personalities. A more or less autocratic family structure appears to be necessary as a preconditioning environment to buy some time for the recovering addict. This time is then used to administer doses of an inner-directed philosophy such as that outlined in Ralph Waldo Emerson's essay entitled "Self-Reliance." If it seems paradoxical that an authoritative environment tends to produce inner direction, it must be remembered that the inner-directed men of the 19th century—viz., Emerson, Thoreau, Oliver Wendell Holmes, Longfellow—were products of an authoritative family structure. It might also be remembered that intellectual, emotional, and spiritual food fed to the recovering addicts while in the climate is rather carefully selected.

"The autocratic overtone of the family structure demands that the patients or members of the family perform tasks as part of the group. If a member is able to take direction in small tasks such as helping in the preparation of meals, house cleaning, etc., regardless of his rebellion at being 'told what to do,' his activity seems to provide exercise of emotions of giving or creating which have lain dormant. As these emotional muscles strengthen, it seems that the resistance to cooperating with the group tends to dissipate. During this time a concerted effort is made by the significant figures of the family structure to implant spiritual concepts and values which will result in self-reliance. Members are urged to read from the classics and from the great teachers of mankind—Jesus, Lao-tse, Buddha, etc. These efforts have been successful to a rather surprising degree. The concept of an open mind is part of a program to help the addict find himself without the use of drugs.

"The sharing of emotional experiences seems to encourage in the family structure a tolerance and permissiveness within rather loosely defined limits in which the addict who wants to recover feels sufficiently comfortable to stay and buy himself time. This permissiveness, of course, does not include the taking of any form of addictive substance. It is stressed, for instance, to everyone that no addictive personality can take anything which will have an effect on his mind. The ingestion of alcohol, opiates, barbiturates, tranquilizers, or psychic energizers is strictly fobidden. Permissiveness in the area of verbal resistance or rebellion to authority is

encouraged rather than discouraged. The insistence is on performance. For example, if it is suggested that one of the boys or girls
help in the kitchen, he is free to 'gripe,' 'beef,' as loudly as he
wishes, but it is required that he comply in the area of action. It has
been observed that the verbal rebellion towards authority seems to
relieve inner tension, and that compliance in the action area seems
to exercise the 'muscles of giving.'

"Another device which in the opinion of the foundation has
been successful, and which is paradoxical in the extreme, is the
'haircut.' The 'haircut' is a session which is attended by relatively
new patients and four or five of the significant figures of the family
structure, during which the patient is 'taken apart' and his performance to date, both constructive and destructive, is pointed out to
him, together with suggestions for his future behavior. These sessions may even contain tones of the 'third degree' and may become
quite brutal, on a verbal level, of course. Surprisingly, the patient's
reaction has been almost 100 percent favorable. As one of our members put it, 'When the word gets around that haircuts are being
given, people seem to get in line.'

"It might be that this device awakens in the subconscious of the
patient a realization that someone cares about him. It may satisfy a
desire to be the center of attention. It may help to make him realize
that a loving father must also be a firm father. Many of the people
who have experienced these 'haircuts' reported a change in attitude or a shift in direction almost immediately. There is, of course,
no policy as to timing, and many times a 'haircut' session will be in
no way critical. They seem to be guided only by intuition.

"Another device which has seemed to produce beneficial results is the 'synanon.' The synanon can be defined broadly as a
kind or type of group psychotherapy. Synanon, which is a coined
word, is used to describe a more or less informal meeting, which
ideally consists of three male patients and three female patients
plus one Synanist who is himself an addictive personality, but who
has managed to arrest the symptoms of his addiction for some
considerable length of time, or seems to be progressing at a rate
somewhat faster than his colleagues in the meeting. The Synanist
acts as moderator and, by virtue of an empathy which seems to
exist between addictive personalities, is able to detect the patient's
conscious or unconscious attempts to evade the truth about himself. The methods employed by a Synanist in a synanon meeting
may include devices or weapons which appear to be unorthodox,

but such surprisingly beneficial results have occurred in an encouraging number of cases that we feel we must further explore the method.

"The Synanist leans heavily on his own insight into his own problems of personality in trying to help the patients to find themselves, and will use the weapons of ridicule, cross-examination, hostile attack, as it becomes necessary. These synanon sessions seem to provide an emotional catharsis and seem to trigger an atmosphere of truth-seeking which is reflected in the social life of the family structure. The Synanist does not try to convey to the patient that he himself is a stable personality. In fact, it may very well be the destructive drives of the recovered or recovering addictive personality embodied in a Synanist which make him a good therapeutic tool—fighting fire with fire."

THE EVOLUTION OF THE THERAPEUTIC COMMUNITY MOVEMENT

During the early years of Synanon, many people, including mental health professionals, visited Synanon and studied its methodology. Many psychiatrists, psychologists, and social workers selected various Synanon techniques and incorporated them into their own private or institutional systems.

The major evolution and development of the TC movement involved the replication of Synanon-like therapeutic communities in other locations by Synanon graduates, and some professionals who believed in the Synanon system.

Jesse Pratt, a former heroin addict, was a pioneer in this evolutionary aspect of the TC movement. Jesse, based on his three-year Synanon experience and his firm belief that Synanon worked, founded the TC Tuum Est in Venice, Calif. Jesse's story is a prototypical case in point of the type of criminal-addict helped by Synanon in the early days.

The fact that Jesse was able to straighten out in Synanon, and then create the first replica of the Synanon TC, is a remarkable dimension of the TC movement. There were many other recovered addicts who later followed in Jesse's footsteps.

Chuck Dederich remembered Jesse from the early days, and how he had become a valuable role model in the club for younger addicts. According to Chuck: "Jesse inspired many addicts to clean up—because they felt that if someone like Jesse could make it, so could they. When Jesse moved in, he had a vague desire to quit using drugs and to get his parole officer's approval. He was a big-time loser, with a lengthy addiction and prison record. He had a criminal jacket of complete incorrigibility in the prison and parole system.

"Around the time he showed up at Synanon, he had just been released from prison. His parole officer got him a job, and Jesse was working about ten hours a day and going home to sit in front of a television set, trying to stay clean. He was in terrible shape as a result of not using drugs. He came down to the club one night, and I told him about our program. He came back the following night and we laid it on the line to him. We said, 'You have to quit your job and move into the club.' Jesse, partly to placate his parole officer, moved in."

In a penetrating interview I had with Jesse later on, he told me his side of his story.

"I was a gutter hype. I have known guys who could fix two or three times a day and be content. Unfortunately for me, I couldn't. I was greedy. I was sicker: my need was greater. I don't know for sure, but I managed to spend hundreds a day for dope, and I had to steal the money.

"I wasn't a big-time gangster-type guy who made his money in lump sums. I was a scared, cautious, short-con, petty-thieving dope fiend and my money was mostly acquired in dribbles or small amounts.

"A typical day in my life started in the morning when, with tears in my eyes, sniffles in my nose, and sweat oozing from my pores, I'd make it to my stash and put my 'get-up' in my veins. When I left the pad, I knew I was on my way to commit a crime to get some money. Most of the time, I didn't have the slightest idea what type of crime it would be or where. Sometime within the next two or three hours I would commit a crime, get some money, buy some dope, and 'fix.' I would repeat this over and over throughout the day, and for months.

"Recreation and pleasures, big or small, are luxuries I could not afford because all my money was set for the 'connection man' and there didn't seem to be enough hours in a 24-hour day.

"I used heroin for about 16 years and I spent about ten of the 16 years locked up in jails and other kinds of institutions.

"Before I came to Synanon, I had given up on myself. I had tried almost everything in the way of therapy and nothing worked. I had private consultation with a psychiatrist, group therapy with a psychologist and a sociologist, and until the day I walked into Synanon, the longest period of time I was 'clean' on the street was for a day or two—or when I was locked up."

After being clean for three years in Synanon, Jesse left, stayed clean, and worked at a steady job. In 1965 he founded the TC he named Tuum Est ("It's up to you") in Venice, Calif. modeled after Synanon. It was started with the help of a psychiatrist, Dr. Thomas Ungerleider, a professor at the University of California at Los Angeles, and several other community leaders.

The direct spinoffs from Synanon residents and graduates include, among many others, Jesse Pratt's Tuum Est; the Delancey Street Foundation started by John Maher, a Synanon graduate, and later directed by Dr. Mimi Silbert, a professional criminologist; and Amity in Tucson, Ariz. founded by three former Synanon residents, Naya Arbiter, Betty Fleishman, and Rod Mullen.

Two Synanon offshoots, Daytop Lodge and Phoenix House, both in New York were founded by psychiatrists Dr. Daniel Casriel and Dr. Mitch Rosenthal. These two TCs were highly significant in the movement because, in addition to their own important work in New York City, they were instrumental in exporting the TC approach to Europe.

These varied replications of Synanon created the impetus that evolved into a national—then a worldwide—movement. These developments culminated in the 1970s with the creation of two significant therapeutic community organizations: (1) Therapeutic Communities of America (TCA) and (2) the World Federation of Therapeutic Communities (WFTC). The TCA organization, among other functions, accredits ex-addict paraprofessionals for staff work in TCs. The WFTC meets annually in countries around the world. Hundreds of TC practitioners attend these world conferences, and present significant theoretical and research papers on various aspects of TC developments. In 1984, the WFTC met in Rome: in 1985, in San Francisco; and in 1986, in Stockholm; and in 1988 will convene in Bangkok.

Two important pioneers in the worldwide movement are Dr. Mitch Rosenthal of Phoenix House, and the director of Daytop, Monsignor William O'Brien. These men and their staffs were vital to the creation and development of TCs in, among other places, England, Sweden, Italy, South America, Australia, and the Far East.

In his address to the Ninth World Conference of Therapeutic Communities in San Francisco in 1985, Monsignor O'Brien, then president of the WFTC, eloquently summarized some of these burgeoning international developments in a snapshot of the world movement:

"There is no doubt that the therapeutic community is one of the most potent treatment modalities in helping individuals achieve change. The elimination of the symptom, be it substance abuse or other disorders, is only part of the treatment and help. We achieve change as a result of meeting the needs of individuals by providing the necessary services. The greatest need is a sense of community, a sense of belonging, and this is what the therapeutic community provides as it effectively deals with the pains of modern man—loneliness and alienation. The key, then, is that the therapeutic community deals with root causes rather than merely treating symptoms.

"As president of the World Federation of Therapeutic Communities, I have traveled extensively around the world visiting programs, and I am pleased to report that I was reassured by what I saw. One cannot help but be deeply impressed by the basic strength of our movement. That strength is reflected in the individual programs, in their dynamic development, and, above all, in their dedicated staff.

"In people like Lars Bremberg and the outstanding job he is doing in leading the TC movement in Scandinavia. In Sweden alone, Vallmotorp and Daytop, the two sister foundations, have a total of 300 beds located in seven different houses and are still expanding. A short-term treatment program will be opening in October, and Lars is now overseeing the training and development of a TC staff in Thailand.

"In the Pacific, Roy Johnston of Australia has been tirelessly and generously working on behalf of the TC movement as president of the recently established Asian/Pacific Federation of Therapeutic Communities.

"In Ireland, we have seen the growth and expansion of Coolemine under the leadership of Jim Comberton and Tom McGarry. Our congratulations go to Jim on his recent election to the presidency of the European Federation of Therapeutic Communities.

"In England, Phoenix House, under the creative leadership of David Tomlinson, now has centers across Great Britain where the age range is 18 to 25 years. They were recently honored by a visit from Prince Charles.

"In Italy, the programs of the Centro di Solidarieta continue to thrive and flourish under the dedicated leadership of Don Mario Picchi and Juan Corelli. In October, there will be the formal dedication of their new center in Rome. In northern Italy, we have witnessed the miracle of Avanzini! Monsignor Avanzini has done a truly remarkable job in developing and directing a thriving, vital TC in Verona. He recently acquired an abandoned airport, and on this site he will soon be opening what has been described as a modern-day 'boys town'. The World Federation can now boast its very own 'Father Flanagan'!

"In South America, through the dedicated work of Juan Alberto Yaria and Miguel Angel Bianucci of Argentina, the Latin American Federation of Therapeutic Communities was recently created, and this bodes well for the movement in South America.

"Under the expert guidance of Peter Vamos, Portage has experienced tremendous growth and is Canada's largest drug-free treatment program.

"Here in the United States, the Therapeutic Communities of America has thrived and reached new heights of achievement under the leadership of its president, David Mactas. Its member programs throughout this country are setting a new standard of excellence which makes us all very proud.

"I apologize that, due to obvious time constraints, I have been able to name but a few of the many individuals and programs generously giving of themselves and contributing so much to the world therapeutic community movement. I wish I had more time to name all of you, but you know who you are. And so, to all of you, for recognizing the problems as well as the potential with which we are faced, I salute you....

"As the 'healing family,' the therapeutic community has the healing power to foster the transformation of our lost, alienated youth into responsible, caring, productive individuals *impelled to help others find the same happiness.* [My emphasis.] It is in the therapeutic community that a true revolution of the spirit takes place, and we must never lose this. Rather than being discouraged by substance abuse and related disorders of our young, we have the opportunity to accept the challenge it presents. As our host program for this conference is Walden House, it seems only fitting to recall the words of Henry David Thoreau in *On Walden Pond*: "'If one advances confidently in the direction of his ideas, and endeavors to live the life which he has imagined, he will meet with a success unexpected in common hours.' With this in mind, together this week, let us advance in the direction of our dreams in our quest for a relevant, dynamic and vital worldwide therapeutic community movement."

INNOVATIONS AND MODIFICATIONS OF
THE ORIGINAL SYNANON MODEL

My research into various TCs around the world reveals that they have incorporated the basic social structure and methodologies of the original Synanon. However, each TC has developed innovative techniques relevant to its leadership orientation, the sociocultural ethos of the home community, and the pattern and types of substance-abuse problems manifested by the TC's residents.

The Amity TC in Tucson, Arizona is an example of the blending of the type of leadership, the sociocultural aspects of the community in which it operates, and the characteristics of the TC's residents. Amity's leaders effected innovations and modifications of the original Synanon model to fit their unique situation. The rationale for the Amity TC system is cogently described in the following communication I received from one of Amity's directors, Naya Arbiter. Naya, a former addict, lived and worked in Synanon for seven years prior to founding Amity in 1981 with two other former Synanon residents, Betty Fleishman and Rod Mullen. She wrote the following statement in response to my question: "In what ways is Amity different from the original Synanon?"

"It has been our perception that for some time the majority of TC programs in the United States are run off a Xerox machine—the early Synanon years serving as the master copy. In the 1977 Chairman's Conference, even Chuck and Betty Dederich expressed vehemently that there needed to be some 'new steps to the dance' in terms of dealing with character disorders. We have tried to develop some new steps based on our past failures...

"In developing Amity we went back to the roots of the movement and reexamined the notion and definition itself: therapeutic community. Since the phrase originated with Moreno, we began to think in terms of a therapeutic community as being an exercise in residential psychodrama. This forced a new level of detail in terms of getting intimately familiar with the details of situations in people's lives; opened doors in terms of allowing and encouraging people to *act out* making amends, *act out* their anger, and their need for family.

"It also makes it safer for people to act out affection and concern. Having people act out their amends instead of only paying them lip service seems to have a particularly beneficial effect on those considered hopeless.

"Einstein made the point that he had little respect for scientists who took a plank and drilled where the drilling was easy. We have tried to drill where the drilling is hard. Starting with the obvious premise that women were underserved, we extended our services to them and then began circling out. Since August of 1981, in addition to accepting those people who have come to our doors in need, we have gone after those people who are considered even within the major treatment communities as undesirable. These include but are not limited to the following: those who have repeatedly failed in other therapeutic communities and treatment centers, including former counselors who are frequently the most cynical and disruptive; Hispanics and native Americans; men who have done five years or longer of hard prison time; women convicts (a hard group to impact, virtually voiceless in our society); severely institutionalized adolescents—boys and girls; women with children; women with histories of prostitution; and men with histories of prostitution and homosexual rape.

"The following is a list of things that we changed that distinguish us from other therapeutic communities.

"1. Female director and predominantly female staff.

"2. Women engaged in extensive self-disclosure, particularly in the areas of sexuality, child rearing, prison and prostitution experiences, and rape.

"3. No rigid phase structure toward graduation.

"4. No staff person could ask any resident to do anything that [he or she] would not and had not done [himself or herself].

"5. Use of animals as pets, particularly for severly institutionalized male convicts with histories of violence.

"6. Inclusion of families, and encouragement for contact *within* the environment of people who knew each other 'from the streets.' In Amity we currently have: a 50-year-old alcoholic with his 19-year-old son (also an alcoholic): a 40-year-old black women (ex-addict) her 20-year-old son, and his 10-year-old son; a 40-year-old man (ex-convict) who had served time for rape and armed robbery and his 22-year-old daughter, 19-year-old son, and two grand-children.

"7. Experimentation with the format of the marathon long-term groups including 'ceremonies.' An effort is made to be as multi-cultural as possible. For instance, we might have everyone gather in a 'prayer circle' and have each person say a prayer from [his or her] religious base, or tell a story from [his or her] culture. Too often in some TCs the TC *becomes* the culture and people feel cut off from their roots.

"8. Eliminated the majority of 'compression/confrontive' grouping in marathon groups or retreats, and substituted formal-ized directed sessions with people telling their personal histories.

"9. The history of therapeutic communities is taught starting with the Oxford Group up to the development of Synanon.

"Observations of note as a result of the above:

"1. The length of stay has increased considerably, and there are fewer splittees.

"2. The more women engaged in self-disclosure and partici-pated in women's retreats, the safer the environment seemed to become for men. (Men began to talk more freely about homosex-uality, and some men began to admit to having raped women.) Men with extensive prison histories seem particularly affected.

"3. Staff increasingly finds itself trying to address the question of fear. Dederich once said that you can 'teach them to stay off drugs but you can't teach them to stop being frightened.' We have tried to do as many things in the environment to represent safety and 'antiinstitutionalization' as possible. This ranges from: the in-clusion of resident's families here; tucking hardened convicts in to bed at night; encouraging physical affection; and a disciplined *lack* of 'King Freak–Head Honcho' symbolism in the environment. Each facility has an outdoor pavillion (chapel) that is a gathering place where confrontational groups *cannot* be held but community gath-erings, commemorations, rituals, and celebrations of life are the norm. These were formed at the request of residents. There is also a history room (the Betty Dederich Room) where any person can go regardless of status in the community and meditate on his or her life. This is by design one of the nicest and more comfortable rooms on the property.

"4. In the marathon group experiences, people have begun to arrange themselves spontaneously into psychodramas. One In-dian male resident who confessed to raping numerous white women and about ten women organized themselves in a group. There was considerable emotional catharsis as each woman who had been raped in her life went before the man, and told him of her rape, she psychodramatically talked to him as if he were the rapist. He sat silently through each encounter until he regressed and began talking psychodramatically to his 'mother', who had substantially abused him.

"5. Residents spontaneously replay emotional incidents that had occurred prior to their coming to Amity; and then move toward a resolution to find mechanisms for forgiveness.

"Our encouraging people to act out these emotional events with each other is fostering more mechanisms for forgiveness of others and self."

NEW DIRECTIONS: 1990

The central theoretical and methodological elements of TCs such as Amity, Tum Est, Delancey Street, Daytop, Phoenix House, the Italian Ce.I.S., and others will be described and analyzed throughout the book. In summary, however, following are some of the innovations and new directions for TCs that I have observed in the process of my research into TCs around the world.

Professionals

Traditional professionals—psychiatrists, psychologists, and social workers—have become more significant figures in the operation of TCs. For example, psychiatrist Dr. Martien Kooymen, after closely studying Synanon in the early years, was personally and professionally responsible for the development of a number of TCs in Holland. Using the original model, he effectively staffed the Dutch TCs with both traditional professionals and ex-addicts.

This professional influence has infused TCs with relevant and viable social–psychological theories, techniques, and methods. The fusion of the classic Synanon concept with contemporary mental-health-treatment approaches has produced a highly successful treatment system.

Leadership Roles

The charismatic, autocratic, male leader, represented by founder Chuck Dederich, has been modified in most TCs. Given the degree of fallout and problems created in some TCs by being dependent on a single powerful male leader, many recent TCs have taken precautions to spread the power among several people — including women. Notable in this regard is the already described Amity TC in Arizona, which is directed by a troika of two women, Naya Arbiter and Betty Fleishman, and one male, Rod Mullen. At Delancey Street the leadership role is shared by John Maher, a charismatic ex-heroin addict, and Dr. Mimi Silbert, a professional criminologist and social psychologist. The Italian TC movement was founded by Mario Picci, a priest, and is directed by Juan Corelli, a former theater arts director, and Tony Gelormino, a former New York addict. In brief, there are many new and different arrangements of leadership models in TCs everywhere.

Preparation for Entrance

In some TCs, notably those in Italy, a considerable amount of TC counseling and group time are spent on preparing the addict for entrance into a TC. In Italy's Ce.I.S. program, the addict begins, while still in the community, to quit drugs; and to acknowledge and begin working on many of the family problems that exist with his or her parents. Consequently when the person enters a TC and moves into residence, he or she is further along in the treatment process, and has a greater chance of becoming a successful graduate.

Another modification in TCs is that the early Synanon tough indoctrination approach, in which the newcomer was grilled about his or her sincerity, has changed into a more sympathetic interactional intake procedure. The tough, "prove you want to change" intake procedure has been modified. Most TCs now use a more analytic approach to examine each applicant in terms of his or her individualistic needs and suitability for the TC program.

Confrontation Methods

The encounter group is still a fundamental group method in all

TCs; however, there is a much greater emphasis on analytic and supportive group and individual methods. In this regard great care is given in TCs to see that every resident has a supportive individual sponsor or friend to whom he or she can turn when emotionally distressed or depressed. In most TCs a considerable amount of time is provided for caring, supportive discussions, one on one, outside of the various group sessions. Although confrontation and encounter are valuable for dealing with nonresponsive and self-deceptive behavior, more than equal time is given to contemplating and discussing personal problems in a caring environment that allows for introspection, and psychological analysis.

Full Disclosure

In some TCs, notably Amity, a considerable amount of time and effort are spent on having people scrupulously examine their lives—and purposefully disclose many of the secrets they have kept about themselves most of their lives. This focus has produced considerable disclosures by both men and women about prototypical physical and sexual abuse and neglect during early childhood years. The exposure of this information is often necessary for helping addicts understand past problems. This facilitates a theraeutic process for the person's "hurt child"—so that he or she can move forward in life with greater trust and freedom from fear in positive relationships.

Spiritual–Religious Issues

Most TCs are not based on any specific religious principles or expectations; however, there appears to be a movement for residents to pursue their personal religious–spiritual proclivities. For example, at Amity, partly related to the Arizona Native-American Indian influence, spirituality is part of the program. There are a number of outdoor chapels where meditation, weddings, celebrations, and personal prayer take place. The strengthening of a resident's spiritual or religious life is now a significant but not mandatory vector in the addict's recovery in contemporary TCs.

Training for Graduation

In the early days of Synanon, there was a general three-phase program: (1) residence; (2) living in and working out; and (3) graduating, working out, and maintaining contact. This was changed at one point to a lifetime commitment to residence in Synanon. The viewpoint now current in almost all TCs is to prepare the resident for his or her return to a life in the larger society upon graduation. This model is the most logical one since most residents ultimately want to assume a viable role, with a traditional family, in their society. Some residents, after graduation, make a decision to work as a paid paraprofessional in the TC they "grew up" in, or another TC. This is also a viable and desirable goal for the ex-addict graduate.

Democracy Versus Autocracy

There was a basic principle in Synanon and some early TCs that newcomers were "emotional babies" who required autocratic control in their first few months in the TC. This concept has a certain amount of logic; however, increasingly TCs are getting addicts in residence who, apart from the alcoholism or addiction, are occupationally and socially mature people. These individuals tend to require a shorter residency—and a more significant role early on in the power structure of the TC. The trend in contemporary TCs is to allocate more power to people in all strata of the organization. There is a logical trend toward greater democratic input into the decision-making apparatus of the overall social structure of the TC by all residents in the organization.

Marathons, Retreats, and Psychodrama

Early TCs, including Synanon, utilized lengthy group and many weekend marathon sessions in their treatment approach. Increasingly these processes, which break down inhibitions and foster greater self-disclosure and awareness, have become significant methods for treatment in almost all TCs. This approach includes marathons, retreats, and psychodramatic methodologies. (These are discussed in greater detail in Chapter 5.)

Family Systems Treatment

A major development in TCs has involved the recognition that the addict's family, in most cases, should become part of the treatment process. In this regard, a resident's family, in most TCs, is encouraged to participate in the program. This takes the form of visits, group family sessions, and parent counseling. This family treatment factor is vital to the resident's future success. An addict, upon graduation from a TC, is bound to have difficulty staying clean—if someone in his or her family is a substance abuser. Involving the resident's family in the therapeutic process is a necessary ingredient in an effective TC program, and the sociometric concepts developed by Moreno are utilized in dealing with the resident's family as an interactional system.

New developments and directions cited here have become integral elements in the growing success of the international TC movement. All of these conceptual and methodological developments are discussed more fully in the the balance of the book.

3

Family Issues:
Intake and Treatment

In an old British B movie there is a poignant and humorous scene where the central character, a professional spy who is seldom home, is saying goodbye to his wife. They have just had a bitter discussion about his wife's past as an alcoholic and the fact that she had become a nondrinker. As he leaves, he turns and tells her, "You know, Sally, I liked you a lot better when you were drinking." Regrettably this type of attitude, which is seldom out in the open, is very common among members of the families of addict-alcoholics. This hidden resistance is only one factor in a family situation that may impede the addict from joining a TC program that will help him or her become drug-free.

There are a number of other family factors that can get in the way of the addict-alcoholic joining a program that may effect a positive change. The addict-alcoholic is often the "identified patient" in the family. He or she may be addicted because of the social forces at work in the family, and the acting out may be a result of these forces. This situation often blockades seeking help because the people involved usually want to maintain the equilibrium of the situation. Like the Indian fakir who sleeps more comfortably on a bed of nails than on a featherbed, the addict and family become accustomed to their difficult condition. Even though it is painful, it is familiar. Consequently the "normal" addictive situation, and a fear of the unknown, may keep the addict from seeking help with the unconscious collusion of his or her family.

The classic example of this is the wife or husband who overtly claims he or she wants the spouse to become drug-free, but on an unconscious level fears this change. As one man revealed to me in a therapeutic session: "If she cleans up her drug habit, what would a beautiful young girl like her want with a guy like me?" The insecure coaddict is often afraid of losing his or her partner.

Another factor that often blocks an addict from entering a TC is that he or she is still playing around with AA's step one—"admitting we are powerless over alcohol and our lives have become unmanageable." Voluntary entrance into a TC involves a clear self-admission that the abused substance is in charge of the addict's life—and most addicts tend to deny this fact, often to the bitter end.

Some addicts simply do not want to disrupt their life-styles in the open community. They may accept help in an outpatient clinic rather than separate from their families and friends. Unless an addict is running the streets, or is in really bad shape, he or she is usually resistant to making the extreme move of entering a live-in treatment center.

The degree to which a person is addicted is often not completely clear. Consequently anything less than having his or her life totally out of control sets up an alibi for not getting treatment.

Therefore, when an addict decides, for whatever reason, to stop using drugs, it is usually not his or her individual decision. There may be family pressure, a pending court case, or suicidal tendencies, or the person may have run into a wall of depression regarding life as an addict. As a result, the motivation to quit drugs at a particular point is usually the result of a variety of factors, which may have little to do with the level of addiction.

When the addict arrives at the entrance of the TC, he or she is not alone, but brings along many issues that relate to the addiction, and foremost in this complex of factors in the network of relationships with family and friends. As indicated, some of the latter are proponents for the addict's drug-free future, whereas others, overtly or covertly, are part of the problem, in the sense that they are coaddicts or enablers who reinforce the addict's drug abuse.

Although the identified patient, the addict represents a network of friends and family who are involved in the problem. Most TCs take these factors into account in their intake process, and they should be considered as the backdrop for all TC intake approaches.

THE INTAKE PROCESS

In most TCs the addict is not automatically accepted into the program. The entering addict is usually forced, in an intake interview, to state the reasons for entering, and to convince the intake committee of the sincere desire to change his or her life. In Italian TCs the addict is often placed in a preentry motivation group for one to six months before acceptance into the program. In most TCs if space is available, an addict may be accepted rather quickly, if he or she convinces the intake committee of a serious intent to become drug-free.

Another factor in the intake process of many TCs is that the interviewers often tell prospective residents that they are not too optimistic about their future. This is in contrast to the optimistic approach of most traditional programs whereby a prospect is told: "Underneath it all you're a wonderful person. If you cooperate with our program, we're sure we can help you stop using drugs." In most cases the addict does not believe the optimistic message. Underneath a facade of volunteering for treatment, most addicts believe that their problem cannot be solved. Therefore, when the intake interviewer is too optimistic, the addict doesn't believe the prognosis, and may not trust the program. The addict is often suspicious of people who see him or her as a "wonderful person" because the addict knows the deceits he or she has practiced with friends and loved ones to obtain and use drugs or alcohol.

Because of these issues, Synanon pioneered and developed an intake interview for TCs that is markedly different from those utilized in most traditional programs in that it makes it difficult for the prospect to enter. First an addict-prospect is told to sit on a bench at the door to await the intake interview, which can sometimes mean for hours. Then the person is taken into a room by an intake committee of ex-addicts and grilled about "why the person wants to quit using drugs and join the program." In brief, the addict is forced to prove he or she is sincere and to fight to get into the organization. This often produces a high level of initial motivation.

I have interviewed hundreds of addicts who entered Synanon and other TCs where this tough, resistant intake approach was used; and the following comment by one ex-addict succinctly reveals most addict's response to this type of procedure. "My real motivation to quit drugs at the point of entry was zero. Mainly I wanted to rest for awhile and lower my need for drugs. I had every intention of using again later on. I just wanted a break from my heavy habit. They saw through my game; and told me they did not want to waste their time on someone who didn't want to go the distance. Also, when they questioned my motives and gave me no real assurance of a cure, I began to trust them. I felt they really knew who they were dealing with. They told me I was probably lying about quitting drugs. They were tough and they were talking directly and honestly to me. This gave me some confidence that maybe I was in the right place. Also, because they had been addicts themselves, I saw some proof positive in front of me that the place worked.

"I, like most addicts, had entered four or five other programs, where I had failed. In those places the professional therapist or doctor was optimistic about curing me. This optimism was a turn-off because I felt he didn't know the real me, and I didn't trust him. In the TC intake interview where they acted like they didn't know whether they could help me, and they weren't sure they were going to take me in, I began to fight my way in. This resistant honest attitude was somehow reassuring, and from the beginning it got me motivated to become drug-free."

The indoctrination, or initial interview, is important in that it establishes a "contract" of conditions for therapeutic intervention. At first some token road blocks are thrown in the way of the person who is attempting to enter. He or she may be given an appointment and made to wait. If even a few minutes late for the appointment, the person is told to come back another time. As one ex-addict professional stated, "I had to begin to learn some discipline in front and demonstrate some level of commitment." If it is indicated, some amount of money is requested as an entrance fee based on the ability of the families to pay. In general, an effort is made to have the individual fight to get into the organization in order to prove his or her commitment and sincere wish to quit the habit— and get well.

In summary, the TC intake interviews are geared to the emotional and physical conditions of the addicts. Those who are very sick from their addiction and thus vulnerable are welcomed aboard more easily than others. In most indoctrinations, however, a tough approach is used in order to inspire some motivation and commitment to joining the program.

Following is a dialogue typical of that in this case in a *tough* intake interview, with a New York cocaine-heroin addict. There are four intake interviewers, all senior members of the TC. They all participate in the interview; however, Jack who is a director of the organization, takes the lead.

"Interviewer" Jack: My first question is: Why are you at the front door of our home? What do you want from us?

Prospect: I want to stay here and I want to get away from New York City and I want to change my way of life.

Interviewer: Why do you want to stay here? Why do you want to stay away from New York? You still have not answered the question.

Prospect: Because I'm sick of the rat race I've been going through.

Jack: What kind of rat race? Do you chase cheese? Are you on a merry-go-round? What do you do? Are you a bricklayer who doesn't like laying bricks any more? Or are you a carpenter who doesn't like driving nails, as I didn't? What do you do that you find so obnoxious? You're unhappy. What makes you unhappy?

Prospect: Well, I'm in and out of jails, taking narcotics. I'm just trying to get off it. I've been trying for years to get off it, in jails and hospitals. Other places accept me for a couple of weeks, they detoxify me, then they throw me back out in the street, and say, 'Go ahead, stay off drugs.' It doesn't work.

Interviewer: How long have you been using drugs?

Prospect: Well, since the first time, it's been close to ten years.

Interviewer: And how old are you?

Prospect: I'm 26.

Interviewer: So you started using at 16, in high school?

Prospect: About 16½. No, I quit school, and right after that I started.

Jack: Why did you quit school?

Prospect: I don't know

Jack: But at the age of 16 you were getting bad marks and running around with the nuts that were slashing tires or stealing hubcaps, kind of like the rest of us sitting here. Right?

Prospect: Yes.

Jack: Were you living at home with your parents?

Prospect: Yes.

Jack: You still live with your parents?

Prospect: No, I had to move to my sister's house. You know, when I'm up tight and I have no place to go, she takes me in. As soon as I have enough money, I go out on my own again.

Jack: But you keep returning to some kind of family life. You keep returning to your momma or a momma substitute. That's one of the things wrong with guys like you and me and the rest of us in the room—the fact that we all have a great big need for momma, one we never really had.

We know that we all have some problems. Your problems are not what you think they are. Your problems are something that will come to you in time. It's going to take six months, maybe a year, for you to learn what they are. Eventually you're going to discover what your problems are. You have no idea what they are at this moment. None. If you knew what they were, you wouldn't be in the shape you're in.

We are a place established for people who can't seem to understand the way the world works. I'm beginning to understand the way the world works. I'm the resident director here. If we accept you, you'll be part of our family. You'll be the new element in the family. You'll be kind of like the new baby, I suppose. We'll talk in terms of family structure; it isn't bad. You'll be told when to talk and when not to talk, for awhile. You will kind of be told what to do for awhile. I guarantee you that if you go through the motions that we describe and prescribe for you, you'll end up being drug-free in time and a happier person than you are now.

If you are accepted here, we'll teach you how to scrub the floor. We'll teach you how to drive a car safely. We'll teach you how to meet people. We'll teach you how to understand others—and yourself, more important than anything else—and, you know, pretty soon you'll start to feel like a real person. This is a new experience for most of us addicts. Another thing we'd better straighten out here at the outset is that we have two cardinal rules. There is no physical violence or threat of it and there is no using of drugs or other chemicals or alcohol. No physical violence and no chemicals whatsoever.

You will find out another thing here in our community. At first, we are in the business of saying no to you. That's part of our business. Pretty soon we expect you to say, "I want to visit my sister." No! "I want five bucks." No! "I want to go to the movies." No! "I want to shoot dope." No! You know, that's the business we're in. We're going to tell you no for a long time. *Pretty soon you're going to learn how to say no to yourself.* Then you're going to find that there is nothing in the world that you really can't do, if you so choose. This takes time. In time you'll be in a position of being able to live anywhere in the United States and be a respected member of the community. This I guarantee you. But it's going to take time.

You know there's a big a chunk missing out of your life. Since the age of 16 you've had some kind of chemical rattling around in your bloodstream. This has caused you to miss all the world's important activities. All of life's stream has just kind of passed you by. A dope fiend is the kind of guy who knows nothing of his environment other than where he is going to get his drugs. We're going to open up your awareness. You may not agree with anything we say for awhile, but you're going to act as if it's all true. Take what we say on blind faith for awhile. Say, "All right, you're goddamned drug addicts yourselves. I'll go along with it, but I don't think any of it's worth a damn."

I don't care how you think. I don't care what you say in our encounter groups. But on the living-room floor or in the everyday business of life here, you kind of go through the motions of behaving yourself according to our rules or you'll get lost.

Join us 100 percent, with everything you got. Please don't bother your brain with trying to figure out a way to smuggle drugs in here or trying to figure out a way to con someone here into scoring drugs with you. Don't waste your time trying to fight the rules of our organization. You will not win. I guarantee it. I know the kind of guy you are, because I was one once myself. I was just like you. You will want to fight all the authority symbols in here.

So, you see, here you are. We offer you life as an adult in comparison with the life of a sniveling, whinning addict from the gutters of New York. You arrived here in a fine suit and a taxi. But I know who you are. You have no money. You have no property. You have nothing of any value. Your mother had to pay your way in here. You see, I know the facts. Work from that point. There's nothing wrong with this if you accept it as being true and grow up from there. You'll become a man. Don't fight the knowledge that's so clear to everyone in this room. Please. It just gets in the way of your progress.

Jack: So how do you like it? What do you think about my little sermon. Is it too tough for you to digest?

Prospect: I'll tell you, in the beginning you got me a little sore, but now what you're saying is making sense.

Jack: We don't expect you to make too much sense at first. In time, if you stay, if you listen, open up your ears, open up your eyes, kind of look around and see what's going on, you'll begin to make sense. Not only to me, but to yourself. That is more important than anything else in the world. You'll begin to make sense to yourself, and you'll find a little peace, a little comfort in life.

After the tough indoctrination, Jack engaged the newcomer in friendly conversation about various matters. This was surprising to him. However, he later learned to distinguish between the contentious, "tough" approach that was used during the indoctrination as part of the TC methodology in comparison with the more general pleasant and supportive atmosphere that was more characteristic of daily life in the TC.

The indoctrination attempts to pare newcomers down to their real emotional size. There is an attempt to get the newcomers to accept themselves overtly the way they really think of themselves inside.

Another characteristic of the indoctrination is to tell newcomers clearly and forcefully what will be expected of them: that they will have to work (at first on a menial level) and that they will have to follow the rules of the TC. In addition, they are given some information about the nature of the organization.

They are further informed that they automatically become part of the staff, because in a TC there is no "we–they" situation involving "prisoners and guards," "doctors and patients," or "inmates and staff." This tends to give newcomers an immediate sense of belonging. In the TC substance abusers can achieve any status in the organization. They can see this as a real possibility, because they know that the individuals confronting them were once addicts themselves.

Another element of a typical TC indoctrination intake interview is to anticipate and prevent rationalizations and excuses for failure. Newcomers are vigorously apprised "up front" of the rationalizations they might use to go out and use drugs. ("Don't even think about smuggling drugs in here.") This seems to have the effect of involving newcomers more quickly. It helps them to become increasingly aware that they are dealing with individuals who know them, and anticipate their thoughts. It engenders elements of trust and respect.

In the indoctrination the assertion is repeatedly made that the newcomer has a limited superego, or ability to control impulses. He or she is told that this self-control must initially be handled by the organization. ("You do not know how to say no yet, but you will learn.") After the prospect's usual low self-image is brought out into the open, he or she can relax about being "found out." The indoctrination has already exposed the prospect in part—and it is not necessary to keep up a "front" that impedes therapeutic progress.

Successful indoctrinations transmit a feeling of hope to new-comers and a belief in their own ability to succeed with people who really understand them because they were once in the same situation. All of this is a new experience, since, in the past, the addict may have been *involuntarily* brought into a prison or hospital, and quickly accepted as an inmate against his or her will.

According to one ex-addict professional, "When the addict arrives in his usual dazed condition, he feels more secure meeting a firmly defined situation. Too much acceptance or affection is something he can't handle at this time. His low self-esteem and enormous guilt about the terrible things he's done as an addict might activate him to run out the open door and smash himself once more."

The "firm hand" of the ex-addict experts the prospect meets in the intake interview is puzzling, and yet attractive and reassuring. It reduces the fear of the unknown, and the newcomer feels a sense of trust in people who have been in his or her shoes. Also, the newcomer's curiosity is often piqued by the spectacle of people with whom the newcomer did time or shot drugs functioning as executives!

Detoxification

In most TCs the addict is detoxified from his or her drug habit without the support of any drugs or chemicals, although some TCs do use a gradual detoxification process. Despite the popular conception of withdrawal sickness, kicking most habits, although quite uncomfortable, is reported not to be an extremely painful experience. This has been attested to by many addicts who have "kicked cold turkey" in TCs. Many alcoholics and pill abusers pose another problem—and some require a medical form of withdrawal before they enter a TC.

The ease of withdrawal from drugs in a TC may be attributed to several factors. In the first place, many drugs sold on the "street" these days have been significantly cut down by each link in the distribution chain, from the major crime-syndicate importer to the street addict. For example, with heroin or cocaine, the quality of the drug that ultimately reaches the average addict has been reported to be, on the average, 8–10 percent drug and 90 percent milk sugar (a white powder that gives the appearance of a drug). Thus, to a great extent, most drugs have a combined physiological and psychological impact, with considerable emphasis on the psychological response.

Despite this psychological factor, in many cases the addict, when drugs are withdrawn, may suffer not only the pain of withdrawal illness but that resulting from diseases of the kidney, liver, and other vital organs. There is much evidence that drug abuse masks physical pain symptoms. Because of this, when the drug is no longer used, a variety of medical problems that were masked by the anesthetic nature of the drugs often appear in the newcomer.

The expectation of pain from drug withdrawal is often compounded by the setting in which it takes place. In most hospitals dosages of drugs are prescribed for the withdrawing addict in decreasing quantities. The assumption here is that the addict will slowly withdraw physiologically. In some traditional hospitals, during decreasing drug withdrawal, the addict may receive the purest and most powerful drugs he or she has ever had. According to one addict, "At this hospital, during withdrawal I first learned about powerful drugs. I was never so well fixed in my life. I floated for two weeks. Just when I began to come to, the doctor would hit me again. I remember at breakfast once I was so loaded my head kept falling into the oatmeal."

In another setting, jail, withdrawal involves several factors in addition to the sheer physical illness associated with drug withdrawal. First, the addict is in a stressful human situation—locked up and confronted with the dire consequences of an imminent court experience. The addict is usually visited by distraught (often judgmental) friends or relatives, and also faces the real possibility of a long-term prison sentence. This set of difficult possibilities seems to blend with the physical discomfiture of drug withdrawal and cannot easily be separated out of the total negative situation.

In contrast with the difficulty of withdrawal from drugs in other settings, the TC provides a unique social setting for withdrawal. The withdrawing addict has already taken the first step by making a voluntary decision to attempt to eliminate the habit. In some TCs the addict is placed on a couch in the main living room, in full view of all members. Also, he or she is in a position to visit with residents, observe the activities in the TC and become better acquainted with the organization. Although he or she can leave at any time, the newcomer usually voluntarily remains because of a commitment made to himself or herself and partially to people in the TC who understand what he or she is experiencing. Moreover, most TCs are reasonably pleasant environments, entirely different from a prison or a cold, antiseptic hospital.

The hi-fi is usually playing, children may be in the room, and the newcomer receives warm drinks (eggnog, hot tea) and is physically soothed with occasional shoulder rubs. People will come over, shake the newcomer's hand, welcome him or her, and chat. Most important, he or she can literally see live successful ex-addicts—perhaps a "clean" ex-addict with whom the newcomer personally used drugs. Newcomers are encouraged to achieve the healthy physical and emotional condition of the people they see around them. They begin to learn about the organization from people who have experienced their current emotions. They see role models of achievable success. They are interacting with people who understand how they feel, many of whom were once in similar situations. In addition to understanding a newcomer's feelings, these people sketch a positive future they themselves are experiencing. These solid reference points provided by other TC members help to minimize the newcomer's psychic and physical withdrawal pains and speed his or her involvement with the group.

During the detoxification process, there is usually a series of indoctrinations and discussion groups for the newcomer. These are not rigorously formalized sessions. Some newcomers go right to work in the TC. At this point the addict is given a job in the TC commensurate with his or her limited ability at the time (for example, washing dishes, cleaning, mopping). This seems to provide a sense of security, satisfaction, and participation. Before the addict's mind can race too far in the wrong direction, toward drugs, he or she is involved in a variety of group sessions that integrate him or her further into the organization.

At the same time that all of this is going on, the newcomer meets a caring circle of friends who try to help and understand. With many newcomers there is an outpouring of deep personal emotion that may have been pent up for many years. In other institutional settings, they often had to maintain a "cool" image to get by. However, in a TC they are encouraged to let their hair down. At almost any time of the night or day, there is a friendly, understanding person available to hear about the newcomer's current and past difficulties. In some TCs, a kind of parental sponsor may be assigned to help the person become better integrated into the TC. He or she is encouraged to develop a caring circle of friends.

In an indoctrination lecture to a group that had been in Synanon for about 30 days, Dederich cogently revealed many of the issues of which a newcomer needs to be aware.

"Here's what we offer an addict, in simple terms. We offer an addict an opportunity to go to work for the Synanon Foundation. When you work for the Synanon Foundation, you get the necessities of life: you get shelter as good as we have, you get all the food you can eat, you get a pretty nice place to live; and if you continue to work for the Foundation for a month, two months, four months, or a year, eventually you'll be a pretty well-integrated human being. You've seen quite a few of them around here since you arrived, whether you recognize them or not. The small amount of work that you'll be required to do, any adult could do standing on his head in a hammock in about two hours a day. Your job will probably run from four to five hours a day.

"You will get the only therapy that works, more often than not, for narcotic addicts and alcoholics. In addition to your work, we demand certain standards of behavior around here for reasons known to us, but not to you, yet. Someday you quite possibly will understand it; you will if you get well, and then you'll see why we are insistent on certain standards of behavior. There is no 'we–they' situation here as there is in a prison.

"The minute you kick your habit, you become part of the staff. You become one of some hundred or so doctors, and then you yourself are a patient and you've got about a hundred doctors around you.

"We insist that you do your work and that you go to group sessions that are designed to help you. We insist that you stay clean and that you, to the best of your ability, behave like an adult human being. We provide group meetings three times a week, where you can have catharsis sessions, and learn why you are self-destructive, and often deceive yourself about your problems.

"You can sit in an encounter group there and ventilate your rage. There you can say to someone, 'How do you stand that guy Chuck who runs the joint?' That's fine. I want you to do that in that situation, but not in the building, at work, or in day-to-day situations. There we expect you to act like a normal person. You will behave yourself and you won't throw your weight around in this place, because you're an amateur. You don't know how to throw your weight around yet. Someday you'll learn how to assert yourself in a constructive manner. Now your behavior is quite obviously still self-destructive. We will teach you how to live constructively and happily here, and then in the outside society."

FAMILY ISSUES

The addict's entrance into and involvement in a TC, among other issues, involves a period of separation from past family relationships and becoming part of a new family and community. It also involves a difficult reorganization of almost all past relationships, especially the substance abuser's relationship to his or her family.

This transition period is often most difficult and complicated; however, it is firmly based on the concept that the TC is not treating an individual, but is treating the addict and the addict's "social atom" of relationships. In the community the addict was "acting out" in a self-destructive way. Some of his or her relatives, and friends were part of this web of relationships.

The typical addict, therefore, arrives at a TC not only with a habit, but also with a social background of some snarled and destructive past relationships. Most of these past associations had a negative effect. Some of the relatives or friends with whom the addict was intimate before and during the addiction were apt to be coaddicts or drug-using enablers. In AA terms a coalcoholic in subtle ways encourages or reinforces the addict's substance abuse.

It is important to note that there are some exceptions where parents, true friends, and relatives had *no* negative impact on producing or maintaining the addicts's self-destructive behavior. In fact they had, somehow in a positive way, been helpful in keeping the addict from totally going under. The following discussion, however, is mainly about the past negative associations and their destructive elements and impacts, because these past relationships played an important role in the substance abuser's life style.

The parents or spouses of many addicts either contributed to or "hooked in" to their addiction problems. In some cases they even used their addict's problem as rationalizations for their own failure. For example, one father, an alcoholic himself, vehemently claimed that he could not hold a job essentially because of his troublesome son. "You drive me to drink." In another typical case, a mother seemed morbidly to enjoy the addiction antics of her "terrible addicted daughter." It seemed to give her considerable material for her daily ritual of commiseration with her alcoholic friends at a neighborhood bar.

Parental Abuse:
Its Effect on Low Self-Concept and Substance Abuse

According to my own research and other research findings, many alcoholics and addicts who arrive for treatment have, in their childhood years, been abused or neglected by their family. As a consequence of this early socialization abusive treatment, they typically have a low self-concept.

In most cases they have used drugs or alcohol to deal with the pain of their family problems and consequential intense feelings of low self-esteem. In reaction to their conceived low self-concept, they tend to put on a facade of confidence and bravado. It is often, at first, difficult to penetrate that facade, and to reach the real person beneath the surface. The encounter groups in a TC in time will get through to the newcomer, and he or she will begin to open up and disclose any "secrets." These secrets usually encompass a feeling that no one, including parents, cares about the person, and he or she feels an enormous sense of loneliness, alienation, and low self-esteem. This last issue is one of the most significant problems that has to be dealt with in the addict's struggle for recovery.

Many individuals who experience a low self-concept were physically or sexually abused. Their substance abuse is often a self-administered treatment for their deeper feeling of low self-worth that was created by their being abused as children. Of course, not all substance abusers are victims of parental abuse. However, for many it is part of the causal context of their alcohol-drug problem. Following are a number of cases that reveal the dynamics of parental abuse and its effect on substance abuse.

Lisa

A prototypical example of such abuse relates to Lisa, whose case history can be summarized as follows.

Lisa, now 18, had one older and one younger brother. Her childhood was spent in the Southwest with her father, a skilled machinist, and her mother, a teacher. Lisa reported that when she was a child, her mother was physically abusive to her, at one point assaulting her in the face and breaking several teeth. Alienated from her mother, she looked to her father for protection. When she was 12, he began having sex play with her; she said she welcomed the attention despite the fact that she felt it "wasn't right." Shortly after this, her parents divorced and her father began living with another woman. Lisa began to run away from her mother's home until the courts granted custody to her father, because her mother stated that she could not control her.

The sexual play with the father continued, until, when Lisa was 14, the father, while drunk, forced her to have intercourse with him.

Lisa told her stepmother about the situation, but the step-mother refused to believe her, stating she was misinterpreting his "father affection." Thereafter intercourse occurred at least monthly for approximately one year, usually when the father was drunk. Lisa sought escape by using various drugs. At the age of 16, she was arrested for possession of drugs and put in an institution for juveniles. When she left the institution, she continued in a life of prostitution and substance abuse until she entered a TC at 18. In the program she learned, in the open group sessions, that many other women who became addicts had lived with abusive families such as this. This helped to reduce her feelings of alienation and low self-esteem. In time she began to like herself better, and later graduated into a healthier drug-free life-style.

Marta

The following case has some similarities to Lisa's. Marta entered a TC at the age of 21. The negative impacts of her parents' neglect and her spouse's abuses had impelled her finally to become a drug addict and prostitute. Marta used the variety of drugs available to adolescents and later became heavily addicted to heroin and cocaine. When she entered the TC her parents were not allowed to visit her for three months. A review of her case clearly reveals the logic of the TC administration policy not to permit such visits from Marta's parents, or her husband, during this period.

Marta had the textbook brand of problem family: a mother and father who were excessive drinkers, continually fighting, separating, then getting back together.

"They were never there when I needed them. They would just go away and leave me when I was a kid. I remember being alone most of the time as a child. They said they would be right back, and then they would go away, sometimes for a day or more. They would be out drinking, and when they got back drunk, there would usually be a fight.

"I still don't know how to explain it, but I began running away from home at the age of two. When I was three, I ran away so much that they made a chicken-wire fence and put me in this cage. I burrowed under it and ran away again. I remember a cop bringing me back on his shoulders.

"When my parents did take me anywhere, it would be to a bar. I remember how the drunks would call me cute. Sometimes they would put me to sleep in one of the booths in a bar while they got drunk.

"I was bad and rebellious from the first grade on, probably to get some attention. I felt very lonely. I wouldn't behave, and my parents were always being called to school. They seldom came, because they were always out either working or drinking. I don't blame them now; they were like children themselves, always arguing and fighting with each other.

"During my early teens, my mother and father separated several times. I seldom saw either of them, since both were dating and drinking. I lived with my mother some of the time and then with my father. I didn't have a home, since we were always moving around. I changed schools several times a year, and I never really got going in any school. It seemed that just when I would begin to get interested in a school, we would move. I began to run away from home and was labelled incorrigible.

"I was finally sent to a great finishing school—the State Reformatory for Girls. In the reformatory I learned about everything I hadn't learned about on the streets. My 'Countess' handle stuck with me. I ran with the toughest girls in the place. Once I got a weekend leave and scored in Los Angeles, ran drugs back into the place, and used with my girlfriends.

"When I left the institution, in no time flat I was back using drugs. That's when I met Bill. He was known around our group as an important dealer. I thought I was in love and latched onto him. We lived together for several years, using all the time. He kept me like a baby. I wore sheer nighties most of the time and just laid around in the pad. I would deal drugs for him if any customers showed up when he was out. He kept me well supplied, and I became totally dependent on him for my drugs. We decided to get married. Shortly after our marriage my husband was arrested and sent to prison for dealing drugs.

"I was all alone and I had to support my habit completely on my own. I began to earn money the only way I knew how. I was still attractive and had clothes. I began to develop a call-girl book, with the help of an older established Hollywood call girl. At first, I had good $50 and $100 tricks. Mostly they were older men in the garment industry. But I was a bad whore. I only earned enough money to keep up my habit. I would miss lots of appointments. I hated what I had to do and could only turn a trick if I was heavily loaded. I always fixed before I turned a trick.

I never tied up with any other person. I sometimes just walked the streets for hours all alone at night. I got busted [arrested] a few times and did some small jail bits. They never really pinned me. Finally I was sent to the Terminal Island Prison for a year.

"When I got out of there, I naturally went back to the streets. It was the only life I knew. I was desperately trying to quit. One day I heard about this TC from a connection. Somehow I got down there, and that was it. I've been clean for almost five years. The main thing I received in the TC beyond the group sessions and other techniques was a new family. I learned how my husband, my mother, my former so-called friends all reinforced my addictive life. I have successfully unloaded all of them and have a whole new set of drug-free friends, thanks to my two-year experience in the TC. It's taken me these five years to get rid of these bad influences and learn how to relate to people who *don't* do drugs. Now I'm remarried to a great guy who I met in the TC and we have a wonderful life."

Marta's family and spousal background clearly reveals the prototypical negative forces that produce an addict. Her drug use was related to her alcoholic parental role models, and her slide into a peer group of "friends" and a husband where drug abuse was "normal" behavior.

Andy

Another prototypical example of this low self-concept substance-abuse syndrome is revealed in 14-year-old Andy's story. He had been emotionally and physically abused, since the age of four, three to five times a week by his alcoholic father. The physical beatings and verbal abuses administered by his father often had little relationship to Andy's behavior. He would be beaten or verbally abused for such offenses as poor school grades or not keeping his room clean. He was beaten whenever his alcoholic father had a need to act out his personal frustrations using his son as a punching bag. According to Andy, "He would hit me or scream at me at times when I deserved it. Like I knew I did something wrong. He would also beat the shit out of me for no reason—just because he was loaded [drunk] and mad at the world. I've always felt like a punching bag, or maybe more like a piece of shit."

There were several consequences of Andy's father's irrational and indiscriminate behavior. The beatings and verbal abuse had the effect of producing low self-esteem in the youth. He tended to feel humiliated and worthless. As a result of these feelings, he felt he was a "loser" and did not deserve to feel he was a worthwhile person. He was demeaned by the most significant person in his life, his father. As Andy stated in a moment of self-revelation in a group: "If my own father thinks I'm a punk and a loser, maybe that's what I am." The result of these feelings of *low self-esteem* were acted out by Andy in self-destructive, substance-abuser behavior.

Jane

Another case in point of this syndrome was Jane who was successfully treated in a TC for adolescents. She had been sexually abused by her stepfather for three years. In addition to her drug problem, one of the fallouts from her sexual traumas was the practice of self-mutilation. She would slash herself with razor blades, and almost died on several occasions. She very obviously had a low self-concept and considerable rage, and did not care what happened to her.

In one encounter-group therapy session I directed, I delivered a diatribe about the deadly destructive effects of drug abuse and in conclusion remarked, "Drug addiction is a form of slow suicide." As I said this, I noticed Jane's eyes light up. I later asked her about her response, and she commented. "You're absolutely right. Now I know why I do drugs. I feel like a worthless piece of shit, and if I had enough courage, I would kill myself. I often feel, especially when I smoke crack, maybe I'll die painlessly and suddenly from the coke."

Pete

Another prototypical case involving child abuse, low self-esteem, suicidal tendencies, and substance abuse related to Pete, a 16-year-old with whom I worked in a TC hospital for substance abusers. Like many addicts, Peter had attempted suicide. He had stabbed himself in the chest with a hunting knife, and had almost died from this self-inflicted wound.

In a psychodrama session I ran with him, he acted out the complex dramatic episode that involved his suicide attempt. A number of dimensions of his feelings about his father, his low self-concept, and his reasons for using drugs emerged in the session.

In Pete's psychodrama a key dramatic episode involved a screaming battle with his father. In the core dialogue with his father, Pete screamed as he brandished a rolled-up magazine that represented a knife he had actually held in his hand during the real fight:

> Pete (to his father): You drunken M-F, you've been beating on me since I was a little kid. I'll never forget that day you threw me up against the wall when I was ten. And I really didn't do anything.
> Auxiliary Ego in the Role of Pete's Father: You deserved every beating I gave you.
> Pete: Bullshit. No kid deserves the things you did to me. I'm going to end this pain now. I'm going to kill you!

I intervened in the psychodrama at this point and used a psychodramatic technique known as a soliloquy.

> L.Y.: Pete, I want you to hold off your next move. Here you are in this terrible situation. Like Hamlet, just say your inner thoughts out loud.
> Pete's Soliloquy: I hate this alcoholic son of a bitch. He's never been a father to me. He doesn't deserve to live. With one move of this knife [the rolled-up magazine in his hand] I can wipe him out of my life, and get rid of all my pain... It's either him or me. [Begins to cry.] But there were times when he was good to me. We went to ballgames and fishing. I guess I love him, and maybe he's right about me. I'm no fucking good. I'm everything he's accused me of. I'm just a worthless punk drug addict. It's never going to work out, and I can't stand it any more."
> Sobbing, Pete stabbed himself in the chest with the symbolic knife in the psychodrama. This was the behavioral act he had

committed in *reality* that had resulted in his placement in the psychiatric hospital.

The session was a classic representation of many drug-addicted youths who have these conflicting emotional vectors at work in their life. They have low self-esteem because they have been physically and emotionally abused. They are full of rage toward the perpetrator of the abuse—in Pete's case, his father. They deal with their emotional pain by a self-administered treatment of drug abuse. Pete's drug-abusing suicidal tendencies resulted in his horrendous self-inflicted wound. In brief, it was almost a tossup between killing his father or himself. Peter believed that either act, killing his father or himself, in the context of his twisted desperate life, would end his emotional pain—the pain he attempted to control with heroin and cocaine.

In summary, child abuse and neglect have a deleterious impact that often results in substance-abusing behavior. The basic propositions that I would posit on this issue of self-concept to help explain the drug-addict consequence has several related characteristics: (1) The child (male or female) is abused (sexually or physically) or neglected by the primary socializing agent—the parents. (2) Because he or she is treated in negative ways with limited respect, the child feels humiliated, demeaned, and unworthy. As a consequence of the pattern of socialization, the child develops a low self-concept and feels self-hatred. He or she thinks, on some deeper emotional level; "If these important, powerful people in my life think that I am stupid, inadequate, and unworthy of love and respect I must be a terrible person," (3) Mixed with this low self-esteem the child develops a rage against the people—the parents— responsible for the abuse or neglect, and this rage is often modulated by drugs.

DESTRUCTIVE FAMILY PLOYS: ON TC RESIDENTS

Most newcomers arrive at a TC with the family configuration I have just described. In many respects the TC becomes for these people the caring, concerned family they never had in their original family. Perhaps for the first time in his or her life, the newcomer is exposed to an empathic family who can be trusted to deal fairly with their situation.

The administrators of most TCs are intensely aware of the potentially destructive relationships in the newcomer's past and try to deter their potential for disturbing the delicate balance of attachment the individual may have acquired in this new social situation. The TC policy of restricting visits by some former family members or "friends" to the newcomer is based on several specified assumptions. A guiding theme is that the newcomer addict is in effect an "emotional infant," and that some prior relationships encouraged, supported, or, at minimum, were incapable of deterring the individual's use of drugs.

Based on these assumptions, in the newcomer's early days in the TC, potentially deleterious social forces are virtually eliminated from the environment. The policy in part operates on the symbolic assumption that the healthy fetus of the newcomer has just become attached to the therapeutic environs of the new family. Any shock to this link could destroy the newcomer's precarious balance of staying drug-free, and he or she would leave and return to the former life-style.

In spite of considerable evidence that they have failed with their "child" (now in a grown-up adult body), many parents attempt, prematurely, to renew their past relationship, and do not fully understand the necessity for the recovering addict to develop a "family" relationship within the TC—apart from them.

Based on my research discussions with a range of parents and spouses who have relatives in TCs, I have delineated several essential kinds of reasons related to why a parent or a spouse is resistant to the TC successfully treating the addict. Following are some deleterious family ploys or patterns for aborting the addict's progress in a TC.

"Please Come Home, I'm Lonely"

In one case in a TC, I observed a mother offer her "child" drugs rather than "mom's apple pie" if he would come home with her. Her child (25 years old) had been clean in the TC for six months. This was the first time in ten years that he had remained clean for longer than a day, without being locked up. On her first visit (the TC had not permitted her to visit him for the first 30 days), she was

overheard telling him: "Please come home, dear. I'm dying of loneliness. You can't drink or use cocaine but I'll give you all the pills
you want."

A Time Bomb of Revenge

For the newcomer in a TC, home visits, as well as parental
visits, can have destructive effects. In one case a young man who
had been clean in a TC for over a year was granted a Christmas
leave to visit his family in Texas. The results were almost disas-
trous. His father began to demean him in his usual style. The
young man came close to physically assaulting his father, and was
tempted to once again use drugs. He still carried a time bomb of
hate and grievances against his father for abusing him as a child,
and he almost exploded during his visit. When he returned to the
TC, he worked out his feeling in a number of group sessions. The
self-destructive time bomb of revenge that ticked in him was almost turned on at his home.

One could infer from this case that he had not fully recovered
from his "illness." On the other hand, he was doing fine in the TC
and there did not seem to be any logical reason for exposing the
newcomer to the former family virus, his father, who originally
helped cause his self-destructive substance-abuse behavior.

"I Would Rather Have Him As An Addict"

In many cases the coaddict or substance-abuse-enabling parent
clearly and overtly does not want the child to get clean in the TC,
but wants "it" home and back under his or her control. Some
coaddict enablers will abort the TC process because they have an
unconscious need to maintain and continue the addict's symptom.
The nonaddict wife of one newcomer in a TC once told me that she
wanted her husband to quit using drugs, yet she admitted that she
had often helped him to get drugs. Near the end of our discussion,
she openly admitted her strongest insecurity and fear: "He's a
good-looking, intelligent man. I'm lucky to have him as my husband. If he really quit using drugs, he would probably leave me,
and find someone who is more his equal. I would rather have him
as an addict than not have him at all."

"Come Home Now or You'll Lose Me"

For some coaddicts their resistance to their "loved one's" becoming drug-free is reflected in a subtle attack on the TC, and an attempt to pull their "love object" out of it. In one case a young man who had been doing well and staying clean in a TC for more than seven months received a letter from his coaddict wife. In the letter she said, "Get well, baby," and then described in great detail her erotic feelings for him. She described her black silk panties and her increasingly extreme passion for him—which, if left unfulfilled by him, would find satisfaction elsewhere.

The letter was revealed by the young man in a group session. It was interpreted by the group as an apparent effort on her part to pull him out of his therapeutic environment and back into their past destructive relationship. In a useful group discussion, the individual involved and the group concluded that if she really loved him, she would give him a chance to complete his treatment.

"I Want Him to Get Clean, But Only If I Do It"

In another pattern the coaddict family member wants the addict or alcoholic to get well, but unconsciously does not want anyone else to help. In the case of one mother who vigorously attempted to see her son against the TC's advice, she expressed deep feelings in the way. "He came to me for help. I couldn't help him. I deserted him, and I don't believe that any mother should have to feel this way." Her comment revealed an apparent preoccupation with her own guilt-ridden emotions rather than her son's needs. She expressed a strong need to expiate her guilt for producing an addict. In order to eliminate this guilt, this mother felt it was necessary that she cure the addict herself; and because of this selfish need to expiate her guilt in this way, she unconsciously attempted to block anyone else from succeeding where she had failed.

The Impatient Coaddict

In another pattern some parental or spousal coaddicts step aside to permit the addict to get well—up to a point. "Impatient" coaddicts are more liberal than the "guilty coaddicts." They permit the therapeutic process to function for a time; however, they revert to type when they see the therapy actually starting to work on their addict's problem. Then they, like the others, attempt to remove the individual prematurely from the beneficial environment. An example of this was the parents who wanted to remove their son after he had been clean for about three months in a TC. Their argument was: "He's gained weight and he's healthy again—we want him home with us so we can help him the rest of the way." They attempted to remove him from the TC environment even though past evidence of their inability to "help him the rest of the way" was crystal clear.

The Visit

An interesting Synanon case that reveals a prototypical enabling parent problem, involving an attempt to abort the process, is what became known in the annals of Synanon as the "Gold affair." In the development of the overall TC movement, there are often such prototypical cases that reveal certain treatment dynamics that have shaped the TC approach.

In the "Gold affair," a resident's mother arrived from New York to "inspect Synanon" and visit her addict-alcoholic son, who had been in the program for 11 days. This, of course, was not permitted, because, as Dederich later told her, her son was "an 11-day-old baby in Synanon and would not survive the visit." The mother caused a scene in the front lobby and hovered around the beachfront, demanding to see her "child." Dederich privately interviewed her son, Jack Gold, as a prelude to talking to the "impatient coaddict mother."

> Chuck: Hello, Jack. I understand your mother is down in our foyer demanding that she be permitted to see you. She appeared out of thin air without calling in advance, and we're not going to permit it. You're 28 years old, and therefore a legal entity, and I wanted you to make up your own mind on this matter.
>
> If you want to see your mother, you can see her—but then you'll have to leave with her. One of the things we have to do in here is train parents in the proper behavior that is of benefit to their son or daughter. So if you want to see her, you can see her and go with her. If you wish to continue to enjoy the benefits of

the foundation, just tell us so, and we will handle your mother. We'll point out a few of the facts of life to her. We don't permit parents to see their children here for at least 30 days. The longer we can stall this off, up to a point, the better it is for you. Before we talk to your mother, I want to find out how you stand on this.

Jack: I would like to continue here. It's the first time I've been sober in over two years—and I don't want to screw it up. When I lived with her, I used drugs all the time.

Chuck: You want to continue here? Then we will explain this to your mother. I don't know how she got out here. She's from New York, isn't she? She came tearing out here to gobble you up again?

Jack: She came out to see me, and she has relatives out here.

Chuck: She does? Well, maybe we'll suggest to her that she should stay with the relatives for 30 or 40 days. Later on we'll permit her to call us and then visit you. We're going to send her on her way. I hear she made a statement, "I will take him with me." Is this the way she treats you at the age of 28?

Jack: This is one of the reasons why I moved out of her house.

Chuck: Very good. In other words, you were almost well when you got here, then, weren't you?

Jack: I don't think so. I'm sure she had something to do with my becoming an addict.

Chuck: There you have it. All right, you can go back to the seminar you were in. We'll handle momma. This is the way you want it? You want to stay her at Synanon, right?

Jack: Yes.

As Dederich was leaving, Jack smiled and said "Good luck" with a sarcastic edge to his voice. Now that Dederich had Jack's consent, he could, if it appeared appropriate, treat the mother as an interloper into his therapy. Because of bitter past experience, he based his approach on the assumption that the woman was potentially destructive in her efforts to remove her son prematurely. The session was taped by Dederich and is presented here in its exact dialogue to reveal some of the dynamics involved in handling this type of situation.

Chuck: Come in. You're Jack's mother. What's your name?

Mrs. Gold: Sally Gold.

Chuck: Sally Gold, these are Reid Kimball, Betty Coleman, and Tootsie Davis. We comprise part of the board of directors at Synanon. Now, what is it you have in mind?

Mrs. Gold: Do you have to run the tape recorder?

Chuck: Yes, indeed, that's what we do here.

Mrs. Gold: Well, these things are very strange, because when I enter any hospital, I investigate.

Chuck: This isn't a hospital.

Mrs. Gold: Well, I say anything; anything that will help my son, I investigate.

Chuck: Very good. Now you're not entering a hospital, are you?

Mrs. Gold: No, but my child is.

Chuck: Child? You mean this great big 28-year-old man that was just in here?

Mrs. Gold: I don't care if he was my grandfather. [Mrs. Gold begins with a tough attitude, and Chuck responds with a louder voice.]

Chuck: Pardon me, Mrs. Gold, you're in my office. I will talk when I feel like it. You're talking about this great big kid I had in here two minutes ago, Jack Gold, as your [sarcastically] "child"? This may be one of the reasons why he's a drug addict, because you keep thinking of him as a child.

Jack has decided that he wants to stay here at Synanon, where he can stay clean and learn how to grow up and be a man. One of the rules we have at Synanon is that we do not permit relatives, particularly mothers and fathers or wives and husbands, to see any of our people for a minimum of 30 days. You evidently didn't bother to inquire about that before you came here.

Mrs. Gold: There were calls made. I will admit it was my fault the way the thing was done. It was done in haste, without checking. I may not be very smart, but I'm cautious. I did oppose sending anyone here or any place without checking it first.

Chuck: Well your opposition is understandable, but your having control over a 28-year-old voter in the United States of America is fantastic thinking. This boy came to Synanon, as far as I am concerned, in order to learn how to be a drug-free young man; and we will, of course, teach him, if he stays. He wishes to stay. I confirmed that, about two minutes before you walked in the office, so I'd be on safe ground. I didn't want to do anything he wouldn't like.

We are in the business of curing addicts; we know how to do it. One thing that we insist upon always is that there be no contact with relatives for about 30 days.

Mrs. Gold: [Sarcastically] Is he in prison?

Chuck: No, he's not in prison, he's learning how to grow up

and stop using alcohol and drugs, at this moment. Now, here's the way he put it to us. We told him that if he sees you, he can go out the door with you. He said, "I don't wish to do that. I wish to stay here at Synanon and grow up so that I can be an American citizen and can vote without being in custody all the time like most addicts and alcoholics are." That's what he told us. He tells me that you're out here to visit relatives. Well, then, if you're going to be out here for another 30 days or so, then maybe we can arrange a meeting at that time. Not today. Not now. Probably in around 30 days.

Mrs. Gold: I was under a terrific emotional strain downstairs, which is over and done now.

Chuck: I understand.

Mrs. Gold: They kept asking me whether I heard what they were saying. I'm very aware of your organization. I'm very well aware of what you're doing. I think you're doing good work, but I think it should be voluntary. [Here Mrs. Gold shifts her approach, apparently in an attempt to gain her objective by more conciliatory means].

Chuck: Mrs. Gold this situation is emotionally charged for you. For me, it's old stuff. If your boy stays here at Synanon, I will make a prophecy that you and I will be very good friends one of these days. Right now, you don't like what I'm saying to you because I'm trying to point out to you...

Mrs. Gold: No, I'm not opposed to you. I understand what you're doing, and I understand what you're saying. And I say it's just unfortunate the way things were done. *He came to me for help. I couldn't help him. I deserted him, and I don't believe that any mother should have to feel this way.* [My emphasis.]

After some further discussion, Mrs. Gold agreed to visit in 30 days, shook hands with Dederich, and left with an apparent better understanding of the situation.

Several key points were illustrated in this attempt by Mrs. Gold to see her son. Her stronger feeling was reflected in the comment, "He came to me for help....I deserted him, and I don't believe that any mother should have to feel this way." It could be speculated that her essential reason for being on hand to pull her son out was an attempt to expiate her guilty feelings of failure.

Her son, Jack, remained drug-free at Synanon for over a year as a cooperative member of the program, and has been alcohol and drug-free in the community for over five years. Mrs. Gold later became a friend of Synanon and a financial supporter of the organization.

TC FAMILY GROUP THERAPY APPROACHES

TCs often differ in their policy concerning visits by relatives and friends. Most, however, make an effort to protect the newcomer from formerly harmful relationships. This policy differs from that of many traditional institutions where the staff often joins with the family vis-à-vis the addict, to commiserate about the difficulty of handling the person or how sick and helpless the "patient" is. This approach tends further to alienate the individual from the "helpers" and may reinforce the relationship that caused the original pathology. This is consciously not done in TCs. Here "staff" members join in and support their fellow members, and attempt to orient friends and family properly to help the resident.

As described, many TCs operate on the assumption that in the early days of exposure to the process, the newcomer is not capable of making too many correct decisions about how he or she is going to relate to these "significant others," many of whom were part of the addict's problem. At a later time, when the TC administration, comprised of former addicts who know the situation, determine that the person's "self" and decision-making apparatus are in better working condition, interaction with past associates is allowed.

"Graduates" of the TC make their own decisions in these matters. Some have gone back into most of their old relationships, and others to some of them, but in many cases they completely cut off all past associations, especially addict or alcoholic "friends."

Because of these varied "family factors," most TC programs have support, encounter, and psychodrama groups that work on the issues of reintegrating families. Almost all TCs have some form of family groups that meet on a regular basis. In these groups, somewhat like the Al-Anon AA family groups, the topics for discussion include such questions and issues as: What was my role in facilitating the addiction of my son–daughter, husband–wife?" How is that person changing and how do I have to change to improve our relationship when he or she is drug-free? What do I do about my own drug or alcohol use? What should I do if the person quits the TC program to return to drugs and wants to move back in with me? The general issue is, "How can a family improve its relationships system for the purpose of staying clean—and becoming a happier more productive entity?"

These are the relatively obvious questions: however, on a deeper level, coaddicts or enablers often begin to understand the nature of their relationship to the addict. Some family members begin to understand that their addict is the "identified patient" and the real problem is the way family members relate to each other—and how this has to change.

For example, Mrs. Gold, after her son had been in Synanon for six months, joined the family group in Synanon called the "Mommas and Poppas." As she participated in the encounter and educational group sessions and became involved with the organization, she began to learn more about her feelings for her son. Her husband had died when her son was quite young, and she felt that her son was all she had in the world. In effect, she was smothering him. She also began to understand that one of the reasons her son abused drugs was connected to his need to "run away" from her because of her efforts to dominate his life, and in her loneliness she kept him dependent on her. She also learned that, in this process, on some covert level, she fostered his use of drugs so that he would stay at home with her. She began to acknowledge that he was a man and not her little boy, and that she had to "let go" if she was going to have any reasonable future relationship with him. As it turned out, both Mrs. Gold and her son grew up and developed insights through the family group, which positively solidified their relationship.

In another case the TC family program changed the resident, Marta's perception of her husband. Marta knew that her husband was continuing his drug use and criminal career. She asked him to move in and join the program, but he refused. In her "treatment work" in the TC program, the more Marta understood her destructive relationship with her husband, the more alienated she became from him. After a year in the program, she finally stated in an encounter group, "The people here are really my friends, I'll never go back to my husband, Jack. I met with him several times and we just don't talk the same language anymore." Marta divorced Jack.

Her relationship with her parents also changed. Her mother and father visited her several times. After having a drug-free perspective for over a year, she concluded the following about her parents in a group session. "They were never there for me—ever. I still have a vague fantasy that they'll turn into real parents someday, but I'm sure now that won't happen. I'm trying to suck on a dry teat—and I'm giving up on them."

Many parents and spouses do not acknowledge any role in the TC resident's addiction. They absolve themselves by maintaining the addict as the identified patient and they do not participate in the TC family program. This has the effect of further alienating the resident from the family. Residents in this instance must come to terms with the fact that they have to work out their future with their TC family without the help of their original biological family and their former friends.

The process of disconnecting from destructive parents is easier for adults than addict-alcoholic adolescents. In a teenage encounter group I have directed for several years with young addicts, I found that most adolescents do not have the same options that adults have in this regard. They must continue to relate, too often, to physically and emotionally abusing parents because they have social and legal power over them. Thus parents who are often extremely difficult because they do not acknowledge or understand their destructive impacts and refuse to participate in their child's recovery process cannot be separated from the negative situation. In such cases adolescents have only two options. They can attempt to gain some insight into the way their parents treat them and bide their time until they are young adults and can leave; or they can opt, when possible, to be placed in a more beneficial foster-home situation. Although both of these possibilities are difficult alternatives, they are better than living with emotionally or physically abusive parents who facilitate drug-alcohol habits.

Another important factor in the treatment of both adolescents and adults in a TC is for them to learn the difference between a true friend and a "drug-abusing friend." In the TC in various groups a resident learns more clearly something that he or she already knows partially from personal experience, that using addicts or alcoholics are quite incapable of being bona-fide friends.

This is a tough blast of reality because most of the resident's past associates were addicts. The road back from addiction, therefore, first involves learning how to relate properly to the ex-addict's family in the TC, and then to reorganize his or her "social atom" in the outside world. This often entails the painful process of disconnecting from people who were drug-using friends and developing beneficial friendships.

THE ITALIAN Ce.I.S. TC APPROACH TO INTAKE AND FAMILY ISSUES

In most TCs the involvement of parents, spouses, and friends usually takes place in the TC process when the addict-alcoholic is in residence or in a support group when the resident has graduated. In my recent research, I have found that the most creative, advanced, and innovative approach to dealing with the addict-alcoholics social atom is found in the 22 TCs that make up the Italian Ce.I.S. program.

The Italian approach involves the family as part of the program along with the addict "child" prior to the addict entering a TC. This preentry therapy process may go on for one to ten months. The family project I studied took place in an enormous old building in downtown Rome owned by Ce.I.S. (Tony Gelormino, an ex-addict, and, one of the directors of the Ce.I.S. program, was my translator.)

At first my involvement with the mass of 100–200 people milling around in the large corridor, spilling out into the street and talking to each other in an animated dramatic way, was difficult to comprehend. However, as I began to focus my research, I learned that a number of powerful and productive family forces and groups were at work in this exciting therapeutic situation.

In different rooms there were alcoholics and heroin and cocaine addicts from the streets of Rome who were participating in so-called "motivation" groups. In these groups the leaders were recovering substance abusers who were already living in a TC and were preparing for reentry into the community. Themes discussed in these groups included "commitments" to staying clean, family problems, and what life in a TC was like. Understanding these issues from someone who had been there helped the preentry addict better comprehend the program, and enhanced their motivation to enter the program.

Across the hall from these intense substance-abuser motivation groups were what was identified to me as "parallel family groups." These consisted of the fathers and mothers of the addicts in preentry who were discussing the parental problems of having an addict son or daughter. Topics discussed in these groups included how the parents felt their drug-abusing children had terrorized them, how they all had practiced a denial that a problem existed, and strategies for dealing with the guilt they felt for the part they felt they played in their child's addiction.

Of even greater interest to me in studying this innovative TC preentry approach was what Tony Gelormino and I labeled "corridor family therapy." This involved small, informal, spontaneously formed two- three- and four-parent and larger groups in the corridor who were intensely, and in an animated fashion, discussing various problems and issues that significantly impinged on their lives. The discussions and debates were at a consistently high emotional pitch and seemed to be productive to the participants.

Most revealing to me was the way one 62-year-old retired Italian police officer I interviewed (with Tony translating) described his family situation—and how "corridor family therapy" and the Ce.I.S. TC had become a significant force in his life.

"I had two boys who were addicts. My wife and I were terrorized by their behavior. They stole valuables from the house. Radios, TVs, hi-fis would disappear. My sons, 18 and 25, would be arrogant and deny they did it when my wife or I confronted them with their thefts. Some nights when they came home late I would feel helpless and paralyzed with terror. My wife and I would pull the covers over our heads to avoid arguing with them. Our life was hell!

"Then I heard about this TC program and I came down here. On my first day here right in this hall, I began to talk to other fathers and mothers who had experienced the same problem we had. My wife and I, at first, experienced some relief in knowing we were not alone with this problem. We began to come regularly and talk about our pain here in the hall, and then in regularly scheduled parent groups. At this time our sons were untouched by the program, but we were beginning to learn about our part in their addiction.

"The first thing we were told by parents and staff was not to worry about who was responsible for the problem. First just admit that it exists. And recognize that you have no power to do anything about it on your own. Stop feeling guilty and humiliated. The knowledge that other parents had experienced what we were going through was helpful, and we began to feel better and saw some ray of hope.

"We began to learn in the parent groups that we did have some power over our boys that we at first didn't realize. We began to talk to our kids about the programs, and that we were working on our family problem. The kids became interested because basically they are good kids and didn't want this pain and grief in our family any more than we did.

"One day my oldest agreed to come here to a meeting with us, and he began to talk about entering a TC for help. The staff here told him they had no room in the TCs now and that he had to be more motivated and committed. He asked, 'How do I do this?' They told him about the 'motivation groups' and he began to participate.

"The next thing that happened was a meeting we had with our son and a staff member from the TC. The subject of the meeting was: How could we make our family life better during this time before he entered the TC? We were asked what we wanted from him and he was asked what he was willing to do. We made a contract with him. If he was to continue living in our house he had to: (1) stop using drugs; (2) get a job; (3) keep his room neat and clean; and (4) come home at a decent hour—among other things. We were amazed that he was willing to try to cooperate. He fell short of some of these goals—but he was trying, and that was certainly better than what we had before coming here to the program.

"This preentry time went on for six months. We all went to groups and began to learn a lot about each other that we never admitted to before. Our younger son had not really changed too much in this time, although he began to get curious about what was happening in our family with his big brother.

"At around six months our older boy went into the San Carlo TC. He's been there now for five months and he's doing very well. Our younger son is now in this preentry program. He's been influenced by his brother and us.

"Sure, along the way we had some setbacks. But our whole family life has improved and we look forward to an even better life. In a way one of the things I learned in the program—and this is a foolish thing for a police officer to admit—I had more power as a parent than I thought I had. Instead of yelling as I used to in the past, I enforced the contract rules we had agreed on by calmly telling my sons that I would no longer support them in any way if they didn't begin to conform. They began to learn that my wife and I really meant what we said. We had learned how we were part of their problem. And when we changed, so did they.

"Why am I here today? As I told you, I'm recently retired from the police force and I come down here two or three days a week and talk to other parents about my experience. See all these people in the corridor? We help each other. A lot of important things happen in our regularly assigned group, but for me this corridor is where people learn to be more effective parents who can help their children get drug-free!"

In summary, whether the TC approach is the traditional one developed by Synanon and used in hundreds of TCs or the recently described Italian approach, some basic issues must be handled in the process of helping an addict-alcoholic join a TC program. One is that the addict and the family must be integrated into the TC program so that they are getting parallel therapy. Second, they must be reconnected in some fashion so that they develop new, more constructive forms of interaction and relationships. Most of these changes are made in the TC process through the use of various types of dynamic therapy groups.

4

Group Methods and Process

The overall anti-substance-abuse environment of a TC is therapeutic. A positive ethos that is both supportive and caring is transmitted to the recovering resident informally on a daily basis in all of his or her individual and group interactions. Everyone experiencing emotional problems or pain has access to another person on a one-on-one basis in order to receive individual caring and counseling, on almost a 24-hour basis.

VARIED TREATMENT GROUPS

In addition to this overall healing environment, on a more specific level, in almost all TCs I have studied there are various groups that focus on specific issues of importance to the recovering resident. These groups focus on such issues and topics as: (1) indoctrinating the newcomer into the TC; (2) family treatment; (3) self-disclosure and nurturing; (4) educational therapy; (5) occupational issues; and (6) social–psychological analysis and treatment.

Indoctrination and Orientation

These groups are primarily for newcomers, and focus on various phases and ramifications of the TC program that will be encountered in the recovery process. These group sessions analyze the structure of the organization and the value and purpose of various methods, such as the encounter group and psychodrama. The goal of these sessions is to integrate the newcomer into the community and serve as a constant reminder to the more senior members who participate in these groups why they are involved in the TC.

Most TCs have a waiting list. As described, the Italian TC system utilizes this waiting time by having applicants and their families attend indoctrination groups, where they learn about various aspects of the TC program. In this way they get a head start on joining the program. Typically, in these groups work is begun on the potential resident's drug problem; and having him or her work out a contract with the family on improving his or her behavior in the family. These orientation and indoctrination groups facilitate a more effective learning experience when the newcomer finally becomes a full-time resident.

Family Groups

Some family-issue discussion groups only involve residents. Other groups also include parents, spouses, siblings, and other relatives. The concept that hovers over every type of family-issue session is that the recovering resident is the nucleus of a familial social atom, and his or her problems are inextricably bound up with the family system. This concept encompasses J. L. Moreno's admonition that "treatment must always take into account the person's social atom, including family relationships."

These family-system treatment groups deal with such specific prototypical issues as: (1) *Denial*—"My parents knew I was an addict but they chose to ignore my problem. (2) *Abuse*—"My mother beat me almost every day of my childhood for no good reason. I killed my rage and pain with drugs, and later when I was older I physically abused women to get back at my mother. (3) *Separation*—"I will not go back to the husband who abused me and my kids. (4) *Neglect*—"My parents were never there for me when I needed them. My father gave me material things, but never showed any love." All of these issues, and others, are focused upon in family groups in order to help the recovering substance abuser and his or her parents understand and resolve the family dynamics that produced the problem.

Self-Disclosure and Nurturing Groups

Many substance abusers have a "hurt child" inside them and have never been able to disclose their painful feelings to another person. As one recovering woman resident told me, "After I was in the TC for six months, I got in touch with my feelings, and I finally admitted that my father had sexually abused me for many years. When it was happening, my mother denied it was going on and I had no one to talk to about my rage and pain. I believe my secret caused me to use cocaine to kill the emotional pain of my problems. I also became a prostitute. This I stupidly believed gave me control over the sex act—and in some ways I felt that abusing masochistic men (tricks) was a real kick. I felt I was getting back at my father. After I discussed these painful things in a group, I cried for days. Other women, and some of the guys, helped me past my painful feelings."

After disclosure in a group, where this is encouraged, the group provides a nurturing environment in the TC for the resident. In this way emotional pain and rage that have been repressed for years surface; and the resident tends to feel less alone and less guilty, and his or her self-esteem is often enhanced by the accepting nurturing response of the group.

Educational Groups

Most substance abusers, while in their drug haze of existence, block out most of the real world. Substance abuse automatically produces learning disabilities. On their path to reality in a TC, they often become enormously motivated to learn, read, and pursue an education. This educational hunger is fed in educational groups that focus on all kinds of subjects, including *philosophical discussions* analyzing such philosophers as Emerson, Plato, Kant, and Spinoza; *current events* related to a range of contemporary social and political events; *social and psychological theories* about mental health, including those of Freud, Moreno, Fromm, and Erickson: the analyses of *biological sciences*; study groups and reading in *literature, music, and art*; and in many TCs, *spiritual and religious* theories and practices as educational subjects.

In brief, TC educational groups cover the range of human subjects. The process often motivates the recovering substance abusers to finish their formal high-school or college education.

Occupations and Work

All TC residents work in and for their organization. Like most organizations there are business-office jobs, housekeeping and kitchen jobs, and manual labor, and these jobs are filled by residents. Many TCs have gas stations, light manufacturing plants, and advertising specialty businesses for the purpose of helping to finance the organization's work. Most of these jobs are staffed by residents. In occupational groups each resident's efficacy and proclivity for meaningful work are analyzed. The group's goal is to help residents, many of whom have had work problems in their past, to clarify the kind of work they would like to engage in when they graduate, and to perform more effectively in their occupation of choice. These groups foster on-the-job-training and clarify occupational goals. The groups are beneficial for the residents in their future occupations later in society.

Social–Psychological Treatment

The overall goal of all of the types of groups delineated here is to help the recovering residents deal more effectively with the emotional problems that are connected to their substance-abuse problem. In this regard various TCs, depending on their social–psychological orientation, have different forms of group therapy. Some have professionally trained psychiatrists, psychologists, or social workers direct the group therapy sessions. Other TCs are more inclined to utilize leaderless rap groups in which people share and discuss their emotional problems, and how they can resolve them. Some TC group therapy sessions are highly analytic, and focus on problem-solving discussions. Also, in most TCs with which I have been involved or have studied, psychodrama and role training are significant therapeutic group methods. In brief, most TCs utilize a range of group methods and techniques, including encounter groups, for resolving their residents' social and emotional problems.

The encounter-group approach is at the core of most group methods in a TC. Consequently the following discussion and analysis will focus exclusively on this important TC group method.

THE METHODOLOGY AND DYNAMICS OF THE ENCOUNTER GROUP

A substance abuser's self-deception about his or her life is a key element in the self-destructive use of drugs, and this compounds his or her basic pathology. A method that is basic to the difficult process of dealing with this problem, and which is utilized in all TCs, is what is variously called the encounter group, the game, or the dynamic group. Although most TCs effectively use the other group methods discussed, the encounter group is at the core of the proper functioning of the overall organization of a TC; and it is a method that is vital for successfully treating an addict or an alcoholic. The basic process involves a group attack on the self-deception that characterizes all substance abusers, even those who think they are facing the realities of their lives. An important consequence of this verbal encounter is that it forces the recovering resident to introspectively examine his or her behavior and lifestyle.

The encounter group, in my view, is a necessary process in all TC work because the addictive personality does not respond to the other, more supportive approaches until the addict's basic self-deception devices are vehemently encountered by the group with the goal of helping the addict encounter his or her own reality. It is harsh to confront a person who is practicing denial and say, "You are suffering from a self-destructive disease—namely, drug abuse—and you have to confront the fact that you are an addict or an alcoholic." The AA experience reveals that the *first step* in dealing with the addict's disease is the addict's clear awareness of the insidiousness of the problem, and acceptance that he or she is powerless over the drug and that life has become unmanageable. The best method that I have seen to get through to an addict-alcoholic on this issue is the cannonballs of truth hurled in an encounter group in the context of a TC.

Encounter-Group Topics

On the basis of my research and personal participation in several thousand encounter groups over the past 30 years, I have here delineated eight central issues and topics that need to be explored if an addict-alcoholic is to come to terms with the reality of his or her problem. It is necessary for the substance abuser in a TC to deal with these issues in an encounter group if he or she is effectively to modify his or her behavior in a drug-free direction. These basic topics are: 1. Addict-alcoholic self-concept; 2. The co-addict or enabler problem; 3. "Friends"; 4. Projected despair: a life without drugs or alcohol; 5. Are drugs fun or self-destructive?; 6. Slippage-Regression; 7. Painkiller and social lubricant; 8. The life and death factor in substance abuse.

1. Addict-Alcoholic Self-Concept

"I am an addict or an alcoholic." Even when addicts enter a TC and openly admit they are "addicts" or "alcoholics," they attempt to deceive themselves about this fact. The encounter group process is vital in order to constantly remind the potentially self-destructive addict about the problem. Any kind of self-delusion in this area can lead them right back into their former lives.

2. The Co-Addict or Enabler Problem

The comment of an addict's wife, "You can take pills at home but no heroin," or a mother's admonition to her addicted teenager, "It's ok for you to drink at home, but don't smoke marijuana," serve as two simplistic examples of the way some co-addicts' family members facilitate or enable the addict/alcoholic to return to their poison. In the encounter group it often requires extreme language and harshness to communicate the way in which a sincerely loving family might reinforce the addict's habit at some time in the fu-

ture—if they are not aware of this possibility. They need to understand how this subtle push towards drugs happens and then they
need to be eternally vigilant in assessing when a "loved-one" or
"friend" is unconsciously facilitating their slide back to substance-
abuse.

3. "Friends"

A teenager in a group I directed remarked, "My best friend
offered me a line of coke yesterday when I was at school, and he
knows I'm trying to quit drugs." It takes an extreme amount of
energy and discussion in the group to prove to a recovering addict
that "no one who uses drugs or offers you drugs is a 'friend.'"
Addict: "But I know him for ten years."
Group: "He is not a 'friend,' if you want to stop using drugs."

4. *Projected Despair: A Life Without Drugs or Alcohol*

One of the most difficult subjects addict-alcoholics must confront in an encounter group is the fact that they can never "use"
again. For most addicts or alcoholics, confronting this fact of life
produces a feeling of gloom and despair, "You mean, later on I
can't have one drink or smoke one joint without falling back into
my habit? That's really depressing." Most addict-alcoholics who
want to stop using continue to harbor a covert self-deceptive idea
that some day, after they are drug-free for a period of time, they can
successfully "use again on a party or recreational basis." The group
has to hammer away at this self-deceptive, self-destructive notion
over and over again in the encounter group. The AA concept of
staying drug-free "one day at a time" is often helpful for the recovering substance abuser to keep in mind.

5. *Are Drugs "Fun" or Self-Destructive?*

The notion that drugs are pleasurable is another issue that requires repetitive group discussion and attack in order to point to
the longer-term effects of being addicted. Many recovering alco-
holic-addicts believe on a deep emotional level that the group is
taking away their main source of fun and enjoyment when they

talk them out of substance abuse. They fight the issue in a variety of ways. They tend to remember their pleasurable "fixes," "smokes," or line of cocaine rather than all of the negative impacts the drug has had on their life. This issue is a special problem with adolescents, most of whom are still in a more clearly early enjoyable phase of their addiction. It is hard to get through to adolescents that they are engaged in a form of deficit spending or a "fly now, pay later" situation, since they have not yet hit the harsh wall of despair and pain that is an inevitable consequence of substance abuse. Often, in order to get through to the adolescent, an older substance abuser who has, in AA terminology, "hit bottom," can communicate what happens down the long-term road of substance abuse. In this regard the encounter group must constantly remind the addict of the real long-term impacts and consequences of drug use—and this requires continuing extremist verbal tactics.

6. Slippage-Regression

Another issue that often emerges in encounter-group discussion is related to the fact that many addict-alcoholics slip at some point in their recovery process, and "fall off the wagon." This is one place in the psychodynamics of drug-abuse treatment where *verbal punishment deters*, if properly administered in a group. "Slippers" should know that if they use a drug, they can expect to be *verbally* brutalized by an indignant group of holier-than-thou addicts in their encounter-group sessions. For the violater a group attack can prove most humiliating, when the group pours out its righteous indignation at the "offender." The fear of this flood of wrath from a caring but contentious support group often deters slippage.

In the context of the issue of drug temptations, I recall a young adult in a TC commenting to his fellow group members, "When I was on pass, I had a chance to smoke a joint. But when I weighed it up against what you guys would do to me when I copped out in this group—something I would have to do—it wasn't worth it."

7. Painkiller and Social Lubricant

"Why do I use drugs?" is a topic that is repeatedly discussed by the recovering addict in TC encounter groups. Two of the most

common responses by addict-alcoholics to these questions are vari-
ations on: "It helps kill the pain of my personal problems," and
"It's the only way I feel a sense of belonging in a group." What, of
course, is pointed out to the drug abuser is "It's difficult, but the
only way you'll resolve your problems is to encounter them head
on, without submerging them with drugs." The group's answer to
the "belonging" sense of alienation issue is that "it is necessary for
you to learn how to relate and communicate with people drug-free,
even though it is a tough task."

It is difficult for the recovering addict-alcoholic to learn how to
confront day-to-day life situations without drugs as a "painkiller"
or "social lubricant." "Addicts" and "alcoholics" in their past iden-
ties had "friends" and a social scene (e.g., the corner, the party, the
bar). They are often resistant to giving up this past identity because
of the fear of having to relate drug-free to another set of friends in a
new social setting. This is an issue of continuing importance for the
recovering alcoholic-addict to discuss in intensive combative group
sessions.

8. The Life and Death Factor in Substance Abuse

An allegation that is often hurled at an addict in a drug encounter group is: "You are slowly committing suicide with drugs." This
forces the addict-alcoholic to assess what Albert Camus has referred to as not a philosophical question but the *only* question: "Life
or death?" This is a critical and often dismal subject for the recovering substance abuser to discuss because many group members are
forced to confront the fact that on some level their drug use *is*
suicidal.

In an adolescent group I directed, a 15-year-old girl revealed
how she immediately went back to drugs when she left the group.
She talked about her despair of ever stopping, "I have no self-
control." The group, of course, in her case was supportive, and did
not attack her poignant vulnerability.

One group member, in trying to pull her out of her abject state
of depression, asked her to "tell us about some of your positive
fantasies." She responded, "I do have one positive fantasy." The
group members eagerly awaited her response, hoping that her
comment on something positive would cheer her up. They asked,
"What's that?" She replied, "My positive fantasy is being dead."

It is obviously difficult for a recovering addict to confront the fact that drug use may constitute an unconscious suicidal tendency. Yet it is a bottom-line issue that must be encountered by all addict-alcoholics in the encounter-group process. The life–death issue can make even the most supportive group seem like an "encounter group" because of the painful nature of the subject. The subtle point here is that the group is seen as being aggressive when its members do not let up on the discussion of this painful subject. When the topic or issue being discussed, therefore, is so delicate and painful, just keeping the person on the subject makes it feel like an encounter-group session to the person on the hot seat. Discussing the life–death factor, therefore, as it relates to the behavior of an addict, automatically makes it an encounter-group situation.

The Encounter-Group Process

The encounter-group approach is fairly standard in most TCs. Three or four times a week each resident meets in a group of eight to 12 people. First everyone in the group settles down, as comfortably as possible, in a circle, facing one another. There is usually a brief silence, a scanning appraisal as to whom is present, a kind of sizing one another up, and then the group launches into an intensive emotional discussion of the kinds of personal and group issues that I have delineated. In most TCs a different person is put on the "hot seat" by the group in a rotation fashion. Sometimes an individual may request the group to discuss his or her problem, but most of the time the person on the hot seat is chosen by a group member. As they say, the game may be on the particular person anywhere from ten to 40 minutes. The length of time spent on a particular person, and the subject, is spontaneously determined by the group, depending on the level of importance and interest in the subject. Another aspect is related to how fast the person's problem is resolved. The group may move on when it feels that it is not making any progress with the person on the hot seat.

There are a number of factors to be considered in the composition of an encounter group in a TC. In some cases the coordinator of the group will receive requests from an individual who wants to be in a group with a particular person in order to work out a special problem, or because he or she has some data on the other person that he or she wants to reveal or discuss. Often two or more people, because of a particular situation, will request admission to the same group—for example, people who work together and have an interpersonal problem. These requests are usually granted, and tend to have constructive consequences.

Some groups are "rigged" in advance. Here a group or some key person is given a preliminary briefing about someone's problem, often with a suggestion as to how it might be worked out. Also, a combination of people with very similar problems may be placed in "fighting range" of one another in the same group. "Big talkers" and "screamers" may be mixed in with "quiet types" in order to give some balance to the group.

Employer–employee problems and on-the-job problems generally are handled in the encounter group. The group provides the opportunity for an employer or employee better to understand his or her work associates' combined "official" and personal roles. When someone is thrown in with a person with whom he or she works, that individual has to relate to the other's role both as a worker and as a person. This provides an opportunity for an employee to confront an employer (or vice versa) on a personal level three times a week.

A person's TC status, high or low, is left outside of the group. This makes the group process more democratic, and enables lower-status people with less power to speak up about issues that are bothering them in the TC. This opportunity is not usually allowed in the outside society. It is a valuable situation for adjusting grievances—and generally gives residents a feeling of power that they probably never had in their former life situations.

The characteristic of random group construction in a TC sets up a mathematical probability that no one specific group will meet intact more than once. This gives all people in the overall TC a chance to meet almost everyone else in the population on a personal basis in the powerful encounter-group situation.

This randomization factor helps defeat the group therapy problem that I have termed a "therapeutic contract." A therapeutic contract emerges in many therapy groups, where the same people meet regularly in the same group over a period of time. The concept involves a conscious and unconscious reciprocal agreement between two or more people not to expose one another's psychological "Achilles' heel." The unstated "contract" might be, for example, "If you don't expose or attack my embarrassing and painful mother problem, I won't bring up your problem with your wife." This type of contract impedes personal growth in the group, since the group is constricted in a search for truth. There is an awareness in TCs of this potential problem—and "contracts" are broken up in the encounter-group process.

Although groups shift, as an individual builds up "group hours," his or her particular emotional problems and weaknesses become well known throughout the TC. This information is often consciously exchanged and passed around the organization for the benefit of the resident. A person may get a "jacket" (or personality inventory) that becomes known. For example, Jack may get a jacket as a "momma's boy," and in various encounter groups this problem is dealt with until Jack has freed himself from his dependency relationship with his mother.

It is standard operating procedure in a TC not to maintain confidences expressed in a group. Personal data are TC property, and an effort is made to use the information for the benefit of the individual involved in his or her encounter group.

This "fallout" of personal information helps to ensure the continuity of an individual's "treatment" in the TC. In groups, on a continuing basis, a person's particular problem may be worked on until it is resolved.

The following example reveals how a session works in the context of the encounter group. This is an oversimplified condensed example of the way such a session can begin and unfold. The subject here is related to a young man's destructive relationship with his coaddict enabling mother, and how he is on the verge of returning to live with her and use drugs.

Jack, age 24, has been in the TC for four months. He is confronted by the group regarding his excessive dependency on his mother. The group alleges that this has prevented him from identifying with the organization and becoming part of the processes that could help him change his dope-fiend behavior. He counters by stating that the accusations are ridiculous and unfounded. "It's a bum beef." It is pointed out to him that he has been observed to do very little else but wait for phone calls and mail from his mother. (The accusation as part of the encounter process is somewhat exaggerated, since Jack has been moderately working and participating in the program.) After about 15 minutes of group cross-examination, he admits to an extreme, depressing loneliness and the desire to see his mother. He claims that she is the only one in the world who truly loves and understands him. He has thought of splitting to go back to New York to see her.

His claim of his mother's exclusive love for him is scoffed at and ridiculed in the encounter process. In reply, as proof of her love, he points out that "she always gave me money for the commissary when I was in prison." This is ridiculed by the group as "guilt money." Jack cites other examples of his mother's love, including the fact that "when I was strung out, she gave me money for drugs." This comment in defense of his "mother's love" is battered by the group. It is pointed out to him how his mother was not helping but hurting him by supporting his drug abuse. In a more low-key rational approach in the group, his mother's enabling role in Jack's addiction is pointed out to him. The encounter process opens Jack up and he is now receptive to learning more about his problem in a quieter, more rational interchange of concepts and information.

He concludes, "Maybe I am sucking a dry tit and ought to let go of my mom. I love her, but I can see how she feeds my problem." The group advises him to "go through the motions" of forgetting her for awhile and forming a "caring circle" of friends in his TC family, where he can receive help on a daily basis. They point out how he can resume his relationship with his mother under better conditions when he "straightens out" and gains control over his problems. Jack admits to seeing his relationship with his mother in a somewhat clearer light. He "feels better" now that his feelings are "out" and agrees to "get on with his treatment." The encounter and its revelations probably prevented Jack's splitting and returning to his deadly cocaine habit, and his mother's home.

This is obviously a highly oversimplified glimpse of a slice of an encounter-group session. However, it illustrates something of the kind of interaction used in an attempt to produce facts about a situation, the types of defenses used, some of the insights into behavior, and some of the suggestions for change. Not all dimensions of a problem are worked out for an individual in any single session. Over a long period of time, however, many members benefit from the help of a group that is familiar with their difficulty, since others in the group have or had similar problems and can identify with the persons and the subject on the hot seat.

Group Role Models

There are usually no appointed leaders in a TC encounter group. This is not to say that a group leader does not emerge in any given session. The leadership, however, evolves in a spontaneous way as a result of a seniority in group experience and the person's effective talent and ability to contribute to the group process.

The senior members of a TC who have logged more encounter-group time are usually more sophisticated in their ability. For example, when they get together in a "senior members' group" (as often occurs), they throw up fewer "smoke screens" to defend and obscure their problems. They waste less time on irrelevancies, and quickly get to the subject under attack. Their senior-member group fighting style is more like using a rapier than a bludgeon. When a point is made, the group does not dwell on it and savor its "great success" but moves into another problem area. At least one senior-group person is injected into every group to facilitate the interaction, pace, and productivity of each encounter-group session.

Also built into the encounter-group session is an awareness of each group member's ability to take a bombardment of truth at that time about himself or herself. The newcomer is often handled lightly (given a "pass") until he or she becomes trained in the method. More experienced senior residents are considered fair game for all-out confrontation. When they are on the hot seat, there is an assumption that their encounter-group experiences have toughened their emotional hides. They usually can defend more capably and are better prepared to deal with the group's unsettling appraisal of their personal problems.

When newly arrived individuals dominate a group, the sessions are more apt to be cathartic sessions that involve excessive "emotional vomiting" and wild verbal responses. As an individual grows and develops skills in the TC organization, he or she usually develops better control and has greater insight. Older members tend to be more intellectual, and in most respects more capable, in encounter-group sessions.

The subject and focus of a session need to be varied, and are often controlled by the older, more experienced group members. One TC leader made this comment on the subject: "There is a tendency, if you don't vary the group's material, to run out of gas. When you shoot your wad with one person or topic, then move on to another, it's a refreshing experience. You have new strength, you have new data to work with. It's very tiring to go on and on and on with one person on the hot seat for too long. After you've talked to someone for ten or 20 minutes, move over to someone else. Everyone in the group can learn more from using a different set of 'emotional muscles.'"

A conscious dimension of the TC group process is the use of the senior member as a role model, and this is often done in the group session. A role model is a person who has been in the situation of the new person and has made progress to a higher level of performance in the TC and in life. The role model is a dynamic example of what the newcomer can become after he or she grows and develops in the TC.

Often a comment is made by the senior person in an encounter group to the effect that: "I remember when I was like you when I was here X amount of time." The role model then shares why he or she no longer feels in imminent danger of returning to drugs or alcohol. This permits the newcomer to identify with someone who has experienced the same internal conflicts, and has resolved these issues.

A senior role model provides some preliminary information about the problems that the newcomer can anticipate when he or she reaches different levels of social functioning. A role model might comment to a newcomer: "I vividly remember telling a group exactly what you just said. I talked about how helpless I felt at the prospect of never drinking or smoking pot again, and in the back of my mind I had this terrible urge to use. I, too, thought that after I've been clean six months, I could smoke and drink 'recreationally.' I've been there. I tried it two or three times, fell right on my ass, and went back to my old habit. Now that I've been clean two years, I know I can't use, even a little. I can't use at all. Maybe you can benefit from my experiences with failure. Take my word for it. You are just like I was, and like me you can't use any drugs 'recreationally.' It's a dumb idea."

This kind of open self-revelation by the senior patient-therapist in a TC is a factor not usually found in professional group therapy. Professionals seldom use their own problems as examples for the patient. In fact, this is counterindicated in most therapeutic methodologies. In a TC, however, it is standard technique for the acting "doctor" to "cop out" and identify with the "patient's" problem. In group, therefore, a recovering resident has pointed out an achievable, positive goal, exemplified by a person who can guide his or her growth from the successful position of personal experience. The role-model concept is openly discussed in TCs as a basic socialization process for developing a drug-free personality.

It is important to note that related to the senior role model concept is the fact that both the senior patient and the junior patient are involved in a therapeutic interaction that is of value to both of them. As Don Cressey stated, "When addict A *helps* addict B, addict A is helped." When the role model is explaining why the junior cannot use again, he or she is reinforcing his or her own resolution to stay drug-free. Therefore, the addict in a TC playing "therapist" is being helped personally by performing the therapeutic role. And since all residents of a TC at various times play "therapist," they are helping resolve their own problems in the process.

The dynamic that should be emphasized in this interaction is that the "junior patient" can perceive what he or she can become by the role model, and the "senior patient" can see where he or she was in his or her earlier approach to life. This constant reminder of the way the senior resident was as a newcomer is important in reinforcing the resolve to remain drug-free.

Valid and Phony Insights in Encounter Groups

An important element in the process of encounter groups is an attack on the "self-deception" of the addict-alcoholic. This attack on self-deceptions and rationalizations facilitates a result of true insight into the addict's self and problems—insights and truths about the problem, family, real friends, and realistic life goals. Therefore, in encounter groups in TCs, *valid* self-examination, self-learning, and insights are most desirable goals, and in this regard parallel the dynamics and goals of traditional professional therapies.

An expression that has emerged in the lexicon of TCs is "the cunning dope fiend." What is implied by this term is that the alcoholic and the addict are too often cunning or devious in perpetuating the self-deception that enables them to rationalize their self-destructive tendency to drink or use drugs. In standard therapy situations, they often employ devious techniques to, as one TC leader put it, "avoid the information that could save their life."

Following is an example of what I would term "the phony insight game" or the "pseudopsychology" that is often employed by addicts in an effort to avoid confronting their *real* problems.

The following incident occured in a professionally directed therapy group in a correctional facility for addicts. A group member heavily involved in the group's discussion made the "insightful discovery" that he used drugs to rebel against his proper, respectable father. The "insight" occurred as a result of a series of interchanges with a "therapeutic-contract" partner, his roommate in the prison who in a later session revealed a remarkable "insight" of his own. The two involved in this kind of reciprocal deception (in some cases, a third person gets a "piece of the action") nurture and manipulate each other over several sessions into revealing their smokescreen "discoveries." These "insights" (even when they have some degree of validity) enable the individuals who have revealed them to get the group off their backs for a time, since they are "obviously making progress" in understanding themselves. They also believe they are making good progress and points toward being released from the institution. In brief, their "insights" are used to convince the treatment people and the staff that they are making progress and are eligible for release from prison.

This kind of phony insight discovery does not usually occur in a TC encounter group, because the group's awareness of this game tends to deter the development or continuation of this pattern of psychological masturbation. Also, most TC encounter group's pat pseudopsychological answers are encountered when they are used as rationales for negative behavior.

In the annals of Synanon, a particular incident helps to reveal the Synanon approach to what I have termed "the phony insight discovery," a ploy used unconsciously to obfuscate the person's real problem. It describes in detail the way Dederich and his associates dealt with this phenomenon.

The episode was described to me by Reid Kimball, one of Chuck's directors, in the following way: "Lefty committed several offenses of the following type. He would bully or threaten another resident, usually a smaller guy. He never used any violence because he knew that he might get kicked out for it. On about his third offense, Chuck and I were in a group with him, and the two of us began to work him over on his problem with the group's help. What happened in this particular case was that we were discussing an incident where he had threatened another resident—his boss, Bill Crawford—with a tire iron he took out of a car. Bill had ordered him to do something in the course of fixing a flat on one of our trucks. Compared with Lefty, Bill is a physical lightweight.

"In the group we confronted Lefty with his atrocious behavior. He began to use a psychological mishmash of terms to rationalize and defend his behavior. He said that he had a psychological block, that he was displacing aggression, and a whole bunch of other rationalizations and bullshit. Some of it may have even been true.

"Chuck and I glanced at each other and mutually decided to put him on. Chuck said something like, 'Well, let's examine the psychological implications of your violent behavior with Bill.' Lefty brightened up, and we went at it. Chuck said, 'Let's analyze it. Is there any significant figure in your earlier life, or is there any situation that comes to your mind when you think about the incident?'

"Lefty's eyes began to glitter, and he said, 'Let me think.' Chuck saw him take the bait and said, 'This may help explain your violent behavior. Think hard.' Lefty pursed his lips, acted pained, wrinkled his brow, stared up at the ceiling, and went off into a reverie of deep thought.

"He then said, 'Gee, that makes a lot of sense. It certainly brings something to my consciousness. At one period, when I was a kid, and I used to wash dishes...'

"'Who did you wash dishes for?'

"'It was my grandmother! She had certain way of talking to me and a nasal twang and...'

"'And perhaps this reminds you of Crawford?'

"'That's it! Crawford sounds just like my grandmother. She used to make me wash dishes and nag at me when I wanted to go out and play. She really use to incite my hostility.'

"Then Chuck said, 'Well, maybe we've hit on it. Crawford, with his particular approach and his voice tone, seems to trigger you, and you associate his behavior with your abusive grandma.' Everyone joined in to confirm Lefty's exciting insight discovery. They further noted that Lefty's hostility toward his grandmother was displaced on to Crawford.

"Lefty picked up on the group's approval and went on further: 'By God, that's it exactly—when Crawford comes on like he does, it's my abusive grandmother all over again. No wonder I blow up and...'

"At this point, Lefty was beaming—carrying on and everything—and then Chuck pushed him right off the cliff, 'You lying son of a bitch, you're so full of shit, it's ridiculous!' With that, everyone in the group broke up in a loud roar of laughter.

"Dederich analyzed the situation as follows: 'Here he was, trying to rationalize away his bad behavior with this bullshit story he had dug out of Psychology I.' Of course, he couldn't get away with it in Synanon. The Lefty story spread all over the club; and from that day on, whenever anyone tried to pull that crap to avoid *personal responsibility for their behavior*, someone would say, 'You're pulling a Lefty!' or 'It sounds just like Lefty's grandmother.'"

The encounter group, therefore, makes it difficult for an individual to hide behind a false insight, complicate a simple behavioral situation with pseudoanalysis, or maintain a "therapeutic contract" for any length of time. "Insight discoveries" are placed under close scrutiny in a TC. If they do stand up after a group assessment, they probably have validity; and in the process, every facet of the insight or situation has been tested and examined.

Professionals tend to lean more heavily on psychological insight. Within the framework of standard professional psychotherapy, insight discoveries (valid or not) are the "bread and butter" of the trade. Professionals may, in fact, encourage insight discoveries to validate their own sense of success. Dederich had this position on the issue: "These insights are, of course, the professional's stock in trade. When someone comes into Synanon loaded with all kinds of psychological mishmash, for awhile we have a hell of a time breaking through to the person beneath. Of course, many psychological principles are valid—and are useful later on in his growth process... But at first we have to deal with the person and his actual behavior at that time. We cannot permit him to use psychological explanations to rationalize his bad behavior. He might shoot dope behind it; and also rationalizations encourage bad behavior and have a negative effect on life in Synanon."

In the TC system, therefore, good behavior is demanded on the implicit assumption that it affects internal (intrapsychic) processes. Most TCs use an approach that is the reverse of that commonly used in traditional psychotherapy. In most therapeutic practice, the starting point for treatment is the internal psychodynamics of the patient. Generally, in professional therapy, the assumption is made that if a person's inner problems are somehow adjusted, he or she will stop "acting out" any "bad" behavior such as using drugs. TCs start with an attack in the encounter group on the reality of overt bad behavior. In the encounter group, and in the person's life situation in the TC, the group demands positive work habits and nondeviant behavior. If the addict in a TC lives positively and constructively drug-free for one or two years, it is conceivable that this will change the addict's inner psychodynamics.

The Encounter Approach in Action

A key issue in the acceptance of the TC approach by many people, especially traditional professionals, is related to their reaction to the encounter group. Many professionals, and people in general, raise such questions as: "Isn't it harmful to verbally attack a person who already has a weak ego?" "How do you know when someone is projecting or ventilating his or her own hostility, and has no concern for the person on the hot seat?" Or the basic question, "How does this approach change the substance abuser's self-destructive behavior?"

My main response to these controversial issues is to point out that in an encounter group what is under attack is not the person or the person's ego, but the person's *behavior*. In addition to this, in an effective encounter session, the group is, through hyperbole and exaggeration, denouncing the self-deception that motivates the resident's self-destructive behavior.

The following example illustrates some of these points in action. In an encounter group in which I was involved, two young recovering addicts—Dinah, 16, and Carl, 17—had developed a relationship. At the time they had been clean around six months. They had "fallen in love" in the therapeutic community, and were both for a time, after they had moved home to their families, attending a drug-addict support group that involved the encounter approach. After a few weeks, Dinah continued attending the group but Carl had dropped out.

In one session the group placed Dinah on the hot seat regarding her continuing relationship with Carl. (This is a summary of the highlights of a 20-minute interaction.)

> Group member: Are you still going with Carl?
> Dinah: Yes.
> Group member: Are you two clean?
> Dinah: I am. But Carl now uses once in awhile. He tells me he smokes a joint with his friends now and then.
> Group member: That's it?
> Dinah: Well, one time last week he really looked high—and

he told me he had done a line of coke. He also had a few drinks.

Group member: In other words, you're hanging out with a lying dope fiend-alcoholic.

Dinah (angrily in defense): He isn't a lying dope fiend. I love him and I resent your bullshit attack on him and me. I know that's all he's using!

Group member: You asshole. This guy was free-basing coke for two years and you're sitting there telling us that he's chippying with a little coke, a little pot, and a little alcohol and it's O.K. with you?

Dinah: You don't understand him. He's really a wonderful person and I resent your attacking us! [Dinah burst into tears and began yelling at and denouncing the attackers. After several more explosive attacks and counterattacks, I summarized the situation, as the group saw it, for Dinah in a quieter, non-threatening and supportive manner.]

L.Y. Dinah, now that you've expressed your anger at the group, let me tell you who you're mad at. You're mad at Dinah. You've been in this place long enough to have learned that a guy who free-based coke for two years and was an alcoholic can't use a little dope. You're deceiving yourself about him—he's using again. Another thing, no one is mad at Carl. We like Carl. He's a nice guy when he's not acting out his dope-fiend behavior.

Now as for you, I shouldn't have to tell you that you're in real danger going with this using dope fiend. You've only been clean six months—and you're very delicately balanced. At this time, going with Carl is not good for you. In fact, it's a dangerous situation.

You really got pissed off at the group and me. You should know that our screaming at you is not an attack on you as a *person*; it's on your current behavior. You were defending and not hearing what this group of ex-addict experts was telling you. So we had to turn up the volume and exaggerate the information we wanted you to hear, for your benefit. All we are saying is that if you continue this relationship, you are in imminent danger of returning to drugs.

Another point that needs to be made, Dinah, is that you've become Carl's coaddict and enabler. You're making it easier for him to use drugs because you are *denying* that he's using again. If you love him, you have to pull his cover and tell him the truth about what he's doing. If you do that, he may have a chance. He might return to sobriety and this group, which he desperately needs. [Jokingly] Now that you've exploded and insulted everyone in the room for attacking you, when we've really been trying to help you, what's your reaction?

At this point Dinah, who had exploded in anger and tears, was smiling, receptive, and listening carefully to what was being said. She began to acknowledge that she had been deceiving herself about Carl and had to do something about either getting him back into the group or breaking off the relationship.

This was a prototypical session that went through six basic phases.

1. The group members put a person on the hot seat for behavior they suspect is dangerous to them.

2. The subject provides a small amount of distorted information. Under attack, the subject's self-deception is revealed. More truth surfaces.

3. The subject explodes at the group in a last burst of denial, where she makes the group the enemy, so that she doesn't have to accept personal responsibility for her coaddict behavior.

4. Someone in the group (in this case, L.Y.) calmly analyzes and explains, now that the subject is more willing to listen, what appears to be going on in the person's life.

5. The subject, after ventilating her displaced anger at the group, acknowledges that she is really angry at herself, for her self-deception.

6. She then accepts the group's consensual opinion on the issue, which is usually summarized by one group member. This tends to lead to a positive change of behavior. In this case Dinah developed more evidence that Carl had returned to drug use, felt that going with him was now contraindicated, and broke away from the relationship.

Random Encounter-Group Issues

I have utilized the encounter-group method in my work with many adolescent groups and have found it to be most effective. Adolescents are usually adroit at confronting another teenager's self-delusions, but are sensitive and vulnerable when they become the target of the group themselves. It takes most teenagers longer than adults to accept the encounter as a technique for their emotional benefit and not to take the verbal challenge as a personal assault. This may be due to the fact that many teenagers, especially those in trouble, have harsh disciplining parents who really do not care about them. These youngsters tend to see criticism as an extension of what they received at home from their uncaring abusive parents. It takes awhile for these adolescents to comprehend the encounter group in its proper perspective.

The most difficult aspect of these tough-love groups for most people, including adolescents, to understand is that in the encounter group the rules that apply in civilized society are modified, so that many facets of an issue can be explored. In normal society, rudeness, insulting language, exaggeration, and ridicule are unacceptable forms of expression for gracious relating. In the encounter group, anything goes verbally. No physical violence is permitted because, among other reasons, a physically smaller person would not be able to tell a stronger person something that might help him or her understand himself or herself better.

It is important to emphasize the fact that after an effective encounter group, as in Dinah's session, the person who was talked to needs, and should get, positive reinforcement. For example, after the group involving Dinah, several people discussed the session with her, over coffee, in a more coherent and sympathetic way.

Many substance abusers who formerly used violence, alcohol, or drugs to insulate themselves from life's realities are thrown onto their verbal resources in relating to others. They learn to interact with words. This facilitates their ability to communicate through a verbal mode of expression rather than with their fists or other possible "weaponry."

The encounter-group approach, because of these factors, is especially therapeutic for formerly physically abusive or violent people. As a result of their training in encounter-groups, they learn how to channel their rage into verbal rather than physically violent behavior.

The power of an individual's confrontation abilities in a TC encounter group appears to be correlated with the emotional strength of the attacker and the attacker's position in the hierarchy. Old-timers in a TC have developed more powerful verbal weapons and speak from a more powerful position in the hierarchy. Their sword has a sharper edge, but at the same time, they have learned to level their verbal encounter with more precision. They are more likely to direct their critique at the person's behavioral problems than the "self," and seem to know when to give a person positive support. They are also less likely to be doing it out of their own emotional needs to attack another person.

An important rationale for the encounter group is that the recipient doesn't "hear properly" in areas where he or she is emotionally blocked. In fact, in sessions that I witnessed, an obvious problem that has been pointed out several times to someone is often literally not heard.

The term "encounter," in a sense, is a misnomer. It is more accurate to view the encounter as an effort to communicate some information useful to the recipient, information that the person appears to have an emotional block to hearing. Consequently ridicule, caricature, exaggeration, analog, repetition, and other devices are used. The volume of the attempt to communicate is turned up at times and down when the person is "rationally" listening to the information about his or her behavior that is being presented by the group.

Sometimes a person in an encounter-group hears relevant data about himself or herself when someone else is on the hot seat. This indirect learning process is referred to as a "carom shot." This involves telling person A what one also wants person B or C to hear and learn. For example, I recall commenting in one session, "You know, Judy, you're just like Mike here and Charley. Like them, you don't listen..." In fact, many people receive effective therapy in an encounter group from listening closely to the data leveled at another person because the message of the encounter applies to them as well as the subject.

Another significant factor in the encounter process is reflected in the "projection principle." Often the person in a group who is "screaming" at another person is talking about himself or herself. People in encounter groups often "project" their own problems onto another person in the process. The projection process is usually pointed out at some later point in the session. For example, someone may say, "You know, Jack, when you were screaming at Mary when she was talking about her feelings about leaving here and going back to drugs, you sounded like you were trying to suppress your own feelings on that issue. How about that?"

The rationale for using ridicule may appear harsh at first. However, as one TC leader described it, "Ridiculous behavior deserves to be ridiculed." The person's behavior (not the "self") is being examined, and if it is ridiculous, the person is ridiculed. He or she is often laughed at by the group for certain past acts. When the person begins to laugh with the group at himself or herself, he or she is considered to be on the road to recovery. Caricaturing someone's behavior is, in part, like holding a magnifying glass up to that behavior so that the person can look at himself or herself more clearly. For example, one of the classic ridiculous comments of an alcoholic or an addict is: "I can quit using anytime I want to." Whenever this is stated in an encounter group, the rationalization will be appropriately laughed at, taken apart, and ridiculed by the group.

It is important to emphasize the fact that the encounter group is always supplemented and enriched in a positive way by later informal discussions in a "caring circle" of friends in the TC. All residents in a TC are encouraged to develop and nurture a caring circle of people with whom they can discuss issues brought up in the group in a more casual interpretive, analytic, and supportive way. These nurturing, supportive discussions with a caring circle of friends are most significant in the overall group process in TCs.

The encounter-group process is an element in another important group method used in most TCs. This method—known as the "marathon," "retreat," or "trip"—involves exploring the personal problems of residents using the encounter-group process, visuals, music, and lectures over a two- or three-day span of time. The expanded time form for self-examination allows more extended coverage of an issue—and additionally opens people up more to deeper elements of their life. People in the marathon group, after a day or two (often without sleep), tend to let down their emotional defenses, and often break into new areas of disclosure, revelation, and insight.

PSYCHODRAMA IN TCs

A methodology that has been effectively incorporated into TC work is psychodrama. My recent research into TCs reveals that most of them around the world incorporate some form of psychodrama or role training in their programs. I have been involved as a trainer and consultant in helping to incorporate psychodrama into the programs of a number of TCs.

Interestingly, many TC directors have told me how the psychodrama method often emerges spontaneously in an encounter-group session. One typical example involved a young woman on a marathon. When her ego defenses were low on the third day of the group meetings, she began talking about her unresolved hostility toward her father, who had sexually abused her. At a certain point in her monologue to the group on her painful and hostile feelings toward her father, she said, "It's weird but Dominic here [another addict] really reminds me of my father." At this point a senior member of the group, who had had some experience with psychodrama, said, "O.K. Dominic will play the role of your father."

What followed was an intense, cathartic verbal outburst of hostility toward "the father," which verged on physical violence. The director of the session placed a pillow in front of Dominic, and the young woman, without too much encouragement, viciously rained blows on the pillow as she expressed her venom about how her father's sexual abuse had caused her a life of pain and how she had used drugs to kill the pain. Her feelings were later shared by other women in the group. The woman's psychodrama experience became the focal point for a valuable, cathartic, and analytic session on how early parental abuse had been part of the drug and alcohol problems of various residents of the TC.

My book, *Psychodrama* (Gardner Press, 1981) describes psychodrama theory and method in comprehensive detail. The following summary of the basic methodology of psychodrama is derived from my book:

Psychodrama is a natural and automatic process. Everyone at some time has an inner drama going on in his or her mind. In this confidential setting, the people involved are the stars of their mental psychodrama session and they play all of the roles. The others they encounter in the monodrama can be their parents, an employer, a God they love, or someone who has forsaken them—a wife, husband, or lover who has rejected them.

Many people are able to act out these internal psychodramas in the reality and activity of their external lives. For such people psychodrama is not a necessary vehicle, except as an interesting adjunct to their life experiences. But for most people, psychodrama can provide a unique opportunity for externalizing their internal world onto a theatrical stage of life; and, with the help of the group present at a session, emotional conflicts and problems can often be resolved.

Psychodrama produces peak experiences—or exciting modes of acting—that often result in individual and social change. In psychodrama a person encounters his or her conflicts and psychic pain in a setting that more closely approximates his or her real-life situation than do most other therapeutic approaches. For example, a young man in conflict with his parent talks directly to a person who, as an auxiliary ego, plays his parent. His fantasy (or reality) of his hostility or love can be acted out on the spot. He can experience his pain (in one context, his "primal emotions") not in an artificial setting but in direct relationship to the "father," "mother," or other person who helped build the pain into him. The psychodrama enactment takes place as closely as possible to the pertinent, specific core situations of a subject's life. The resolution of pain or conflict does not necessarily require an extensive analysis or discussion because the subject of a session is experiencing the emotions in action. Often when someone has had a deep psychodramatic experience, there is no need for lengthy group discussion—sharing—or analysis. The protagonist has learned about the mystery of the problem in action; he or she feels better immediately, and it is not necessary to go beyond that point.

In most sessions benefits can accrue to members of the group other than the central protagonist. Group participants are encouraged to witness aspects of their own lives that became manifest in the session, as if watching a dramatic play that projects their own behavior onto the stage in front of them. This kind of personal participation, either as a subject or a member of a group in a live psychodrama, produces maximum emotional impact and the therapeutic benefits.

A session I directed with a young man named George helps illustrate the dynamics of psychodrama as utilized in a TC setting. In George's case psychodrama became a valuable adjunct to other group methods from which he was benefiting in the TC. The fact that George had an intense hatred for his father had surfaced in many group sessions; and it appeared that George's drug abuse was an effort to kill the constant pain of this extreme hatred. George's hostility toward his father was displaced onto other people in the TC, and despite the fact that he had discussed his problem in many encounter groups, he seemed to be stuck with his problem, and this impeded his therapeutic progress in the TC.

In the session George went back in time to a basic and traumatic scene in his life with his father. He acted out a horrendous situation that occurred when he was eight: his father had punished him by tying him up by his hands to a ceiling beam in their cellar—like meat on a hook—and then beat him with a belt.

After George had physically acted out much of his rage by retaliating in the psychodrama against his father with a padded encounter bat, I finally improvised a psychodramatic vehicle that facilitated a conversation between George and the auxiliary ego "father." I put a table between him and his "father." At the same time he talked to his father, I gave him the option and the freedom to punch a pillow that he accepted symbolically as his father. This combination of psychodrama devices enabled George to structure in thought and put into words his deep venom for his father. He blurted out much of his long-repressed hatred in a lengthy diatribe. Finally we removed the props, and after his rage was spent, he fell into his "father's" arms and began to sob, "Why couldn't you love me? I was really a good kid, Dad. Why couldn't you love me?"

In a later psychodrama session in the TC, I had him reverse roles and play the role of his father, and for the first time he began to empathize with the early experiences in his father's life that brutalized him. George's grandfather—who beat his son—was the original culprit, and George was indirectly receiving the fallout of his father's anger toward his father, or George's grandfather. When George reversed roles and returned to himself, it diminished his hostility toward his father because he was able to understand better why his father was the way he was; and he, at least psychodramatically, that day forgave him.

A central point in explicating George's extreme psychodrama experience is to reveal that the learning in action on his part, combined with his encounter groups, was effective. It was not enough for George to just talk about his anger or yell at others in encounter groups. He required a vehicle such as psychodrama that gave him the opportunity to reenact, physically and psychologically, the scenarios of his father's abuses of him in their bizarre details, and then dispel his rage in a role-playing session.

Most people require an active vehicle for expression, either exclusively or as an adjunct to another approach. It is apparent to many individual therapists that many people, when embroiled in the discussion of deep emotions, either have the urge or actually get up out of their chairs and begin to move around physically. It is precisely at this point of action that psychodrama comes into play. There is a resonance between encounter-group work and role playing, and there is ample psychodramatic evidence that most people can benefit from some form of learning in action as an adjunct to their verbal-discussion therapy. The psychodramatic method has become a method utilized in many therapeutic communities everywhere.

In recent years I have conducted a number of week long training sessions with Italian TC leaders who have effectively incorporated the psychodramatic approach into their programs. In particular, since 1983 I have directed hundreds of psychodramas several times a week with adolescent addict-alcoholics in a TC-oriented psychiatric hospital. Psychodrama blends well with other group processes and has proved to be an extremely effective method for treating the recovering residents of TCs.

CROSS-COMPARING GROUP PROCESSES IN A TC AND IN TRADITIONAL TREATMENT INSTITUTIONS

In concluding my discussion of group methods and processes in TCs, it is of value summarily to cross-compare the varied group processes that are utilized in a TC in comparison with professional group therapy in most traditional clinics, hospitals, and institutions. TC group sessions often operate within a social scheme and under a set of conditions different from those of standard professional group therapy.

1. The group sessions in TCs are administered by a group of peers who have similar problems. Because of a similarity of life experiences and identifications, a fellow TC member is more likely to be acceptable as a "therapist" than the usual professional. Also, compared with the usual professional therapist, the TC member is not seen as an authority figure in the usual sense.

2. The TC member can and does reverse roles as "patient" and "therapist" in TC group sessions. The person who plays the role of a therapeutic agent in an encounter group expects, and often does obtain, some insights into his or her own problems in the process of helping the other person. He or she often projects his or her own problems into the situation. This kind of cooperative therapy is the essence of a true total therapeutic community.

3. TCs involve a democratic approach to "psychological interaction." There is an absence of the usual status differences between "patients" and "doctors." This condition of equality among group

members seems to facilitate a deeper intensity and involvement than the process involved in standard group therapy in a traditional institution.

4. The emotional growth of each person in the TC is of concern to everyone in the TC society. Everyone's success and personal growth are part of the TC's overall development. An enlightened self-interest in helping another member is a significant motivating force for all participants. There is a "gut-level" recognition that "no man can be an island" in a TC. Involvement entails helping other members, and this is fostered by an *esprit de corps* that does not exist in most other institutional settings.

5. The group session material is timely, pertinent, and important to all members of the group, partly because they live together in the same community. In contrast, in professional group therapy in the open community, group members usually come from various walks of life, convene for a session, and then return to their private worlds. This kind of treatment can become a therapeutic game, not closely related to basic life situations, since the group members do not live in the same social environment. In TC groups a person locks horns with others who are part of his or her actual primary group, or family. Everyone is a "significant other" to residents in the TC life space. The "other" confronting a person in the TC group may be a roommate, an employer, a lover, or a spouse. Having the other person understand or get a "correct" self-picture of himself or herself is of crucial importance. When a decision is made in a group session, the person has, to a large extent, acted. The encounter group or the psychodrama in a TC is therefore a live potent situation, and the outcome of a session has real meaning for all participants in the organization. This primary-group "family" factor makes all group sessions more intense since they are vital to the resident's recovery and the overall success of the TC program.

5

Dealing with Crisis

In one context, the overall society can be perceived to be in a war over drug abuse. There are people vehemently opposed to substance abuse, moderates (people who don't care), and proponents of drug abuse. Most TCs, despite the fact that they are supposed to be "antidrug societies," have all of these same complex forces at work in their community on both an overt and a covert level.

On the surface everyone in the TC is committed to staying drug-free. On another, more subterranean level, however, the drug/nondrug war rages, and it is a serious life-and-death struggle for all individuals in the community.

THE DRUG-ATTITUDE RATING SCALE

When an addict is drug-free in a TC, the number of consecutive "clean days" is important. However, more important is the person's covert attitude regarding drugs. By "drug-attitude" I am referring to the addict's true commitment to quit self-destructive substance abuse (including alcohol) for life. The ex-addict who has been drug-free for a year may be more vulnerable to imminent regression than someone who is clean 90 days if he or she has a poorer drug attitude. This is due to the fact that the 90-day clean addict has a a greater anti-drug attitude than the one-year-clean person.

A drug-attitude is difficult to measure because it operates on both the overt and the covert mental level. For example, the newly arrived addict may overtly seem to be voluntarily committed to totally quitting drugs; however, the commitment may only be word deep. Their attitude may be related to the fact that he or she is badly addicted; is ill; has an imminent court appearance and wants to look good; or the addict has hit the wall of final rejection from an employer or family and has to demonstrate a zealous overt commitment to becoming drug-free. The underlying drug attitude to truly quit their addiction may be at the zero level; however, temporary circumstances force him or her to enter a TC and put on a show of serious intent.

On a drug-attitude scale, people who are using drugs and are committed to drug use are obviously zero; and a person not using drugs (or alcohol) with total true commitment *never* to use drugs is a 10. The recovering addict's drug attitude may, therefore, be analyzed on a scale of 0 to 10. A drug attitude of 0–3 is a low level; 4–7 is a good level; 8–10 is an excellent attitudinal level.

In TC groups, a person's drug attitude ratings is a useful topic for discussion periodically during an addict-alcoholic's recovery. There are two perspectives on the drug-attitude assessment: how recovering addicts assess themselves and how the group rates them.

In my work with adolescent drug addicts in encounter groups, I often periodically assess their drug attitudes and find it is a useful ritual. Some teenagers functioning at a low-level drug attitude (around 2) openly admit, "I'm staying clean only because I'm in this program and I want to get the heat off me. I don't want to go to the state reformatory. As soon as the heat is off and I'm out, I fully plan to get stoned." Those with a high drug attitude (8) say, "I really want to quit, but it's a struggle. All my old friends at school use and it's hard to say no." Still others, on an excellent level (10), have stated, "I'm still tempted when I'm offered some drugs. But I'm really enjoying life now without any shit—and it's a good feeling. I've been clean now for six months and I think I'm going to make it O.K. I'm especially enjoying having very few hassles with my parents."

When I have my groups perform the drug-attitude exercise I first have an individual rate himself or herself, and then comment on why he or she has come to this conclusion about himself or herself. Then I have each group member in turn rate the individual, and comment on the person's subjective rating. Sometimes the group's overall rating is consonant with the individual's assessment. In other cases the individual may rate himself or herself lower or, in a self-serving way, higher than the group's assessment. This usually leads to an interesting, heated, and productive discussion.

When a person overrates himself or herself, he or she is often shot down by someone in the group. For example, one adolescent, Mike, gave himself a 9. When I went around the group, a friend of his said incredulously, "A 9!! When I went on pass a few days ago, you asked me to bring back a joint for you. You're a 2!" It was apparent to the rest of the group that Mike, in terms of his drug attitude was operating at a level of 2, and was inflating his degree of change.

STAYING WITH THE PROGRAM

Staying drug-free in a TC, dealing with regression, and managing the various crises that normally emerge in the recovery process are complex issues. Dealing with the recovering addict's crises is an ongoing problem. An important crisis issue is related to the drug-attitude level; however, a more fundamental issue is staying in a program where there is an open door, and the resident can leave at will.

A viewpoint I have used in my substance-abuser group discussion is to perceive the drugs formerly used by the addict as "bad friends." The "bad-friend" drug was helpful in sedating emotional pain and creating a false aura of fun and pleasure. The substance abuser, however, paid an enormous price for the "friendship." In certain respects, in the recovery process, the addict has lost the "best friend" drug—something that could be relied on to carry him or her through difficult times. In this analog of the "lost friend," the recovering resident feels a certain amount of grief for the loss, and goes through a kind of grieving process. It is difficult to give up a friend, even a bad one like drugs or alcohol. After the grieving process is over, the recovering substance abuser must learn how to deal with his or her problems, emotional pain, and life situation in a clean and direct way. A major step in the recovery process is to use the TC program by making positive attachments to the people and the group methods available in the TC instead of leaving the program and returning to reliable but self-destructive "old friends."

At first the newcomer's positive attachment in a TC is quite fragile. The longer he or she stays in the drug-free environment, the more he or she is drawn into and becomes attached to the hard core of older residents who are devoted to an antidrug posture. At first it is important to "buy time" for the newcomer. Research into TCs reveals that when the recovering addict-alcoholic stays and gets past the three-month mark, he or she is most apt to "make it."

The commitment of the ex-addict leaders is usually greater as they are further away from returning to an addict existence than the newcomers. The newer people are closer to the periphery of the circle of involvement. People at this outer fringe tend emotionally to have one foot in and one foot out of the organization.

When someone slips or leaves the TC, the newcomer is more apt to be shaken by this split than an old-timer, since the involvement in the organization is quite fragile, and his or her drug-attitude rating is lower. The member who leaves the TC prematurely, produces a measure of crisis for those members who have an emotional tie with the "splittee." A split results from a recovering addict-alcoholic's personal crisis, and also produces varying levels of crisis in the organization.

Newcomers fail and leave the program for a variety of reasons. One type of potential splittee is the person who cannot be induced to "believe" that the new environment in which the person finds himself or herself is "for real," and that he or she can trust people in the TC. This "limited-belief" feeling is often found in newcomers who have tried other organizations for help and failed. Upon arriving at the TC, they are apt to encounter many individuals whom they knew in another institution. Despite the overwhelming weight of visual evidence of the differential quality of the TC as an organization, they still, as one TC leader remarked, "have a high level of mistrust."

Individuals who have been in prison bring a special type of mistrust. Such splittees sometimes become so engrossed in perceiving the TC as a custodial structure that they may leave in a ridiculous fashion. For example, one such person left by way of the building fire escape in the middle of the night. He could, of course, simply have walked out the front door.

The case of Bobby, who in the past had been in prison for many years, reveals the prison syndrome. In a group session it was pointed out to him that he acted like a prison psychopath. He continued to have a self-image of being a "stand-up guy" (someone who upholds criminal values). Reference was made to a situation in which he withheld information about another resident who had confided in him his intention to split. His confusion about "squealing in prison" and telling the truth in the TC was pointed out to him by a TC leader who had once been in his shoes and had himself done a lot of prison time. "I would agree with you that maybe a guy should not rat in prison. In the joint he gets few enough privileges. So if he has some contraband in his cell or has some Mickey Mouse homosexual deal going for him, why snitch? Life is hard enough; why should he have to go to the hole? However, in here when you 'tell' about someone's bad behavior or, in the case of Joe, his plan to split, you're helping the person, not squealing on him. It may be a kind of therapeutic first aid. The minute his symptoms begin to flare by bad behavior or a desire to leave this place that can help him, your revealing this fact may help save his life. Instead of his splitting, and going back to drugs, if we learn about it, someone may be able to point him back into the right direction. If you squeal on him in here, you're helping to save his life."

The newcomer who has not established any significant "caring-circle" relationships with other people in a TC is also a potential splittee. The "loner" who is not drawn into the group has less chance of making it. The relationship he or she vitally needs may come from an old-timer, another newcomer, or a clique of several people. The person needs to find someone or a subgroup in the TC organization with whom he or she feels free to discuss intimate momentary or long-term problems. It is of particular importance to have this kind of caring circle of therapeutic friends when an inevitable personal crisis appears, since crises of this kind are par for the course for recovering addict-alcoholics.

The attraction and motivation to leave the TC and return to drugs may be related to a coaddict spouse or someone who is not a TC resident who is attempting to pull the person out of the TC. The following discussion from an encounter group depicts an individual close to becoming a splittee from a California TC. It reveals some of the cross-pressure crises that the person who is a relative newcomer faces and how he or she can productively discuss them in group, and in this way avert sliding back into drugs.

In this encounter-group session, Al, a former heroin and cocaine addict, appeared to be "in trouble" because of an extreme concern for his wife, who lived in Chicago. He wanted to stay and "do something for himself." However, outside pressure from his wife was building.

Al: Since I came here two months ago, I keep thinking about my wife and I can't handle it. I'm always considering my wife. I'm always considering her, man, like in the future, you know? I can block her out of the now for awhile, but she's on my mind all the time. I feel like I got to do something about her.

Nancy: What does she want you to do?

Al: Well, she wants to be with me, and I guess I want to be with her. I really don't know; I know that this it the only broad I think about. I ask myself how bad I want her here. Do I want her to come here and see how I really am? I know she's got some real distorted image of me. To her, everything looks real swinging—beautiful. And right now I feel pretty shitty about myself.

It's pressing me, man. Sometimes I feel like the only way I'll ever make it with my old lady is to cut out—to split. Then I realize that it wouldn't work, and I'd probably start using drugs again. I'm real confused. I just want her to think I'm sort of a great guy, you know, who is curing himself. I guess I would like to maintain my macho image with her as a heavy-duty drug dealer. I don't want her to see this helpless baby side of me that comes out in here. I'm caught in the middle.

It never worked when I was with her. When I was with her, I used drugs, and probably would again. But I still want to be with her.

Pete: You know what? I think you're some kind of morbid asshole or something, man. About a month ago, you were telling me the same goddam thing over at the dorm next door, when we were living over there.... Your wife and all those words that you said tonight. You've been carrying this on for three months. You know, she's on your mind and blah, blah, blah, you know, on and on and on, man. How long are you going to carry this shit on?

Al: Well, that's the point.

Pete: Yeah, it is the point.

Al: I feel that I've got to get it straightened out somehow. It's in my gut—I can't understand it—but, you know, I got to get it straightened out somehow in my gut.

Wilbur: Al, you don't have to feed yourself a lot bullshit. You want your old lady?

Al: Yeah.

Wilbur: Start from there.

Al: Yeah, I do, but then I always go through the same shit—I can't help that, man. That's how I think, man. I go into a real long extended debate—the pros and cons—and I argue with myself.

Wilbur: After two months in here?

Al: Since the day I walked through the door, if you want to

put it that way. Yeah, I got a tie with the broad, man.

Pete: Well, why don't you work toward getting her here to see how you feel about that?

Al: I am. I've got it worked out.

Pete: No, why don't you do something toward getting her here?

Nancy: I thought she was coming here for the summer to stay?

Al: Well, that's a possibility. I gave myself like a minimum of a year, you know, before I would see her again. The thing is, I want her very much, but what I want is for her to come and live here and be with me. This is what I want. All the other problems are secondary. But I also feel that it's an awful short time, and that's where the conflict comes up. I'm afraid that if she comes down in a year, I don't know what I'll do—I went into a hell of a thing when she was here for a week. And I got both of these directions pulling at me. I'm afraid to have her here, yet I want her here.

Wilbur: In the meantime you're obviously in pretty bad shape. Why don't you cut her loose, Al? After all, you've both always used drugs together—and that's what will happen again if you got back together with her. She's still using drugs, isn't she?

Al: Yes. You're right, Wilbur. If I go by the past I have to think here's a broad I probably don't really want, and isn't good for me. I was forced to marry her because she was pregnant. Most of it is just guilt, and it's going to drive me out the door back to drugs. I know she's still using heroin and cocaine. I can't handle a dope-fiend wife now. It would be destructive to me and her.

Al worked on his difficult conflict over several months. The odds on his going back to his wife and remaining drug-free were slim at that time, and this was reinforced by others who had been through a similar experience. He resolved his crisis conflict by constantly talking about it in groups. This enabled him to resist splitting for another six months and to develop a resistance to regression.

At a later point, his wife, who had been using drugs, saw his successful recovery, was impressed with his progress, and joined him in the program. They "graduated" and left the TC about a year later. They maintained a supportive contact with the program, and both of them had been successful in resisting drugs, at last check, for over five years. If he had left when he was going through his crisis of feeling, both Al and his wife would have failed.

In general, the longer a person lives drug-free in an antidrug TC, the more likely that person is to develop the social skills and emotional maturity necessary for living a drug-free life in the larger society, without the "bad friend." Consequently staying power is a significant issue. Dederich's commentary on the issue of splitting is helpful in understanding the group process. "Here's the phenomenon we have in Synanon right now. There is now a hard-core center of antidrug people, who have learned to live their lives without drugs. They are not likely to split and go back to drugs. There are concentric circles and an ever-widening core of people who, we are sure, will stay no matter what happens. You could call these core people 'positively cured,' although I do not like to use the concept of 'cure.' Let's say the core will, at minimum, never use drugs or get into trouble again. These people are our healthy center, and their numbers are growing all the time.

"Let's look at Synanon as a dynamic organization that whirls like an atom or a molecule. The centrifugal force of this whirling dynamic may throw off a chip, but this has no particular effect on the stationary hard-core antidrug people. Crisis at Synanon affects a little segment of the perimeter. It usually consists of one person. Crisis is now represented by all the members of Synanon trying to hold the one chip, the newcomer who has not yet properly been integrated into the organization.

"Another factor is the way we do our work here. When the groups get too routine, or when these vital group sessions are not used properly, there is an important loss of necessary self-examination. When we get off kilter from our basic therapeutic processes, we lose people.

"A return to first principles is always good to get back into the center of things. We need constantly to reassess our posture, our emotional condition, and get back on the track of our main job in Synanon: helping people help themselves to learn how to stay drug-free."

REGRESSION AND "EMOTIONAL HAIRCUTS"

Regression on the part of ex-addicts does not always take the form of drug use in the TC or splitting. Regression often takes other, more subtle forms of negative behavior.

In situations in which blatant signs of potential regression appear, a member may request a counseling session, or may be called in and given an "emotional-haircut," as Dederich puts it, in an effort to save his or her life. The tools of attack therapy or gentle counseling may be brought into play to help the person see the direction of his or her life. A TC leader must decide on the best, most appropriate approach for the recovering addict-alcoholic's momentary emotional needs. Most TCs use some form of haircut in their programs. The "emotional-haircut" method developed in Synanon in the early days, involves a kind of tough emotional father-to-son straight talk.

The following portion of a longer session is an example of the kind of haircut that is administered to residents who show subtle signs of regression. The haircut was delivered by Chuck Dederich and Reid Kimball in the earlier days of Synanon to two married "second-stagers" (living in Synanon and working outside), Phil and Muriel.

In his criminal-addict past, Phil had run with a Mexican gang, dealt drugs, and was known as El Gato. He earned the nickname in the criminal culture because of his proficiency as a "cat burglar." He had a long record of addiction and criminal behavior and had spent considerable time in different prisons and jails. At the time of this haircut session, he had been clean about one and a half years. He had married Muriel, and both worked and were doing reasonably well—Phil as a cab driver and Muriel as a hairdresser. At the time, although they both worked outside, they lived near the main Santa Monica Synanon building. The session was requested by Muriel, who saw signs of regression in Phil, and felt they were headed toward a crisis. Her concern led her to seek help from Chuck and Reid. After about a half hour of preliminary discussion, the session seemed to arrive at the crux of the problem.

> Muriel: First of all, I am concerned about his not attending support groups anymore in Synanon. To him I'm just kind of a nut. I have to avoid arguments or discussions of this kind with him. Then he began to grow his thick Mexican moustache. The first thing that hit me was that it was a throwback to his old Mexican-gang environment. I couldn't discuss this with him. I said I didn't like it, and he got annoyed with me. When he said, "I'm going to grow a moustache," I made the mistake of saying, "No, you're not!" About an hour or two later, he said, "Nobody tells me what to do!"
>
> Chuck: You have to be awfully careful about how you handle this dope fiend here. There are many things that you can't talk with him about in the privacy of your own home. You can't even bring them up in groups because he doesn't attend them any more.

I can understand, it must be a very tense business over there in your house. Can you talk about politics in your home, or does he forbid you to talk about politics too? He says, "Nobody tells me what to do!" Well, there you have it, the classic remark of the dope-fiend criminal. This is his great cry as they bust him, lock him up, put him in jail, shake him down, and delouse him. He stands at attention and shouts, "Nobody tells me what to do!" [To Phil] You are a figure of fun, Buster, you really are!

"Nobody tells me what to do!" This is the one that I like better than his brush, when somebody comes up with that perfectly ridiculous comment.

Now, Buster, I'm going to tell you what to do. And I'll show you. You either do it or you'll get the hell off Synanon property. [Phil and Muriel live in an apartment rented by Synanon.] You shave off the moustache, you attend groups, and you behave like a gentleman as long as you live here. You don't like it here? God bless you, I'll give you the same good wishes that I gave other people like you when they left and went off to jail.

That's the way we operate in Synanon; you see, you're getting a little emotional surgery. If you don't like the surgery, fine, go and do what you have to. Maybe we'll get you again after you get out of the penitentiary or after you get a drug overdose. "Nobody tells me what to do!" Nobody in the world says that except dingbats like dope fiends, alcoholics, and brush-face-covered El Gatos.

That's an ultimatum; there it is. We know what we are doing, and if you don't think so, test it out—test it out. Try it your way and see what happens to you. We'll pick up a bad statistic. That's what we'll do.

What a magnificent atmosphere that must be to live in over there. "We don't discuss my moustache." What else don't you discuss over there because nobody tells you what to do? [To Muriel] Do you have other verboten topics? Dare you discuss his drastic need for attending the groups he so desperately needs to save his life? You can't do that, can you? Things are getting pretty tight over there, aren't they?

I wonder if he's been messing around with an occasional little benny [Benzedrine]? You know, to keep awake while he's driving his cab. A little phenobarbital at night, you know, kind of to ease the tension, to clear the head so he can be very careful about picking out the things that you can discuss between yourselves? Maybe an occasional little shot of vodka to kill these long hours at night when he's wheeling his little cab around? Actually, all of these things I'm mentioning are symptoms. They are actually no more dangerous than the symptoms we've been discussing, like the fuzz on your lip and your attitude. "Nobody tells me what to do! I'm going to grow a Pancho Villa moustache." You have a dope-fiend attitude. You belong leaning up against the wall tickling your ribs. You know, "Get over here, get over there, get out of the car, come with me," —the history of your life. You're headed for it. That's what's happening to you, Phil. Boy, I hate to see it. It's such a waste, such a complete waste. You have the world by the ass and you're throwing it out the window.

Let's get with it. Find out what the hell's going on over at the cab company where you work and get a day job instead of working nights. Let's have a nice, courteous report of the status of your progress toward a day job delivered to Reid in the next week. Reid likes to hear these things. And get that damn moustache off.

In the meantime, while you're trying to get your day job, you better scurry around here and see if you can get together a group in the afternoon. We have a lot of newcomers down here who would be tickled to death to have a little afternoon group session once or twice a week under the auspices of a boss Synanon therapist like you can be. You know, they are just longing for this. They need your help. Put something back in the pot—not for them, but for your own sake. Helping some newcomers, and being reminded of how you were, will help you stay clean.

The sharp "haircut" helped Phil and Muriel over this difficult period. They later saved enough money to buy a modest home and move out on their own. They had a child and appear to be doing fine. Phil and Muriel maintain a continuing affiliation with Synanon as a support group.

In dealing with crisis or "regression," the haircut type of counseling session is tuned to the needs of the person in a TC. In the case of Muriel and Phil, Chuck believed that a tough line was required. The later evidence of Phil's "straightening up" supports Chuck's hypothesis in that case. On other occasions a softer counseling approach is used in coping with the crisis of potential regression, especially when the person involved is "delicately balanced" emotionally. The handling of the following situation reveals the quality of this softer counseling approach for resolving a personal crisis.

Janet, in her early 20s, began using drugs in her teens, and had been in several juvenile institutions before coming to Synanon. She had been addicted to pills, quaaludes, and cocaine. She had been in and out of Synanon three times. On her third try at the time of this session, she had been in Synanon a week, had just kicked her habit, and was about to leave again and go back to drugs. Chuck heard about this, and the following counseling session took place. (I was present and recorded it.)

Chuck: I'm kind of at my wit's end, Janet, but I'm going to try somehow, if it is possible, to help you through this rough spot. You're pretty sick now. You're not as sick, of course, as you will be when you start using again. You made a real all-out effort to get into this place over a period of something like two or three weeks. You came down repeatedly. You really knocked yourself out. Now you want to throw that all away and go running out the door again. You're playing with death. You keep doing this over and over again. You're going to reach the end of the line, and this could do it. You're in no danger right now, except you don't feel very good. You've felt worse in your life, haven't you?

Janet: Yes.

Chuck: Did you live through it?

Janet: Yes.

Chuck: This is ridiculous. Nobody's mad at you here. We want to help you do something for yourself and you won't let us. What the devil did you want three days ago when you made it back into Synanon? Janet, when you said that you wanted to do something to take care of yourself, we believed you. Now we believe you again. We act as if we believe you, and we hope it will work out.

We can't turn it over to the gods. What we do is turn it over to you. It all depends on your guts. We can't give you any-thing...nothing...nothing...you have to give it to yourself. Now I understand you want to run off again.

If you're trying to prove that you can get along without Syn-anon, you can prove that, too. Of course you can. There are people all over the country just like you getting along without Synanon. They're using drugs and they're locked up, but they get along. They dream for awhile of a better life—but can't make it. Why don't you just hold on? We have signs all over the place saying, "Hang tough," and all this cornball stuff. It works, it works.

Why don't you stop fighting it? Why don't you let other peo-ple do your thinking for you for awhile? Look at the mess that your thinking always gets you in. You keep trying to use that decision-making mechanism of yours, and, baby, it's no good at this time. You're not a bad person. You're like someone they send to the hospital. They take everything away from him. They put him in bed. They bring food and drink. They tell him when to turn the lights off and go to sleep. They give the person a little pill and say," Now go to sleep," and then they wake him up. This is the way to treat an illness. Just because you're ambulatory and you can walk out of here doesn't mean that you're not helpless. You are helpless.

Why in the name of God don't you let somebody help you? That's all anybody here wants to do for you. Why do you want to go back to drugs? In another couple of days, you'll fully kick the habit you came here with and you can begin to eat and live again.

It's at times like this I almost wish we could confine you and make you kick your habit. You know, tie you down, and then in three or four days it would all be over. But, you see, it wouldn't work that way. This you've got to do for yourself. Nobody can have a baby for you. There are certain things people have to do for themselves, and this is one of them.

I don't know why in the devil you have to keep punishing yourself. What are you so guilty about? Why do you have to go out and try to kill yourself all the time? You don't have any fun out there do you? Do you have any fun out there?

Janet: No.

Chuck: Are you living when you're out there, Janet? I don't think you are. You're just a sick little helpless girl at this time. And you want to go back out there into the jungle again.

Give yourself a chance. Why don't you do me a favor? I think we've all been pretty good to you the times you've been here. I'm going to put on the spot, and if you turn me down, you can just add this to your ball of guilt. I'm asking you, as a favor to me, to stay here one more week. Pay me back for everything that I've tried to do for you.

You stay here one week for me and you can wipe the slate clean. Then you can go. You can either face up to that debt or put it down with all the rest of the unpaid debts that you've built up in life. You can wipe this debt clean in one week. In seven days, we'll be even.

If you walk out of here now, too bad...too bad. On the other hand, if you pay me back, it would probably be the first person you ever paid. There's a deal for you. Stay here a week for me and we're all even. You can go now, you know, and say, "Thanks, Chuck, but I don't want it." Or we can make a contract and start in even across the board. That's all I have to say. I'm asking you to stay one week. Go on downstairs, think it over, and make your own decision.

Janet thought it over, and stayed. Chuck traded on the relationship he had developed with her. It was possibly the only approach that would have kept her from going back to drugs at that time. She decided to stay. A year later she told me, "I felt for the first time that someone actually cared about what happened to me. I think I'm going to make it this time." In fact, the last time I checked, she had been clean for over five years.

In the process of learning how to lead a drug-free life in a TC, many people slip back to drugs along the way. A basic reason for this is that they lack impulse control. When they are sheltered by the TC, they can stay clean. However, when an opportunity presents itself to "use," they are so delicately balanced that they slip. The manner in which "slippage" is handled in a TC is critical to whether or not the addict more fully returns to drugs.

It is apparent that automatic ostracism or expulsion is too harsh a response; however, some action is required. If the "slip" goes "unpunished," it opens the situation up for other delicately balanced members to slip, or totally go back to drugs.

The group process for dealing with a slip can become a focal point for strengthening a TCs overall organization. Following is a case example of how a slip was handled in the early days of Synanon. The process reveals some of the basic dynamics of Synanon's organizational structure, methodology, and group support. This group method is used in most TCs in one form or another to deal with deviant behavior.

Ted, a two-year member, stole some pills from the medicine cabinet of a donor's house while visiting to collect a donation. This was reported by the donor, and upon intensive cross-examination by the staff, Ted admitted to the act. A general meeting was called for all TC members and the offender. Ted stood before the entire TC population, in front of the living-room fireplace, acting guilty and contrite.

This form of all-out haircut, the "fireplace scene," is seldom used, except for extreme misbehavior. The fireplace scene involves a situation where the group can choose to impose its ultimate punishment and eject the "offender," although this harsh discipline is seldom carried out. The fireplace session was conducted by an ex-addict director, Reid.

Reid: We have to expose people in this house who are working against themselves and the organization, the people here who are carrying on all the phony-baloney stuff that kept us all in jails and nut houses. This has been going on with this nut here. This is going to be a good opportunity for everyone here to examine his part in this type of behavior. Examine whether you are contributing to this by your apathy or just what your role is in this. We have all failed in some way with this guy.

You can learn a lesson for yourself by looking at this guy's problem. You can derive a benefit from it. You can get a good clear look at the vicious disease that you suffer from if you're a dope fiend, and perhaps you can make an even more determined resolution or effort to get away from anything that is that depraved or that has a hold on you and can cause you to do such things.

I am going to enumerate these things in a moment with reference to this guy. Some of you will use his vicious behavior as a rationalization to go shoot dope. You may think, "What's the use trying? If a two-year resident can't make it, neither can I." I suppose if you want to do this, you are a loser, in front, and you're only waiting for an excuse to go back to drugs.

We sort of anticipate losers and take for granted the fact that in this particular corporation or factory that produces cleanmandays, we have, at different levels, people who cannot make it. We have some poor devils who have been here for a long time and are back in the dishpan [demoted in their job] because they couldn't abide by the simple little rules of good behavior we lay down here. We do not use dope or use physical violence. We ask for good behavior whether or not you feel like it, and whether or not you place any value on it. We ask you simply to conduct yourself sort of like a human being.

The same thing, apparently, can happen to older persons who are over the honeymoon. They are over the thrill of not living with a big knot in their stomachs, doing nasty things to their family or waiting for the police to knock at their door. For them the enjoyment of living like a human being has lost its initial impact. It becomes sort of ashes in their mouth. The honeymoon is over, and they have been blasé about living like real people.

We have some people in this group who have never really made it. Any improvement, change, or reformation in them was really only on the surface. Underneath they maintain a dopefiend attitude and mentality. We lose some of those. These are some of the calculated losses that we have to operate with. I guess we have to expect it.

Some of these losers have an inherent viciousness. The viciousness is manifest in this guy Ted. We took him in here a couple of years ago when he was flat on his back. The state parole department jerked him out, because to them we were out of bounds on a zoning violation. We fought like dogs for him. The administration here sat up night after night composing letters, making phone calls to all the authorities, and knocked themselves out trying to save this guy's life. We finally got him to stay.

After a time we gave him some responsibility and the privilege of getting his driver's license back. We insured him for driving one of our vehicles. We entrusted him with visiting our donors—the people who keep us alive, who feed us, who pay our rent, who put food in our bellies and clothes on our back.

Ted here chose to go into one of our donor's houses the other day and steal some pills out of a medicine cabinet. I don't know if this is the first time. He claims it is. He's, of course, only copping to what we absolutely have on him. He stole some pills. He did this while, at the same time, we have people out all over this country knocking themselves out for our organization. These citizens have come to our aid and defense. Donors like this lady and her sister go out on a limb for us and this punk violates their home. She's a registered nurse, and she has been telling other people of the miracle they've found and the good work that's being done here in our little experiment for cleaning up drug addicts.

Teddy said to me before, "I don't know, it just happened. It's just one of those things." You know, kind of an all-inclusive cleanup. You know, like a blackout; he doesn't know what prompted him.

I don't believe it would happen to a lot of other people in here. It happens to a real vicious ingrate. I don't know how else to describe him. [Reid in his diatribe reinforces the positive behavior of some of the others in the group.]

This woman suspected her pills were missing on trips prior to the other day. As painful as it was to her—and she was very distraught about it—she said she had to know. So she put an exact number of pills in two different bottles. Four were missing out of each one. Ted denied everything when he came to my office, but after I told him the exact facts, he copped to that much. We don't have any more details, so I guess he's not copping to any more at this time; but I guess you all know now what kind of a situation he puts us all in. Tell us about it, Ted.

Ted: I don't know what to say, Reid. I guess the reason I'm still here is because it's not easy to be here right now.

Reid: Why don't you go into more detail about how it just happened...It just happened that you went into this woman's home, asked to go to her toilet, went into her medicine cabinet, and stole her medicine. To you it's dope, but to her it's medication.

Ted: I went in and took the pills. I took the pills. The state of mind I was in, Reid…I don't know what state of mind I was in. I couldn't control myself.

[A lot of accusing questions are now asked by the group.]

Jeanne: I want to ask you some questions, Ted. I'd like to ask you how you could take any pills at all, being completely clean, and come home and not be totally wiped out [loaded]? I'd like to know how you could do this?

Ted: Jeanne, I don't know.

Jeanne: I don't see how you can be clean, Teddy. I don't believe that you just got loaded once yesterday. I'd like you to tell me if there is anything stashed [drugs] at our house, where we have children and other people who could go to jail behind your bullshit behavior.

Ted: No.

Jeanne: I don't know whether I can believe you or not.

Ted: I didn't know what I took until I was told. I didn't know what they were.

Ray: How many times did you steal from this woman?

Ted: This is the only time.

Tootsie: You were asked a question—how did you know where the pills were?

Ted: I went to the medicine cabinet.

Arline: Do you check every medicine cabinet in every house you visit?

Ted: I don't make a habit of it, Arline.

Reid: Are you telling us that you didn't know what the pills were when you took them?

Ted: No, I did not.

Reid: They could have been vitamins. You just dropped some pills?

Ted: I knew they were pink ones, but I didn't know what kind of pills.

Henry: Ted, you went into the toilet when we were there?

Ted: Yes, and washed my hands.

Henry: You didn't open the medicine cabinet then?

Greg: All of a sudden you started to look into medicine cabinets yesterday, and yesterday you got caught?

Charley: [Another person who was with him] Teddy, was I sitting in the living room when you were doing this?

Ted: Yes.

Charley: Thanks. Thanks a whole lot. You could have screwed me up too.

Bob: You haven't got guts enough to make it out on the

streets. You've been sucking on this tit around here for two years. Don't tell us you're here for any other goddam reason. You're just here to whine and cry a little bit longer.

Ted: What I've done concerns everyone here and I think I owe myself and everyone here this much—to stay.

Jeanne: You don't owe me anything, Teddy, except a big fear that I've got drugs in a house with four or five children and other people who could all go to jail. [She lives in the same house as Ted.]

Reid: Let me get one thing clear. Your inclination is to leave, but because they think you can make a contribution to us by this demonstration, you're staying? Is that what you're saying?

Ted: I'm thankful for the opportunity to stay.

Reid: Why don't you leave?

Ted: I don't want to go. I'm afraid. Look at me. Where could a guy like me go? For Christ's sake.

[Several group members shout, "Back to jail!"]

Reid: How come this is a different answer than the other one? That "I felt I owe this to you to stay."

Ted: I'm pretty confused right now.

[There are a lot of questions and shouting at this point, two or three or more people talking at the same time. Ted is accused of other offenses. He is accused of different "funny" actions at his home.]

Dave: [He had slipped six months ago.] I was sitting right up there where you are six months ago, and I know what you're thinking. You're thinking, "If I just cop to just one little slip, I'll probably be able to make my recovery a little bit faster." Yeah, don't deny it, buddy. I've been there. You're thinking, "This is just one little thing. If I make it look like I just got out of touch this one time, they won't all hate me out there quite so bad." That's what you're thinking. I want to tell you something, buddy. You better get it out. You better use this opportunity to get all that shit out of you or you're a dead son of a bitch. If you don't cop out [be totally truthful] you have about as much chance of making it as a snowflake in the Mojave Desert. You better pour all that shit out of you.

Reid: You remember our contract upstairs, Teddy. If we find out anymore you're lying about, we're going to kick you out of here.

[There are more questions, more accusations, and there is more defending by Ted.]

Arnold: I'd like to say one thing. This is a good time for anybody else who wants to cop out and save their lives right now. I know there are people in here who think they are putting something over on us. Now is a good time to save your life by getting any crap out in the open.

Greg: [Heatedly] I would like to ask everybody to hear this here right now. If there is anybody in here that has anything going on, let's hear it. I don't care about saving lives and all that. That's good for Arnold or others. But, you know, do us a favor. There are some of us here who would like to get ahead and make this place grow and help ourselves. Do us a goddam favor. Either get up and do the thing and maybe save your life or, you know, walk!

Please! This is an appeal from me. I don't want anybody to smash our home. We've got bastards like Ted running around in here stealing dope out of medicine cabinets and thinking he can get away with it.

Reid: The people who are playing funny little games in here — the tough guys in the halls, the people who are stealing from each other — you jerks, here's your end point right here. [Points to Ted.] Here's your end point! You know who you are, the ones that are playing these funny little phony-ass dope-fiend games in here. Asking for our help, professing to be one thing, then trying to rank it. You start with these small phony games, but here's your end. Ted here is a real big punk. You little punks keep it up. You can grow up to be Ted's size before too long.

I hope you don't cop out to your phony nonsense. I hope some of you make a decision to end it right now. You know who you are. Just ask yourself, "Am I so goddamn hopeless that with the whole world out there, I come in here to rank this place?" This is a place where dope fiends like you can save your life. Boy, you're a real son of a bitch if you're playing any phony little chicken-shit games in here. Don't call it by any other name. That's what you are. The people pulling this nonsense in here are real punks, believe me. Ted here is only one example of the insanity in here that undermines our work. Think it over. Whose side are you on in here? Are you on Ted's side, which involves self-destruction, or do you truly want to change your life and stop using drugs.?"

I was present at this fireplace scene, and I interviewed various people who were present to analyze the impact of the "demonstration." There was a range of reactions to the fireplace scene. For many there was a feeling of threat and fear that Ted did not come clean about all his offenses. It seemed that he was still lying. An underlying fear expressed was: "If Ted could lie like a dope fiend, I could too."

An assumption in a TC is that if an individual does not clean out his or her emotional wounds by telling the truth, guilt and anxiety will fester and eventually "kill" the person by driving him or her back to drugs. The notion is that ex-addicts and alcoholics cannot handle any degree of dishonesty at all. They must tell the truth completely or return to drugs.

Here was a two-year failure. Some old-timers were disturbed on the grounds that if it happened to Ted, it could happen to them. Some newcomers expressed the fear that they might not make it. It also gave some newcomers an excuse to seek to leave and validate the "once-a-dope-fiend-always-a-dope-fiend" assumption in which they still believed.

Ernie, a 35-year-old past offender with more than ten years of prison time in his past, expressed another type of reaction: "How could a guy two years in here do that? If I was going to shoot dope, I would go out of the building." In part he was expressing his fear of the possible spectacle of himself in Ted's shoes. At the same time, he was expressing a loyalty to the TC. He indicated in his comment that he would not "foul up" the organization that had provided so much hope for him and others like him. If he were going to shoot dope, he would go elsewhere.

Ernie somewhat reflected the position of the "old-criminal" ethos by identifying with the group. His moral commitment, despite the fact that it involved illegal ends for many years, was to his group. His reasoning was that since this group was now "his gang," and since its existing norms were "no drug use and no violence," he would cooperate and adhere to these norms while there. If he were going to misbehave, he would go elsewhere.

One female newcomer used the episode as a possible rationale to split. Her comment was that "if this type of slip could happen to a two-year person, it could easily happen to me." She appeared extremely disturbed and discouraged by the event, and this shock stayed with her for some time.

One of the women directors admitted to a feeling experienced by some other senior people. She admitted that during the fireplace scene she regressed in her thoughts to feelings of self-inadequacy: "I identified right there with him as a lying dope fiend, unable to cop out. It shook me" Although this director had been in the TC for more than three years, she still found a part of herself identifying with Ted.

The fireplace mass meeting appeared to be a learning experience for many members. For some it helped to clarify their position vis-à-vis the organization. The episode produced a greater motivation to work harder for themselves and the "club." They attributed Ted's failure to their own unawareness: "We should have been aware of his problem and helped him." Many felt that they had let Ted down by not being aware enough to have prevented his slip. And in some respects this was true. It heightened the members' motivation to talk to each other more and to keep in touch for greater cohesion.

Greg's comment, "If there is anybody in here that has anything going on, let's hear it," revealed his concern and motivation. Greg, in addition to his dedication to the club, was getting married at the time. The experience of his fellow two-year member shook him deeply, since it threatened his new security as an ex-addict who could make it. The incident clarified for him the fact of his close ties with the organization. The "no-man-is-an-island" theme had proved to be a reality that could go two ways: A person who makes progress helps all, but a member who fails in some way diminishes everyone.

Over the long run, the impact of the incident on Ted himself had constructive results. At my last check, he had been clean for more than seven years, and he seemed to be functioning well in the community. His later comments reveal how deeply affected he was by the fireplace scene: "I was never so humiliated in my life. I felt terrible at the time. However, a little humiliation is a small price to pay for saving my life."

THE RESOLUTION OF CRISIS

Recovering residents of a TC can "live or die" on the basis of a crisis. It is often a situation in which all the positive and negative forces at work in oneself and in the organization are marshaled. In some respects a fireplace scene or a haircut is a battle between the internal constructive and destructive forces in the residents and the organization. In the fireplace scene, Reid was the protagonist for positive behavior; Ted, by the nature of his act, enacted the role of the compulsive addict personality. This combination of forces existed in all of the people involved in the general meeting to different degrees.

Many people who participated in the fireplace scene later told me that some of their inner feelings were clarified by the crisis. Some came away from the session with a greater resolve to succeed.

In various groups there is usually a central person on the hot seat; however, other recovering addict-alcoholics feel the barbs directed at the central protagonist and learn something for themselves. Janet later told me that the counseling session with Chuck related to her crisis convinced her for the first time in her life that someone cared. Crisis situations help to articulate and surface new information and emotions, both for the central figures in the crisis and for others less involved but in the same emotional situation.

A side effect of many crises appears to be a greater insight into the dynamics of the individual's problem and a closer identification with the total group. Crisis situations often force an examination of each person's degree of commitment to become drug-free and to improve his or her drug attitude. It parallels the more generalized drug-attitude exercise.

In many cases, after a slip on the part of an individual, he or she "grows up" and becomes more involved in the organization. The person involved attempts to demonstrate his or her dedication to become drug-free more intensely and, at the same time, places himself or herself more firmly into the group's guidance, scrutiny, and evaluation. This increased attention is most useful for the recovering addict.

Some slips or signs of regression are flares put out to get attention. [Bill's moustache, for example, which he grew and shaved off several times since the haircut, seemed to be a barometer of his emotional condition.]

The misbehavior of a member sometimes (as in Ted's fireplace scene) also gives the overall group a right to react as "righteous nonoffenders," attacking bad behavior. This somewhat holier-than-thou position seems to reinforce the group's own positive behavior. Witnessing the ridicule to which they themselves might be subjected if they misbehaved serves as a partial deterrent and control of their negative behavior.

A crisis placed under a microscope also raises a significant question for all TC group members to examine: "What have I done to help produce this failure in my brother or sister?" Individual failures or crises are considered to stem from dislocations or from problems within the total community.

In the wake of a crisis, the administration and many members review and analyze the group's patterns in an attempt to locate the source of the failure. All related people are asked to examine their roles in allowing the person to slip. The reasoning is based on the assumption that no person in a TC is a separate entity, and that everyone has a responsibility to everyone else.

This theme of everyone being part of everyone else was discussed the next day at the noon intellectual seminar, after Ted's crisis. The concept placed on the blackboard and discussed by the entire group was taken from Kahlil Gibran's *The Prophet*.

Oftentimes have I heard you speak of one who commits a wrong as though he were not one of you, but a stranger unto you and an intruder in your world.

But I say that even as the holy and the righteous cannot rise beyond the highest which is in each one of you, So the wicked and the weak cannot fall lower than the lowest which is in you also.

And as a single leaf turns not yellow but with silent knowledge of the whole tree, So the wrong-doer cannot do wrong without the hidden will of you all.

In the substance abuser's past life, crisis was almost a normal daily experience. A whole host of breaking-point crises and emotional experiences were par for the course. The crisis episodes in his or her past, however, usually pushed him or her further down and were deleterious in life. He or she had a limited ability to learn from the crisis experience. In contrast, in a TC, an attempt is made to explore and *exploit* crisis situations fully for each member's and the group's therapeutic advantage.

A basic assumption is that human growth almost naturally involves a series of crisis incidents. The standard comment during a crisis in a TC is, "Let's examine it; we may grow up behind it." Crisis situations are manipulated and useful in a TC to help the individual and the group grow.

The process of growth is recognized to be a natural cause of crisis. Giving up one attitude for a better one usually entails a degree of emotional disturbance. An attempt is made in the TC to convert the crisis situation from a destructive to a constructive experience.

Some of the methods employed in a TC may appear harsh at first glance. However, the consequences of certain behavior, when there is no intervention (or the wrong kind), for a recovering alcoholic-addict can be deadly. The only price the recovering addict has to pay for growing up is, at times, a form of group pressure. And this pressure is inflicted on his or her behavior not on the "self." The reward can be a life free from the enslavement of drugs.

The eminent French sociologist Emile Durkheim cogently pointed out how the societal process of punishment was an act that was often more significant for solidifying and validating society's norms than its effect on the offender. In a similar way, the total process of crisis management, when carried out effectively in a TC, appears to identify the group more closely with positive values and beneficial behavior patterns. Dealing with crisis in a TC properly, in effect, involves an intense and sharp appraisal of the rules of the community, and living by them. The group's solidarity in attacking self-destructive behavior gives all residents an opportunity to examine the norms of the TC. This usually produces a greater overall *esprit de corps* and a more cohesive, truly therapeutic community.

6

The Struggle for Recovery: Changing, Growing, and Graduating

The encounter group and other aspects of a TC are designed for the emotional growth of residents. The basic process involves teaching people how to live their lives productively and happily—without drugs or alcohol.

In the early period of their stay in a TC, newcomers are considered "emotional infants" in certain aspects of their personality who require protection and support. For awhile they are given a "pass" in the groups. The groups go easy on newcomers recognizing that they are delicately balanced, and could easily split and go back to their past self-destructive lives. This period of grace gives newcomers an opportunity to become accustomed to the new family. They open their eyes to their new possibilities in life, make friends, and increasingly become attached to the organization. This process takes place in the groups, at work, and in the continuing supportive caring-circle informal conversations that take place in TCs almost around the clock.

After several months, the recovering addict-alcoholic's new family, in groups, at work, and elsewhere, begin to zero in on some of the newcomer's emotional disabilities. They begin, slowly at first, to help the addict assess his or her strengths and weaknesses. Without drugs the ex-addict begins to see life differently, and to relate in new ways with people.

As the group sessions begin to reach the newcomer, he or she starts freely to express many feelings that were bottled up inside for a long time. Typically the recovering addict shouts and screams back at the "attackers," who very often are perceived as psychodramatic auxiliary-egos or stand-ins for a problem parent or spouse. After a time the newcomer begin to recognize and accept others in the TC as real friends trying to help him or her change in a positive direction and grow out of the need for drugs or alcohol. Most addict-alcoholics during this early phase require the understanding and sympathetic environment that a TC can provide.

REMOVING THE MASK

Residents of TCs come from all walks of life, and have become addicted for various reasons. However, there are in the mix of most TCs some individuals who are encrusted with years of tough behavior to cover up their deeper sense of insecurity. They are "cool," "hip," and often present a tough-guy mask to the world to cover up their underlying more sensitive selves.

Addicts-alcoholics from upper socioeconomic positions in the society, some of whom are people of social eminence, have a different kind of mask. Their masks relate to the disparity between the strong images they present to the public and the insecure, unhappy people who exist underneath this facade. Drugs serve the same function for these people as they do for lower socioeconomic group criminal addicts; they facilitate a self-deception of feeling strong when the person underneath is full of doubt and insecurity. In this context a basic reason why high-status people, entertainers, athletes, and corporate executives become substance abusers is that some drugs (especially alcohol and cocaine) give them a feeling of competence when underneath they are frightened and insecure. For all kinds of drug addicts, regardless of class or background, learning how to feel competent and improving one's self-esteem without drugs is one of the most difficult tasks that needs to be accomplished in the TC process.

A prototypical example of a high-status person's drug problem is revealed by Liza Minnelli's experience at the Betty Ford Center, a short-term TC for the treatment of chemical dependence. She described this experience, in an interview, as involving an intense self-examination that shattered a well-constructed false shell that she had formed around herself in over 15 years of pills and alcohol abuse. "You just don't get fixed at once," Minnelli commented. "You constantly work on yourself, constantly. I must deal with my real feelings at all times. The encounter-group process at the center did not allow me to bury feelings that are going to come up and mug me later."

Her sense of humor remains; however, she has given up the glib banter that let her slide through life without encountering her deeper feelings. "In my self-deception, I didn't equate my feelings of dying with the drugs I was taking. I thought I had mononucleosis or hypoglycemia. I didn't know exactly what was wrong with me. Valium nearly killed me. I was taking five milligrams a day for 15 years. Some doctors throw it at you like candy. I was like a little kid those 15 years trying to act like a grown-up."

The drugs helped Ms. Minnelli keep up her mask of "being a grown-up" and facilitated her performance as an entertainer. The main cost to her was to give up the real "self" that could make her truly happy. Her problem was characteristic of the dilemma of many high achievers in show business, sports, and industry who require the bolstering of drugs in order to perform under the pressure.

The criminal addict in a TC does not usually have the talent or the social training of the higher-status addict, but he or she has a similar image problem. The criminal addict maintains a tough-guy mask that must be peeled away if the person is to grow up in a TC.

Both the high-status addict and the low-status criminal addict share a common problem. This problem is referred to in TCs as an "attitude problem," one that masks their real selves. Their external presentation of self to others is not congruent with their usually negative underlying feelings and emotions about their real selves. Their drug use was helpful in balancing these two incongruent self-concepts by bolstering their low self-esteem. When the drug is removed in the encounter-group process in a TC, the real person beneath begins to appear.

When criminal addicts drop their tough-guy masks, they usually become sensitive and vulnerable. At times the addict even feels free to cry and reveal the frightened child that usually hides underneath the tough-guy facade. Childish tantrums are tolerated sometimes, even encouraged, in the groups or psychodramas in order to release these long-pent-up emotions. What takes place might best be described as a "resocialization process." The addict is forced to give up the old patterns of relating. It is continually pointed out that these old attitudes were the ones that drove him or her to become, and stay, an emotional child—using drugs as a coverup. The evidence is powerful, since it is presented by people who themselves went through this process but successfully changed to a better way of life.

Removing The Mask: John's Story

An interesting case in point of this removal of the false criminal mask and growing up drug-free in a TC is revealed in John's story. John, after "growing up" and graduating from Synanon, founded an innovative, successful, and effective TC. John's early attitudes and life-style gave little indication that he would grow up to become a powerful, intelligent man and one of the most prominent leaders in the TC field.

John arrived at Synanon in 1962, at the age of 22. He was a thin, baby-faced young fellow. His pale, ascetic face had an almost religious quality. In his neighborhood on the Upper West Side of Manhattan, he was known by some of his peers as Whitey the Priest.

He received this nickname from an addict who was kicking a habit. As John relates it: "Once, in jail, some Spanish guy who was kicking a bad habit came to for a minute. He saw me and began to scream hysterically in Spanish that I was a priest. Later on it was picked up by other people who knew me around the city. Some of the whores on Columbus Avenue would even 'confess' to me as 'Whitey the Priest.' First I made sure they gave me a good fix of heroin, or money for a fix, and then I would actually listen to their 'confessions'! They weren't kidding; they were dead serious. After the 'confession' took place, usually in some hallway or in a bar, after they had poured out their tragic story, I would lay a concept on them—something like, 'Into each life some rain must fall.' I'd bless them and cut out."

In his adolescent years John worshiped gangsters and criminals and wanted to be like them. In his neighborhood there were many to imitate. A criminal he especially admired was Trigger Burke, who, according to John, "went to the hot seat without a whimper."

When John was 12, he took his first fix of heroin in the course of his delinquent business. "I use to run dope and deliver heroin for some of the pushers in the neighborhood. One day I delivered a package of heroin to some guy, and out of curiosity I asked him for a little. He fixed me, and that was it. I began using from then on. It's hard to describe my first feelings about heroin. The best way I can describe it is that it's like being under the covers where it's nice and warm on a cold day. Of course, now I don't recommend it to anyone except as a mercy killing."

John was first institutionalized at an early age by his parents. He does not remember why. From then on, for many years until he became drug-free, he felt extreme hatred for his parents, especially his father. In the institution he "always felt a need to protect the underdog in a fight." He had several fights each day and found in the "home" he was placed a "house of horror."

When he left the institution at about the age of nine, he began running with various young kid gangs on Manhattan's West Side. They were involved in petty thievery. John ran the streets, used drugs whenever he could, and received more training for a life of crime. "In my neighborhood, when I was 12 or 13, I was considered a 'cute kid.' The whores liked me, and once in awhile, for a gag, they would turn a trick with me. I admired the stand-up guy gangsters. They were my idols. I had two heroes at that time—the Mafia boss Frank Costello and General MacArthur."

"I took my first real fall at 14. I was sent to the reformatory at Otisville. I hated everyone there and wanted to kill the director and some of the guards. I was always fighting and spent a lot of time in the hole [solitary confinement]. This gave me a chance to think and plot different ways to kill the guards and the man who ran the joint."

From Otisville, John, at age 16, was transferred to another reformatory for older boys. From then on he spent time in various institutions. These included several trips to Riker's Island Penitentiary, Lexington for a "winder" ("You wind in and out"), New York City's Riverside Hospital for young addicts, and various New York City jails.

"The last time I got out of jail, at 21, I degenerated. I became ragged and dirty. I preyed on anyone I could get to. I stole dope from other junkies. I broke into slum apartments and took toasters and radios in poor neighborhoods. I began to really hate myself and what I had to do to keep using shit [drugs]. I began breaking into four or five apartments a day. I remember, in some of them, seeing a shopping bag or a poor old lady's black coat, and it would kill me to steal the radio or toaster. I couldn't understand what had happened to me. I always thought I was going to become a big-time operator. I wanted to become a good, respectable professional thief, and instead I had to look at myself and admit I was a common run-of-the-mill street hype."

It seemed that when John no longer could maintain his illusion of being a stand-up guy and "boss" criminal, he tried to quit drugs and the life. In desperation he voluntarily went to Lexington, and then to Riverside Hospital. Nothing worked for him. He heard about Synanon from a sociologist, Dick Korn, whom he had met on Riker's Island. Korn sent him by plane to California with money out of his own pocket.

"When I got to Synanon and saw guys like the Greek, Middleton, and Reid doing something for themselves, it got to me somehow," John told me. "There were no authority figures I could really hate like I did in the joint. I immediately liked Chuck. Somehow he struck me as a nice guy. In a way he became one of my heroes."

In his third month in Synanon, it was revealed that John had a court "hold" on him from a prior offense. He had to appear in court in New York City. Synanon and John's mother put the money together for his round-trip flight. I happened to be in New York City at the same time on other business, and I appeared in court on John's behalf. I told the judge about Synanon. I related that John had been clean for three months and that his prospects were reasonably good. John was given a suspended sentence and directed to return to Synanon.

Right after we left the courtroom, I knew I had a tiger by the tail. Synanon's hold was light and the lure of the streets was powerful. I could almost feel John salivating for a fix.

I decided to hang on to him any way I could manage it, until his scheduled midnight flight to Los Angeles. To kill the afternoon, I called a radio announcer I knew and made arrangements for John and me to tape a radio program. This held him for the afternoon, but he slipped away from me in the early evening to "attend to some business." I was helpless to hold him any further except by force. That, of course, was out of the question.

Somehow John made the plane to Los Angeles on his own and got back to Synanon. Of course, before taking the plane, he had slipped. He said, "Yes, I got some money together, scored, and fixed. I couldn't control myself in New York. It was too much for me."

I asked him how he managed to make the plane. "The only thing that got me back to Synanon were the promises I made," he said. "I told the Greek and Jack Hurst I would be back." The same criminal loyalties and image that originally had almost destroyed John had, in this situation, helped him to return to his Synanon lifeline!

The criminal mask and the attitudes John had held on to for many years had to be removed as a first step in his Synanon treatment. This was accomplished by a barrage of verbal surgery in encounter groups and emotional haircuts.

CHANGING ATTITUDES

The attitude change and the behavioral growth process that John and other tough addicts are exposed to in a TC were delineated by Dederich in a lecture to a graduate class in social welfare at UCLA that I taught at the time. "First you remove the chemical. You stop him from using drugs, and you do this by telling him to do it. He doesn't know he can do it himself, so you tell him to do it. He doesn't know he can stay and have a little job, as long as he doesn't shoot dope. 'You want to use dope, fine, but someplace else, not here, He stops using drugs. Then you start working on secondary aspects of the syndrome. Addicts live under the control of drugs, therefore, they talk about this all the time. So the next thing you do is attack the drug language. Eliminating their addict language is very important. We get them off the negative language by initially giving them another. Since there is some vague connection between their personality problems and the social sciences, we encourage them to use this language. The language of psychology and sociology is great stuff. Whether or not the recovering addict or alcoholic knows what he's talking about is exquisitely unimportant at this time."

"Very quickly, in a matter of about 90 days, they turn into junior psychiatrists and sociologists. They become familiar with the use of about 20 words related to social psychology and misuse them. Who cares! It doesn't make any difference. Now they're talking about 'hidden superegos,' 'transferences,' 'role models,' 'displacement,' 'primary and secondary groups.' This is all coming out, and they're not discussing drugs. They get off that, and they talk about 'ids,' 'superegos,' and 'group structure.' They make another set of noises.

"First they substitute this sociological–psychological language wholesale. Eventually, when they come to learn something of the meanings of the words, they stop using them. Of course, like any intelligent adult, you don't interlard your social conversation with technical terms. No one does this."

Language is, of course, the vehicle of culture and behavior; and in TCs it is instrumental in changing attitudes and the behavior patterns that the addict has used in the past. The resident begins to use a new, still-undeveloped set of social-emotional muscles. The addict-alcoholic's past behavior and thinking are modified by the various group processes in the TC. The individual is blasted, then supported in various groups and learns to change his or her attitudes and behavior.

An important goal of the encounter method is to change the addict's "attitude problem." The false self-image held by the recovering alcoholic-addict is attacked and punctured with this approach. But is is not only applicable to criminal addicts. Upper-status cocain–heroin addicts and alcoholics in their substance-abusing days often glorified getting "stoned" or "loaded." Everyone, at some time, has heard an otherwise sensible person—perhaps a corporate executive, a teacher, an athlete, or a celebrity on TV—make such idiotic jokes as, "Boy, did I tie one on last night," and then go into a stupid story of getting so intoxicated he or she doesn't remember what happened.

A good example of this stupendous stupidity is revealed in various films that depict people under the influence as being humorous. For me, there is absolutely nothing funny about these films. They are as funny as the disease of cancer. A generally stupid and ignorant "attitude" about the glory of drug or alcohol abuse is too widely held in our society. The encounter approach attacks the addict-alcoholic's stupid attitudes related to the disease; and it is as applicable to the high-status addict as it is to the criminal addict.

An example of this important issue is the encounter group that was administered in the wake of a bad attitude that affected the behavior of 12 young New York "gangsters" who had come to Synanon for help in the early days of the organization.

The group of so-called "little gangsters" was brought into Chuck's office as a result of bad behavior on the beach on a Christmas morning. They were called in for cursing and "crime talk" within the hearing of an elderly gentleman who was passing. Chuck later told me: "Since Reid and I were already going to give our time to the youngsters who had committed the offense in question, we called in all the young people in the club at that time for a mass haircut on this subject. With the same set of motions, we were able to work on the larger little-gangster symptom we find in many of our young newcomers."

In addition to the relative newcomers who were on the carpet, a six-month member and some older Synanists were in the group to add to the discussion. They represented role models of the change that could take place in the group present if the young men straightened out their attitudes.

The elements of exaggeration and artful ridicule are revealed in this session. The pattern of attack and then support is also demonstrated. A typical session of this type goes beyond the bad behavior of the moment and into a more serious problem—necessary attitude change; and this is revealed in the session. Unlike the encounter group, it is not interactional. It is a one-way "educational sermon" usually delivered by several older members to younger members. Chuck and his main aide Reid dominate the scene. (I was present and recorded the session.)

Reid: I don't know what you'd call this meeting. I don't think you'd even call it a haircut. I think we're going to make some observations on the attitude of stark, raving stupidity that keeps people on self-destructive drugs. Think about this—we actually have some guys in this room who are representing themselves to each other and other people as New York gangsters. I have an idea that Legs Diamond or Bugsy Siegal would have never wound up in here, even if they became junkies.

These punks sit around here and discuss in the back toilet how you hit a guy with a pipe. I doubt if any of you hit anybody. Maybe you've been slapped a couple of times and you think of this as gang violence. This group was just out in the front of our building talking about boosting and dope and managed to say something like "I don't give a fuck" as one of our neighbors and taxpayers passed by. These little gangsters, all sent out here on momma's money, haven't even observed that their little clique is made up of dishwashers and service-crew men who haven't even been here long enough to get any of the treatment they so sorely need to change their stupid attitude and grow up. Here you are, little punks, who have the idiotic attitude about representing yourselves as gangsters or hard guys. You get around our pool table downstairs and I guess you think you sound like Al Capone. You sound like one of the cheapest, phoniest pool-hall gangs over on the East Side, where they chip in 15 cents to play a short rack of pool.

This is really kind of funny. We always figure we have a disturbed ward. Part of the disturbed ward gets in front of the jukebox and they stick their ear against it and they snap their fingers. We stand at the doorway and we laugh. It's all right—they're insane. But when it starts messing with our business, we have to knock it off.

For a short period of time, we don't mind if you stand in front of the toilet and signify to each other how bad you were or how much dope you shot. You were all such big shots that your mommas put you in Metropolitan Hospital [a New York hospital for addicts] three or four times, then a couple of trips to jail, and then you're shipped out here. We are not going to permit you to stand out in front of our beach and insult our neighbors. You are all so stupid that you don't even know how funny you are. You tell each other about all the dope, all the big scores, how bad you are, and yell "fuck" out in front of our building. Your stupidity is pathetic. I met a few gangsters. They used guys just like you to go to get their sandwiches. And if they were big peddlers, they gave you a cap [capsule of heroin] for delivering something.

Chuck: The lunatic fringe, the disturbed ward, the punks from the sidewalks of Azuza, New York, Akron, Ohio—they're all the same. They all saw the same TV shows and movies. When they come out here, some of them get with what we are doing, stay, and grow up. Others go back and wind up once again in a hospital or some penitentiary or the county jail or sitting in some filthy bar. We know that we have to put up with this insane attitude and behavior for a period of time, until you work out of it.

When you get out on our beach and can't behave yourselves like grown-up human beings, we have to take steps. You can't use the beach, you can't do this, you can't do that. You see, everybody else in the world that ever got into this business of cleaning up dope fiends and punks realized they they were bucking something that was absolutely impossible. There's one thing that's peculiar about punks like you—they inevitably foul their own nest. If you get them in a penitentiary and lock them up and you decide, 'Well, now let me see; we'll try to give them just a little bit. We'll give them dessert on Thursdays, or we'll give them three eggs a week instead of two." You know what they'll do? They'll throw the extra egg at each other. Not even at the guards!

This is the stupidity of the young punk that has made every single agency give up on this problem. Well, we're not at that point any more. The first two or three or four years were pretty rough. But we know now that some punks can grow up. We give them just so much time around here, just so much time! This time comes to an end, and you either fish or cut bait, you either grow up or get lost.

Reid: Let's consider another angle. If this place was San Quentin or Sing Sing, I might agree with your tough-guy attitude. In prison I suppose you have to let it be known that you were a hot shot on the street and that you're a bad guy inside the walls. This is what you do to get status in prison. But think of how ludicrous it is when you come here to this place and you try to be tough guys or gangsters. In this place, if you make progress, you act like an adult. If you are gangsters, let's at least concede this, you're the very dregs of gangsterdom—the very dregs.

Chuck: When this thing hits you and you begin to just get a vague inkling of how absurd your behavior has been, later on when you grow up you're liable to get hysterical laughing at yourself. This is the beginning of growing up, when you see how extremely and ludicrously funny you are. This is kind of a young group. The old gangster, of course, went out of existence before most of you guys were born. There are very few of them left any more. I'm talking about tough guys that really made big scores. I would venture to say that in the last five years, all of you in this room, if you took every dime that all of you scored and put it on the table, it probably wouldn't support Reid's old drug habit for six months. You see, the thing is too absurd even if you want to use that frame of reference.

Let's look at some of the hipster's stupid attitude behavior. We have the jukebox syndrome. That applies to people who use the jukebox not for what it's intended, not to listen to music, but to put on an act. The jaw kind of recedes and drops a little bit, and you have this bit [snap, snap]. That's the jukebox syndrome. Healthy people listen to jukeboxes to hear music.

Then there's the pool-hall syndrome. Men go to a pool table to play a game of pool. Nuts go to the pool table to make shots this way [backward], when it can be done much better the other way. They use it to give it this cigarette bit. They leave their cigarettes there until the eyeball is all full of nicotine.

Reid: You guys aren't vicious or anything. You're like every one of us was. None of you in this room was as stupid as I was.

I'll guarantee it. You couldn't have possibly been. I was so dingy, dumb, and had a terrible attitude problem. I still hold the god-damn record for working on the coffee counter. When I first got here, I was on the son-of-a-bitch washing cups for ten months. Nobody's talking about you as exceptional cases. When some-thing happens, when you get over this idiocy, you will look back and think, "What were we trying to prove? What the hell is there to prove? Nothing!"

Chuck: Let's think in terms of your attitude problem, if you can actually get down through your funny little image and say, "Where am I?" Let's list where you are not: You're not in the streets of New York. You're not in some big yard at Sing Sing. You're not in the county jail. You're not in a private sanitarium or hospital. You're not in a pool hall. "What am I?" You get those questions answered. This involves growing up. It's a much more comfortable way to live, boys, let me tell you. It really is.

Reid: Let's look at the phenomenon of drug addiction. All of us, I think, in here are agreed that we might have had the attitude one time that it was pretty hip to be a dope fiend, or even an alcoholic. I think it's pretty lame to use dope now, don't you? In other words, you're kind of lame if you're willing to use a little white powder that will put you in a cage for five or ten years. That's where your current attitude will put you, if you don't change it.

Remember that everybody here was just like you, including me. As an example, I'll guarantee you I'm a hell of a lot further from ever sitting in a mental hospital or a cell for the rest of my life than you are. I'm probably a hell of a lot more comfortable, and I'll guarantee I was just as nutty or nuttier than you when I arrived.

Chuck: Let's accelerate this program. Would you rather be like Reid is today than like you are? [They indicate "yes."] What's stopping you? You can beat him in this race for sanity.

Reid: Think about either lining yourself up on the side of a sensible attitude or lining yourself up on the side of insanity. When you stand around and you agree by not making any com-ment when some real dingbat is raving and slavering, I guess you've got to face the facts that you are on the side of insanity. There are two camps in here, really. We've always had a bunch of lunatics at any given time. Are you with them or with the sane people who have given up the drug bullshit, have changed their old attitudes and are growing up?

Do you realize, if you can change your attitude, there isn't anyone in this room who ever again has to sit in a cell or stand on some cold goddam corner waiting for the man to come back with his shit [drugs]? You don't have to go to any more lunatic asylums. You don't have to go through kicking another habit. You don't have to do any of these things. Nothing in the world is going to make you do these things if you don't want to. This is true only if you decide to give up the attitude that keeps getting you back into trouble.

Chuck: We can bring it a lot closer to the moment. Do you realize that you never even have to have another "haircut" in Synanon? You don't even have to have anybody talk bad to you ever again. This session is business for Reid and me. This is work. Who wants to work? There are many more pleasant things that we can do than to pull a kid in and try to teach him how to save his life. You don't ever have to be on that end of a haircut again. You can keep your mouth shut, do your work, and try to behave like a gentleman. In a very short time, you're in a position of trying to help another guy who comes in here sick. Then you can turn to some other guy here and say, "Was I like that? Is that the way I acted? Is that the way I appeared to be?" And he will say,, "Yeah, that's right—that's the way you were." You won't be able to believe it. You just won't be able to believe it. None of this stuff has to happen to you again.

You know, a little verbal attack in here is the highest price you can pay, a little humiliation. There is no punishment; we can't strap you to a chair and knock out your teeth as sometimes happens in police stations. We can't do that, and we don't want to. We can verbally humiliate your bad attitude in an effort to save your lives. That is all. After you get a few of these haircuts, you'll learn how to do it pretty good yourselves, so that you'll be able to help some other guy see the light. But you really don't have to go through this ever again. I mean at this moment, right here, you can walk out the door of this office right now and it doesn't have to happen to you again as long as you live.

If you can absorb this little lesson we've just delivered about your attitude, this could be the best Christmas present you ever had. You really couldn't have a better Christmas present than this little Mickey Mouse haircut we just gave you. This is a good one. This is a Christmas haircut. Merry Christmas fellows!!

Several weeks later the "little-gangster haircut" audiotape was played back and was analyzed in an interchange with Chuck, Dr. George Bach, a noted psychologist who was an authority on the positive aspects of verbal aggression, and myself. (see George Bach, *Creative Aggression*, Doubleday, 1983).

Chuck: First of all let me make one point clear. This is not a regular encounter group, this is a "haircut." Attack is, of course, used here, and it is delivered against bad behavior.

George: I was impressed with the approach. However, there is a part of this that requires clarification. You had some warmth in your attack. Some of the others were, I felt, too harsh.

Chuck: The extreme lead-hammer attack technique is a natural approach for an alcoholic or an addict fresh off his medicine. He is so frustrated and full of hostility that the lead hammer comes naturally. In training a group leader in a TC you have to teach him to use his hostility properly. From my own experience, the haircuts that I gave four or five years ago were almost 100 percent totally vicious, with very little warmth. But as my own hostility diminished, I used the haircut as a teaching device, and I wouldn't, so to speak, black out personally in the middle of one. I would always have my eyeball rolling and reflect to myself, "I'm pushing this kid too far. I better come over here and lift him up." It's easier for me, because I do haircuts now with my ego. I don't do it out of my id or out of my personal hostility.

George: Why didn't you let the "little gangsters" speak or talk back?

Chuck: Let me clarify that for you, George. Again, the important point is that this is not a regular group. Our people do a lot of their talking in a group interchange. This is a haircut, directed at changing a bad attitude that led to bad behavior.

In the context of a seminar, a drama class, or our encounter group, they can yell back and forth all they want. But when we are trying to correct a bad attitude, one that led to negative behavior, we don't want to hear any reasons for it; this could become symptom reinforcement. We don't allow them to talk about or rationalize their bad behavior. We know that it's bad behavior to yell "fuck" on the beach. I don't want to hear any reasons why somebody did it. All we want to do is tell them graphically, clearly, with dramatic imagery the way we want them to behave in the future. I'm not interested in why they want to behave badly. The way they behave is what brought them here in the first place. We attempt to correct stupid attitudes. Call it therapy if you want to. We point out their stupidity in the hope that they will learn how to grow up and function like adults. We stress this education for life.

George: The way you do this, I noticed, is to use a few principles from basic conditioning theory. First of all you use the principle of repetition. Second, you use the principle of analogy, saying the same thing many different ways to avoid monotony. If you constantly said the same thing all the time, "You have a bad attitude, you have a bad attitude," you would soon lose them. Instead you described their bad attitudes with a variety of metaphors, and very dramatically.

You also used what I would call a "relay system." I think it's a very important contribution to technique. Both you and Reid take up the attack in tandem, each using his own strengths. In professional group therapy, we encourage our cotherapists to express different approaches. The reason for this is to tell a patient different things with different therapists. He cannot quite take all the dishing out from one therapist. When we sense that, we call one the "stick" and the other the "soft." You don't smash the ego; you are paring it down to the reality of the individual involved. You inform him of things he can't see for himself. You are letting him know how he comes across to others, and this is helpful to him in changing his negative attitude and behavior.

L.Y.: A good encounter-group therapist is a master of smashing the excess negative ego. Without letting his own ego get in the way, he pares the person's self down to its reality. He also has to be an expert and master at uplifting the person. I believe there is a correlation between one's effectiveness as a smasher and as an uplifter. In a sense you are not attacking the person himself or the ego, you are attacking the person's bad attitude and behavior. It's a subtle, but important point. You don't attack the person: you are dealing with the bad attitude that leads him in a self-destructive direction.

Chuck: There is another angle to be clarified. For example, one of the defenses that many addicts and drunks develop is humor. If there is a spark of humor in the person, he will develop that facility to its fullest potential. Humor is one of the defense mechanisms that he used to defend himself for years when he was a sick alcoholic or addict. We can train him to use his humor and his sense of the ridiculous as a therapeutic tool. Not only that, but humor makes all of our group sessions more fun. We don't take ourselves too seriously.

Many alcoholics and addicts have developed exaggerated humor to a fine art for their own defenses over many years. People who are subject to or washed in an environment of this kind are not going to lose this ability. I'm a very good fencer and bludgeon man because I had to use my tongue to keep me alive when I was a crazy alcoholic. The people who come in here are potentially masters of ridicule. But only potentially, you see; they need to be trained to use it as a therapeutic art. Not only have many addicts and alcoholics developed the art of ridicule, but they also led a pretty ridiculous life. They can draw their absurd life experiences and use them, once they get past their pathology. The addict or alcoholic's past absurd life provides a very rich resource of absurd situations that can be dramatically used to help others change their negative attitudes and grow.

THE "MORAL" POSITION OF THE
EX-ADDICT-ALCOHOLIC THERAPIST

The ex-addict therapist often operates from a stronger position with peers than a professional therapist. In some respects the professional therapist's viewpoint is not as acceptable to the recovering addict or alcoholic as is the experience-oriented ex-user's perception of a situation.

The ex-addict's power in attacking the recovering person's attitude partially emanates from his or her own life experience. He or she has been in the other person's shoes and worked out of that situation. The ex-addict has traveled the tunnel back and has necessarily learned something about the pitfalls that happen along the way. His or her own successful resocializations and honesty are powerful weapons, and can be used skillfully and effectively to attack the addict's bad attitude and help the addict's growth process.

The ex-addict has a perspective on the addict-alcoholic behavior that is different from that of most citizens or professional therapists. After a time the drug world holds no charm or attraction for the ex-addict—who has concluded from hard-won truths that the attitude that leans toward such behavior is stupid and self-destructive; and he or she is inclined vehemently to present a viewpoint that will help others to recover.

For example, Reid's approach in the little-gangster session served to attack any latent negative beliefs in himself. At the same time that he went at his "clients," the process of attack clarified for him where he had been and gave him still another look at his own past behavior. An ex-addict like Reid sees nothing particularly attractive about this past "criminal dope-fiend" pattern, but is inclined to be disdainful of this type of behavior and to look upon it as "stark, raving stupidity."

TC graduates have paid their dues of having "been there." They feel fully entitled to view addict behavior in a totally negative way. Many traditional professionals who "work with addicts and alcoholics in some respects have less of a right to attack the behavior in the same way." In addition many professionals, in contradistinction to the committed ex-addict therapist, are intrigued by, and even take vicarious interest in, their patterns. Professionals are necessarily required to be more conservative in their *judgments* and *disapproval*, since they are usually only tourists in the foreign land of addiction. Many professional therapists admonish each other in the literature on therapeutic practice with the dictum to "be non-judgmental and withhold value judgments on deviant behavior." Ex-addicts, on the other hand, feel entitled to express a totally negative emotional and ethical commentary on what they perceive as the "stupidity" or "insanity" of the addict-alcoholic's attitude and behavior.

Reid's commentary during the haircut was unalterably opposed to the little-gangster criminal attitude. The objects of Reid's intense criticism of their behavior were receptive to his discourse. They were, at minimum, accepting of his right to give his sermon since he was one of their own. (The little gangsters would probably not sit through the same kind of diatribe if it were to take place in a professional establishment and administered by professional therapists.)

In my work in hospitals with adolescent addicts, I have utilized the therapeutic services of recovering ex-addicts who reside in a TC. I find that these young people respond most effectively when the older ex-addicts speak from their own experiences of past problems and necessary attitude changes. One of their most effective opening phrases includes: "When I was going through what you are experiencing, I felt just like you do." This kind of commentary is very helpful to young addicts in their growth processes. They do not feel as alone in their movement toward personal growth when they see older people who have been where they are now and who have changed in a positive way.

In my experience with adolescents, I have also found that the ex-addict teenagers who grew up in our program were most useful. They were listened to more attentively by the kids than were the imported older ex-addicts. The experience of their peer "therapists" who had the same problems, had changed, and were now staying clean had a profound impact on their own growth process.

THE SOCIAL GROWTH PROCESS

There are various phases of social growth a resident goes through in a TC. When the "mask" of the past and the addict-alcoholic's negative attitudes are changed, in a next phase recovering addicts go through what can be referred to as a "honeymoon period," when they have metaphorically "found salvation." They tend to accept all of the TC concepts, and begin to parrot TC language, even when they do not fully understand the principles they are espousing. Everything they learn is learned at gut level. They say such things as, "I feel comfortable for the first time in my life," and recite all the phrases that have evolved to explain the new feelings experienced by recovering addict-alcoholics in TCs. Other semantic forms that have evolved in TCs include: "going through the motions" or "sitting on your hands and hurting" (behaving properly even though one feels terrible); "gut-level insights" (understanding one's self on a deeper level); "goes through 'things'" (anticipated emotional upheavals and depressions); and "does what one has to do" (behaves with great resolve to "straighten out" and grow up).

The honeymoon phase of growth is considered a crucial and delicate period. A newcomer, after a few months, may give a surface appearance of being adult and healthy; however, the TC administration is aware, based on past experience, that underneath he or she is still a most fragile and vulnerable person, who is apt to split and go back to drugs or drink unless properly handled through this early emotional learning obstacle course.

The pattern of this dangerous honeymoon period of more overt than real growth is not a new experience for most newcomers. It is likely that at some time in their past addictive histories, before coming to the TC, they were successful in detoxifying and in not using drugs for a period of time. However, invariably when they were on their own, their successful abstinence would be short-lived, and they would slip back into drug use, often without really knowing how it happened.

The basic reason why the newly recovered addict is vulnerable to slippage and regression is that all that has happened at this point is that he or she has been clean for a few months. The person feels a certain euphoric respite from a past life where he or she was emotionally or physically involved with poisoning his or her system with drugs, and in a state of combat with family and society. For the recovering substance abuser, this peaceful break with past wars is a major self-satisfying achievement. However, this is a deceptive period because cleaning up and joining the program is only a first step. What the recovering addict is now confronted with is the arduous task of restructuring relationships and learning how to work and live without drugs—those bad but reliable "friends."

Effective TCs are constructed to take the addict through the total emotional reconstructive process required to achieve the changes necessary to function properly in the outside society. Regrettably, in many communities around the country there are spurious, highly advertised "treatment programs" that do nothing but detoxify the addict for a time, project the addict into this first honeymoon phase, and then put him or her back into the same societal configuration that caused his or her addiction.

The basic problem is that all these programs accomplish is to render the substance abuser clean for a brief period. What they do not accomplish is the necessary arduous social–emotional individual and group processes required for addicts to really change their personality and behavior. Phony "TCs" waste the addict's time and money because they do not get the addict past this first phase of the recovery process.

Several months is usually not long enough to bring about any marked changes in a person who has lived many years of destructive life experiences using drugs. The TC people recognize this early appearance of sobriety as only a first step toward a more stable drug-free personality development. The newcomer is given some modest approval for this growth. He or she may be assigned, in a carrot-before-the-nose fashion, to a more demanding job than he or she is equipped to handle. However, the newcomer is kept under close appraisal, since the early honeymoon period is a vulnerable time in the growth process, and the "feeling good" part of it may give the substance abuser an excuse to run off and reward himself or herself with their preferred drug or drink.

Although the newcomer may receive rewards for these early steps up the TC ladder, he or she is seldom given, in groups or in informal discussion, any approval for *not* using drugs. This absence of approval for abstinence appears to be a key element in getting the person past the honeymoon period onto firmer sober ground.

Care is taken not to overapprove this baseline of expected behavior: staying drug-free. The reasoning in a TC takes the following form: Most addict-alcoholics have attempted to quit using drugs and have succeeded for a time. When they have done this, very often in other settings, they have received too much approval for their abstinence. In the TC when they are voluntarily off drugs for a period of two, three, or four months, they begin to look around for the approval they have usually received for not using drugs when they were in the outside society or in other programs. It is not forthcoming. The point that is driven home, in a realistic TC, again and again is: "Why should we approve your not using drugs? Millions of people do not. You shouldn't use drugs, and there's no special reason for us to reward you in any way for staying sober." This tends to break the vicious circle that in the past put the addict-alcoholic back on the "poison." (This nonapproving approach has some parallels with the old saw of giving someone approval for not beating their spouse.)

The vicious circle that needs to be avoided, often operates in this way with respect to the addict's or alcoholic's past life situation:

Phase one involves the drug or alcohol addiction syndrome. There are no social rewards for this behavior. It is generally condemned and produces the painful results of family conflict, job difficulties, hospitalization, physical pain or discomfort, and so on. In any case the temporary euphoria gained from the drugs or alcohol does not counterbalance the longer-term pain.

In *phase two* of the vicious circle, the individual stops using alcohol or drugs for a time. He or she then begins to receive some approval or reward from some others for not carrying on the self-destructive behavior.

Phase three emerges when the individual no longer receives approval or reward for not being an alcoholic or a drug addict. People in his or her life at a certain point stop congratulating the addict or alcoholic on being such a swell person for not "getting loaded." When former addicts or alcoholics begin to be judged on the basis of regular adult demands (which they often feel inadequate to fulfill), in their sensitivity they begin to feel that no one cares if they remain sober and they then return to their original syndrome of drugs or alcohol abuse.

It can be speculated that, in some measure, the addictive person resumes the "bad behavior" of substance abuse in order to stop again later, and once again receive reward and approval. This vicious circle does not operate with all addicts or alcoholics. However, it appears to be the case with many.

The departure or break from supporting this described vicious circle in the TC is that newcomers do not receive approval for not using drugs in this first honeymoon phase. In the TC they are expected to *not* use drugs. During this phase of development, a newcomer is thrown for a bit of a loss when he or she does not receive the usual approval for not using drugs. This helps to break the vicious addictive circle for many. Moreover, if the newcomer makes a childish threat to go out and shoot drugs, no one *overtly* seems to care. The correct TC position—one derived from the AA experience—is: "If you want to go out and kill yourself or wind up in a cage, go ahead."

In the TC the staff is aware of the delicate complexity of this stage of potential failure and consciously and unconsciously attempts to help newcomers over this difficult early period of adjustment. Approval for not using drugs never fades out, because it is never given in the first place.

The TC's anti-addiction posture is clear and persistent at all times in all situations. Approval is given to residents for constructive work habits, positive attitude changes, and emotional growth.

The TC social environment helps many people who formerly failed to get past the difficult early phase of abstinence by providing a community of experienced and understanding ex-addicts. Residents have people with whom they can communicate and who understand during this trying period of transition from drugs to a clean, constructive life. Help is provided in the variety of structured groups. There are also many informal situations in the TC where addicts communicate with their important caring circles of friends, and have endless casual conversations at meals, over coffee, and in recreational situations about the issues and problems vital to the struggle for recovery.

One recovering addict, Sally, who was 20 and a resident in an effective TC, told me how her other attempts to quit drugs always seemed doomed to failure because she had "no one to talk to" about her feelings, and she poignantly described how her newly found caring circle of friends worked for her.

"I remember one time, when I got out of one of the many institutions I went to for my problem, I went for three days without using. I really wanted to stay clean. Then I began to get lonely. I realized when I looked through my old address book that the only people I knew to call and talk to were addicts. I didn't have any nonaddict friends, and I surely didn't know any person who would admit to trying to quit using. Finally, I broke down and called some addict I knew, out of sheer boredom and loneliness. Naturally, I was back on cocaine in a few days. I probably should have gone to

AA or Cocaine Anonymous." (Attendance at support groups is highly encouraged by most TCs for their graduates.)

In her first several months in the TC, Sally found the change of language and discussions confusing but different. "In the TC I was at first surprised when people were jumped on for talking about drugs. Not only was there a ban on talking this trash, there was a ban on newcomers' talking alone to each other. I remember being told not to talk to Paula, who had been in the place for a few weeks. I was told: 'She can't tell you anything yet but how to free-base. Go talk to Betty. She can tell you how it is in here.' We were just not permitted to discuss drugs, and that was so common in this six-week wonder-cure place I had been in before that didn't work for me. I found that the TC was a refreshing change. I always had an inner desire to talk about art and intellectual matters, and this kind of talk is approved of here."

"Another thing about this place is that, night or day, in the living room there is always someone with whom you can discuss the real problems you are having at that moment. This is not true with your average professional therapist—the 50 minutes and goodbye sessions that I found useless. I have had four- or five hour-long intense and valuable talks with other people in the program over a coffee cup that really straightened my head out on many important things in my life. And they knew what they are talking about because they had been through it just like me.

"The other amazing and wonderful thing about these informal talks in the TC is that you can talk about the terrible downside of getting and using drugs. When I would talk with some of the same people on the outside, all you were allowed to talk about, because they wanted to seem cool, were the good things about getting high. Here, for the first time, I can unload about the bullshit part of using drugs.

"For example, in one informal conversation with another woman who had been through the same experience I had, I finally could see and admitted I was a 'coke whore.' On the outside we saw ourselves as glamorous, young ladies happily free-basing coke with exciting successful guys at swinging parties. Over a cup of coffee in talking with this girl, who had been at a lot of Hollywood parties with me, we both admitted that our former glamorous life really involved putting out for creepy guys we didn't like—just like any prostitute—to get our beloved cocaine."

WORKING TOWARD GRADUATION

Most TCs provide a positive social atmosphere that points addicts in new and constructive directions of long-term social growth. They discover a different language, different ways of relating, and the new possibility for exciting and interesting growth. At about a four-month point, a resident becomes sufficiently aware of the TC's social structure to become involved in status seeking and climbing the organizational ladder. Status seeking in the TC hierarchy is a process that is encouraged because it is a developmental process that parallels life in the real world. The recovering addict at this point is in a position to look around and select some role model, a senior person whom he or she would like to emulate, and also begins to go after what appear to be interesting and worthwhile status jobs in the TC. He or she is encouraged to do this and to attempt to "manipulate the environment" to acquire status in the organization.

The process of successful upward mobility in the social structure of a TC requires, as in any organization, a knowledge of its structure. Residents are motivated to try to understand something in depth about the social structure and organization of the TC. A healthy side effect of this positive status seeking is that it is a useful learning situation for "growing up." Since the structure of a TC compares in many ways to that of other human organizations, learning more about how it works fosters a greater level of sensitivity and empathy in the recovering person.

To succeed in status seeking in the TC, one must learn how to relate effectively to others. This requires a degree of empathy, or the ability to put oneself in another's place, to understand the other. The recovering addicts then become more involved in the world around them. They begin to learn how to see themselves as others see them. This process takes place not only in the formal TC community per se but also in the intensive encounter-group sessions and psychodramas. Newcomers find that their self-image begins to have a degree of reality. They begin to see personal weak spots and strengths through the group's eye, and they try to change dimensions of themselves that they feel, and others feel, are defective and self-deceptive. Their work and personal development are measurable by the progress they make in the occupational organizational hierarchy. The TC becomes a real life training experience that is useful for the recovering substance abuser outside of the TC.

In most traditional treatment or correctional settings, growth in the institution often disables the "patient" or "inmate" from developing successful social skills useful in the outside society. In many of these organizations *dependency* is encouraged. The more manipulative and dependent the persons become, the better he or she is able to function in most hospitals and institutions. In contrast, social growth in a TC involves a clearer perception of the organization and the development of skills for assuming self-responsibility and greater independence.

The upper level of most TC organizations comprise individuals who have acquired these self-reliant skills and are potentially capable of functioning at the administrative level in other organizations. Their job and social skills are often transferable to work and life outside the TC organization.

Most TCs I have seen delineate some general levels or stages of growth that define where the recovering addict is at in the path toward graduating drug-free from the program. For purposes of analysis, an arbitrary division of first- second- and third-stage residence has been formulated in most TCs. These levels of growth are not nearly as cut and dried as they may seem, since each person's rate of growth is different. Some people who have been in residence for six months are further ahead of some two and three-year residents. The person's level of growth and position in the TC are different in each individual case; however, the following three stages reflect the general growth and status position of members in a variety of TCs I have studied.

First Stage:

Here newer members live and work in the main building. Newcomers are watched closely to ensure that they will stay clean and that someone from their past will not tip them in the wrong direction with a phone call or visit. When going on a walk, or out on a pass the newcomer is often accompanied by an older member. It is assumed, that newcomers at this time are relatively incapable of handling productive associations with the outside community. Their relationships are closely watched and regulated for their own benefit and personal protection because they are very vulnerable at this stage to regress into the past addiction patterns. They feel good, however, and are in a kind of honeymoon phase.

Second Stage:

Here recovering addict-alcoholics live in TC residence, and they work or go to school in the community. Those who work for the TC in administrative jobs have considerable freedom to conduct relationships outside the TC. Second-stagers are assumed to have learned how to conduct such relationships on their own. They are usually around six months or a year away from their problem and are considered to be reasonably resistant to relapse. This more independent phase of growth calls for considerable freedom and an enlargement of the scope of outside associations, work, and personal relationships.

Third Stage, or Graduation:

This applies to individuals who live and work in the community and to residents who work for the TC. These members have complete freedom to come and go as they please. The graduate level of growth implies a sufficient emancipation and distance from the original problem for an individual to conduct his or her personal life plan on his or her own terms in an independent fashion. The graduate may chose to continue as an employee of the organization, or to live and work in the community and attend support-group sessions for a time after moving out.

It is apparent that "graduates" who have developed therapeutic skills in the process of their own recovery are enormously valuable people as leaders and administrators in TCs. Many stay on and work in the TC that helped to save their lives, and become very dedicated professionals who strengthen the TC program. Others go on to work in other TCs. "TC professionals" or graduates are a vital source of power for the worldwide TC movement. The Therapeutic Communities of America organization has developed procedures for certifying TC graduates as paraprofessional drug counselors.

It should be noted that in many TCs there is no special label or stamp placed on so-called first-, second-, or third-stage people.

These are only convenient categories for descriptive purposes. As indicated, in a TC freedom is a correlate of personal responsibility. As the members grow and begin to move up both in the organization and in outside relationships, their increasing maturity is encouraged and rewarded. Graduate status does not usually involve complete disaffiliation from the TC, even for those who choose to live and work outside. Almost all the people who have benefited from a TC voluntarily maintain an affiliation. The involvement often takes the form of a weekly support group. It may also take such forms as giving financial contributions to the TC, providing goods and services, or counseling newcomers.

The type of comment often made by bona-fide graduates is, "I want an opportunity to put something back into the pot. The TC saved my life, and I want to help in any way I can." What has become apparent is that this kind of contribution is as significant and beneficial for the benefactor, who has matured, as it is for the organization. The graduate's tie and involvement enable him or her to see the route traveled and indirectly to receive a continuing physical and emotional checkup by people who know the graduate well, and can read him or her clearly and sharply. The graduate has also developed important friendships with others who have had a similar self-destructive problem and successfully made it out of the morass. Friendship bonds are often developed in a TC that last a lifetime.

I have observed in some cases that a person who has grown up in a TC and then moves too far outside the range of the organization sometimes regresses. There is some comparability between this phenomenon and that of diabetics who are removed prematurely from their insulin or patients with heart disease who overextend themselves physically. It seems indicated, therefore, even for those who move into the community, that some contact with the organization is in order. The contact helps graduates maintain a perspective on their life-style and seems to be beneficial.

One of the most important aspects about maintaining this recommended contact with the TC is that graduates are in a position to see newcomers. In meeting and talking with a newly arrived addict, the graduate is reminded of the past, and this is something an addict should never forget. Most TC professionals perceive this interaction as a necessary and useful continuing experience for all graduates. Graduates see in discussions with newcomers the gross manifestations of their own past problems. Seeing this glaring past picture of themselves enables them to remain aware of the possibility of vestiges of self-destructive behavior. Even when these negative forces are dormant or latent, they might flare up. In the process of talking to newcomers, older members not only see themselves as they were but are in a strategic position to attack any negative components in themselves that may still be potentially operative. This is useful even though these negative aspects are latent and held in abeyance at the time.

For these logical reasons, graduate TC people who live or work in the community are encouraged to maintain some type of affiliation with the organization in their own self-interests. When they do not fulfill this requirement, they run the risk of regression. The graduates who regress to drugs are often people who cut off their lifelines. It may seem to some an unnecessary dependency to maintain a lifelong tie with a TC. However, using the medical model as a parallel, it seems necessary for many diabetics and heart-trouble patients to keep in communication with their doctors. In a similar fashion, at this time a "lifeline" with their TC seems indicated for people who have arrested a problem that can be perceived too often as a terminal disease.

For the same reason that AA has adopted its "once an alcoholic, always an alcoholic" philosophy to prevent regression, TCs need to operate in terms of a similar concept. The general belief of "once an addict, always an addict" reminds graduates of their lifelong vulnerability, and I believe it is a valid operational concept.

Growing up in a TC has been described as a "circuitous and torturous tunnel back into humanity." It seems to be different for each person. Some stumble on the way, split, come back, and finally make it. Others join, stay, hold on tight, and travel the route back from their past lives in a steadily rising curve of personal growth, and graduate into a positive, happier way of life.

7

Success Stories: How and Why Therapeutic Communities Work

The original TC, Synanon, was developed and cut its teeth on the most difficult addict and alcoholic cases. The hundreds of TCs that have emerged in recent years utilize and have been built upon the foundation of most of the concepts and methods developed in Synanon and the earlier TCs. The more recent programs are uniquely adapted to the changing patterns of drug and alcohol use in a younger and more diverse population of substance abusers in contemporary society. Also, the spread of drug–alcohol abuse around the world has produced TCs that have been adapted to the special cultural conditions that exist in different communities and societies.

Notable in the recent TC efforts to combat drug–alcohol abuse is the fact that increasingly programs are constructed and directed by a new coalition of TC graduate ex-addicts and university-trained professionals. This combination of leadership has had a profound positive effect on the movement.

Also, as previously discussed, the harsh-attack group approach has been tempered, and more standard psychological personal problem solving has been incorporated into a variety of programs. Moreover, the general figure of two years for treatment has gone down for some addicts who have a reasonable level of personal and occupational competence in society to six months. Some residents never fully "graduate" because they have taken jobs in TCs and thus devote their lives to treating other addicts.

Following are three case histories that I have selected from the hundreds of TC residents I have interviewed. They represent different types of addicts treated in different TC programs. These cases describe the basic theory and methodology that have emerged in the context of different types of TC programs. These scenarios reveal, in context, how and why TC programs effectively treat a wide range of people from the viewpoint of three addict-alcoholics who successfully kicked their habits in a TC program, and are now happy, competent, and productive citizens.

THREE CASE HISTORIES

Bob

Bob had been a cocaine and heroin addict for over 13 years when he entered a TC at the age of 33. He had tried many other programs and several professional therapists in individual counseling, and nothing had worked for him.

During a period of a year that he was in a TC, I had many research interview and informal discussions with him, and had observed him in encounter-group sessions. He came from an upper-middle-class background, and in spite of his addiction, he had managed to almost complete a college education that included courses in psychology. After college he had had some success as a producer and director in the theatrical profession in New York.

Given Bob's unique ability and background as a student, a producer-director, a drug addict, and a "patient," I invited him to give a talk to a graduate university seminar of mine on his TC experience. In his presentation he cogently described his feelings during his first year in the TC. His perceptive statements document many issues involved in the process of recovery in a TC program. The following statements are excerpted from his one-hour lecture to my class, and a number of additional in-depth interviews I had with him.

"Today in my talk I will try to give you the benefit of my contact with various institutional approaches to my disorder, which has been labeled by psychoanalysts as 'constitutional psychopathy, complicated by drug addiction.' I guess, in your frame of reference, 'sociopath' would be more applicable. At any rate this diagnosis was made 14 years ago by Dr. Abraham Kardiner, a pretty reputable Freudian psychiatrist, after I had spend eight months in therapy with the man.

"Over a period of 13 years, I wound in and out of private, public, state, county, and federal institutions for drug addicts; as well as private hospitals for people with the whole spectrum of emotional and psychological disorders. What I think is relevant to examine here today, in the light of my experience, is what happened to me in the 13 months that I've been in the TC that has made it possible for me not to behave as I did previously.

"There is no evidence, as yet, as to whether I have been changed on a deep and meaningful level. But there is plenty of surface evidence that my behavior has manifested a change so drastic from what it was 13 months ago that, to me and the people who knew me before coming to the program, it's almost unbelievable.

"What I wanted to point out to you, in brief, is that what happened in the TC program did not happen for me at the Menninger Clinic in Topeka; the Institute of Living in Hartford; three times at Lexington, KY.; at New York Metropolitan Hospital; at Manhattan General; or at the Holbrook Sanitorium. It also didn't happen for me with a number of individual shrinks.

"When you think of an addiction history of 14 years, many people have the image of 14 years of constant drug use. The thing that makes people drug addicts, to me, is the equation that they learn after their first detoxification. Drug addicts become drug addicts not when they just become addicted to drugs, but when they learn this equation. They kick their habit physiologically, they have decided consciously to change their behavior, they are going to manipulate themselves in every way that they know in order not to repeat what they've been doing, and—bingo—they repeat exactly those processes that got them to the point that they didn't want to get to. This, to me, is the person who has taken his first cure and then gone back to dope. The usual institution he goes to is also part of his addiction process.

"Certain circumstances force people to enter a TC. The AA always uses the phrase, 'You reach your own bottom,' So, let's assume that I had reached a 'bottom.' I had tried everything else in the Western World. I think, just about everything else; you know, chemical cures as well, which I didn't bother to mention.

"Anyway, I entered the TC. At first something very strange happened to me. I came into this place early in the morning. I had just gotten off the plane. I'd flown 3000 miles. The usual reception at a place where a person has volunteered for a cure is 'Welcome aboard!' This was not the case, I was told to sit down and shut up, in just about those words; you know literally, 'Sit down; shut up.' [In this TC other applicants received a more cordial intake interview. The intake staff, however, felt that in Bob's case it would be useful for him to battle his way into the organization.]

"I figured I was talking to a disturbed person who didn't understand who he was talking to. In the first moment of contact, instead of being told 'welcome aboard,' you're told to shut up and sit down. Whereupon, being loaded on a variety of opiates, I explained that I had just arrived in California; that I had flown in from New York; and that I had talked to a board member—whereupon the magic words 'shut up and sit down' were readministered. I began to realize that reason has nothing to do with the behavior of these people. These are not reasonable people, obviously, because I had no alternative. If I'd had an alternative, I would have said, 'I'll come back another time.' But I was 3000 miles away from my connection. I didn't have that resource.

"I sat down for a number of hours, and then I was called by some people into a room. Oh, first of all, my luggage was taken away from my possession. And one of my pieces of luggage contained a variety of drugs, nonnarcotic in nature, that were prescribed for me by my psychiatrist. When I left New York, I said, 'I'll be gone for six months,' and he wrote five prescriptions for six months' worth of five different kinds of medication...you know, to ease withdrawal...nonnarcotic—psychic energizers, tranquilizers, sleeping medication—a whole satchel full of it.

"The intake interview...I've been subjected to many intake interviews, by social workers, psychiatrists, psychologists, and charge nurses, you know. And I was usually asked a variety of questions, and I had my pat answers: Am I white or black—'I'm white.' In this instance I wasn't asked anything. They didn't even want to know my name. I mean, literally, they did not say to me, 'Who are you?' They proceeded to tell me who I was. Their only contact with me had been a phone call from Westport, which lasted maybe a minute, and then my contact with the guy at the desk, who didn't listen to what I was saying. So they were telling me who I was.

"They told me things like I would 'never make it,' I was a 'momma's boy,' I was 'spoiled,' I was 'probably incurable,' and that if I didn't shut up, they would throw me out; that they were not interested in learning anything from me, because I had nothing to teach them—which, of course, to me was absolutely absurd, because, you know, I had come there to enlighten the West Coast. This was a shocking experience. I'm making it humorous, but it shook me up; it shook me down to my feet.

"In the intake interview there were five addicts staring at me. One said, 'There's an accumulative 37 years of sobriety in this room and 82 years of dope addiction, and your three seconds of sobriety doesn't count.' Now that was reasonable to me. So you see, I was being hit on a reasonable and nonreasonable level as I saw it.

"So they were talking about me as if I weren't there, after this thing happened. You know, 'Let's take him downstairs, let's do this to him...' I wasn't being consulted, and the first thing I thought, when I heard about the TC concept, was, "There won't be any 'we' and 'they' alienations, because these are folks like me, and they know how sick I am.'

"I was then taken outside by a large man. A gargantuan character whom I would never have an opportunity to communicate with, even using dope. I found out he was a street hype from Detroit and he looked very tough. Outside of the TC, it would just be a matter of conning him, or him hitting me over the head. He proceeded to take my little satchel with medicine in it and led me downstairs to the basement of the building, which was pretty grim. It looked like the 23rd Precinct in New York. He took the satchel and opened the bottles and proceeded to pour them into the toilet. I said, 'Now, wait; you see, you don't understand. These are non-addicting drugs—none of these drugs are addicting drugs, and they're legitimate. See, my name is on them.' And while I'm saying this, he is like grunting and pouring my medicine out.

"This is another important aspect of a TC that is different from other institutions. The first thing I picked up in this indoctrination, being a manipulative type of guy, was this: When people didn't want me or didn't seem to want me, I, of course, wanted them. The appeal to me was somewhat like a fraternity appeal in a college. The fraternity that is most difficult to get into is naturally the most desirable.

"Well, what had been communicated to me immediately by 'sit down and shut up,' you know, as if I were rushing the house, was that this club was rather exclusive. They were not particularly impressed with me, so naturally they must be pretty good—because my self-esteem was pretty shitty, although it didn't look that way.

"Then my personal property...I think a person's property represents who you are—you know, your resumés. For people in the theatrical business, your eight-by-ten glossies [pictures] and your theater programs—you know this is who you are. I had a few pieces of clothing and an electric shaver, things you picked up that are pawnable. These things were taken away from me, brusquely. And I was given—'schmatas' [rags] is the only word I can think of. I was given unseemly clothing.

"There was nothing institutional about the clothing. There was a plaid shirt that didn't fit. And I was very specific in asking for cotton because my skin gets sensitive during withdrawal. I was given a wool plaid shirt, because I asked for cotton, and a pair of khaki pants that didn't fit, and rubber go-aheads or flip-flops, or suicide-scuffs, which were very uncomfortable. And then I was taken upstairs.

"There I was. My luggage was gone, my resumés, my identity, my drugs...my pride. I also had my hair cut, just because I protested too much. I had my hair cut off rather short, and by a guy who didn't particularly care for the cosmetic value of a haircut. I didn't need a haircut. The day before I had been to Vincent of the Plaza in New York and had had a haircut.

"I went into the living room and was introduced to a few people. I recognized a couple of them. I recognized a couple as drug addicts. Like I saw scar tissue on their arms. I saw that they were—like maybe they really were drug addicts.

"Kicking my habit in the TC had a big effect on me. It was a process which, again, was very different from other institutions. The institutions I had been to all had detoxification procedures of one kind or another. All the detoxification procedures that I've ever been involved in, although they may be medically necessary for people with heart conditions or for people who are over 93, really were not necessary. In all of the settings I have been in, the bit was to exaggerate your symptoms so that you could get more medication. If you get medication, you feel better; if you don't, you feel bad. I don't think there is anything pathological in this kind of behavior. So the thing to do, of course, is to get medication.

"I was told, with the flushing down the drain of the medications I had brought, that I was not getting any medication. And I said, you know, 'I'm going to get quite sick—I'm not feeling very good!' 'You will not get any medication.'

"I said, 'You don't understand. You see, I'm going to be really sick. You see, I'm from New York, and they've got good heroin and cocaine in New York, and I'm strung out—and I'm going to really get sick.'

"They again repeated, 'You will not get medication. If you want medication, you can leave and get medication. But here, you won't get medication.'

"This immediately stopped a whole process that would have gone on for two or three weeks if medication were given. This is another important thing: I had my biggest manipulative device taken away from me, because there was nothing to manipulate for, except maybe a glass of water. That's about it, you know? And how much of a con game would I have to run down to get a glass of water?

"Then the guy assigned to me as a sponsor started his therapy. He was a big black guy who sure knew his job. The second day I was there, I started to get sick. The drugs held me for 24 or 30 hours. He came up to me and said, 'Little brother'—he referred to me as 'little brother,' which offended me to the quick—'when are you going to get sick?' I was sick, and he knew I was sick. So he came over again and he said, 'Little brother, when are you going to get sick?' Because his attitude was ridiculous, as far as I was concerned, I said, 'Oh, I'm all right.'

"Now what he had done by this simple little intuitive thing of 'When are you going to get sick?' is that he let me know that he knew that I knew that he knew. He immediately stopped the possibility of—you know—he didn't give me sympathy; he didn't give me any kind of 'understanding'—and yet he gave me understanding on a very deep level. Like it became a challenge to me to see how unsick I could be in withdrawal during the next four or five days. And I noticed another thing. There would be some people in the house who would come over and kind of be concerned about me. I'd get a back rub. If I wasn't vomiting, I'd get a milkshake, and sometimes I would drink the milkshake so that I could vomit and show them how sick I was. There were still these things that were going on that weren't getting me anywhere.

"And then they did something to me that was very important. They made me think they had a secret. They made me think that they knew something that I didn't know. I snapped to this, and it was quite true; they did know something I didn't know. They still know many things I don't know. It wasn't just a mystique. They really had information I didn't have. And they weren't willing to share it with me, particularly, at least at this time. This got my nose open. I became quite curious about what it was. My sponsor would drop a concept on me—you know, an incomplete statement—like a zen cat and run off in the other direction. He would say something like, 'Just stay,' You know, like a zen master would clap me on the head and I'd have enlightenment.

"Well, this is what was going on during the period of detoxification, TC style, which is a cold-turkey withdrawal, which is unlike any other cold-turkey withdrawal because it's bad and it's wretched, but it's not all that wretched and not that bad.

"I was up off the couch in four days. Now I had been kicking habits. I was a specialist in observing myself kicking habits—you know, reading Cocteau as another frame of reference in kicking habits...how he kicked his habit—and all of my evidence crumbled. You see, all of my evidence was destroyed by the experience that I was sleeping by the seventh day, and I hadn't slept without medication, in or out of a place, in seven years. I had not been able to sleep. I was now sleeping within seven days.

"On the fifth day, I was rewarded for kicking my habit by receiving a mop! I thought the least I deserved—you know, the least—for what I'd been subjected to was a week at a country club. Instead I was not rewarded at all. Because there really was not any reason for a reward. I heard things like, 'Not shooting dope is not worthy of a reward. People don't shoot dope! Therefore, not shooting dope doesn't earn any reward.' It's like saying, 'Congratulations for not beating your wife.' or 'Thank you for not murdering my sister.' You know, one doesn't do this, so naturally you're not going to get a big hand.

"No one in the TC is going to applaud you because you're not shooting any dope and you're mopping floors. Somebody's got to mop the floors, and you're constantly told you don't know how to do anything else at that time. You begin to think that maybe they're right because, at this point, you're pretty vulnerable psychically and physically—so maybe mopping a floor isn't a bad thing to be doing.

"And then the magic thing begins to go to work, this thing about the secret. I think this is what motivates you to mop the floor well. You begin to see that if you mop the floor well, you won't feel as guilty as if you mop the floor badly.

"In most institutional settings, and in most psychoanalytical or socially oriented or tradition-directed treatment centers for addicts, your guilt is usually ameliorated: 'You're a sick fellow; you can't help yourself; you have an acting-out disorder; together we'll work this thing out, resocialize you, and everything will be great.' So, of course, what people like myself do is, they take all this ammunition, they fuel themselves with the fact that they are acting out a disorder. What can they do? They have all the data, so they go and act out.

"Here they lay guilt upon guilt. In other words, every time the energy flags a little bit—like mopping the floors and the corners aren't done—instead of being told, 'Well, you know, he's still sick; he hasn't really kicked yet; he's new and he hasn't done much floor mopping in his time,' you are made to feel that the dirty corner represents a dirty corner in your psyche, your gut. You think that you really are ridiculously bad at mopping floors, and you get guilty, you see, and your guilt is fueled.

"Now, whenever you are in an institutional setting, your guilt and problems are analyzed and explained away—they are lightened. The burden of guilt is lightened. In this TC whenever things begin to get buoyant and you permit your insanity to return as self-compensation for your low self-esteem, you're told you're not unique in nature and get smashed on the head with a verbal velvet mallet. It doesn't crush the tissue; you still feel the impact of it, but it really doesn't hurt.

"I soon learned that there were people in the TC without the social status I had in the outside world, without the resumés and the eight-by-ten glossies, who were not smashed quite as hard as I was. They came in with a birdcage on one foot, a boxing glove on the other, and, like, they were in bad shape. You can see that they don't have any totems of success or any illusions, so there's no reason for them to be ridiculed the way I was ridiculed; and they are treated in a more caring way. But they still will not be able to get rewarded for bad behavior.

"For instance, I think this is significant in looking at the total picture. A friend of mine arrived from New York about three months after I got here. My friend, Herb, was addicted to barbiturates and cocaine as well as heroin. He got pretty damn sick and began to act pretty crazy. This is interesting. One of the directors came down and told Herb that if he acted like a nut, they'd have to ask him to leave, because they couldn't handle nuts. In other words, 'Herb, you'll have to go to Camarillo or someplace where they handle crazy people. We don't handle crazy people, so you're not allowed to be crazy here.' Now I've been in three psychiatric hospitals with Herb, and I know how crazy he is. Now, literally, this happened to work. 'Don't be a nut.' And, you know, he wasn't! He just couldn't act crazy if he wanted to stay, so he didn't.

"Herb was a pretty sick guy physically, but he was able to curb his emotional symptoms because of this direct approach to him by an understanding ex-addict.

"Here is another significant thing in terms of an institution, and in terms of understanding the TC thing. About three or four weeks after my arrival, I began to notice that the place was full of me. In other words, in every other institution I had ever been at, I had a very schizoid feeling. There were the doctors, and I was kind of like them...but by some fluke, they became doctors and I was an addict. I'd look at them, and because I knew a lot of psychology, I felt like I kind of had a foot in their camp. And yet I was with the addicts because I am an addict. There was a kind of 'we–they' thing, and I kind of felt that I was straddling them both. I knew that my soul was with the addicts because the doctors did not know where it was at. They really didn't.

"In the TC, in contrast, I saw a million manifestations of me, in everyone, because despite their background and status in the TC, they were addicts like me; and I truly trusted them.

"The contract I had set up all my life with other people was a 'we–they' situation: my father and me, my psychiatrist and me, the warden and me, the teacher and me. This contrast was smashed by the TC situation. I became aware that the place was run by a hundred Bobs, different aspects of me. Different aspects of me were all there. So when I hated somebody's behavior, I disapproved of me. My sense of alienation with the 'we–they' equation—the hip and the square, the culture and the subculture, the ingroup and the outgroup, the Jews and the gentiles, the whites and the blacks— and all of the 'we–they' equations that I had learned primarily were destroyed in the TC. I had nothing to rebel against but myself.

"I began to see what Lew Yablonsky articulates as 'social mobility' in a TC. [I had discussed this issue in introducing Bob.] We don't have a caste system where my upward mobility is restricted to being a patient or an inmate. We have a kind of class system, based on clean seniority, productivity, mental health, talent, and so on. I've begun to climb this status ladder, and I'm beginning to understand now that I'm hooked into the organization and want to move up. The side effect of this status seeking for me has been growing up from being a baby to my chronological age of 33. In the process I, of course, have stayed clean, and I plan to remain drug-free for the rest of my life."

Bob remained in the TC program for two more years, working as a counselor with newcomers. He left the program to resume his career in TV and film, but maintained a constructive connection by participating in a variety of TC and other support groups.

Bob has been drug-free for over 20 years, and along with his work as a successful TV and film producer, he has continually worked effectively in the TC movement in sharing his group-therapy expertise and antidrug posture in the war on substance abuse.

Jill

Jill was 17 when I met her in an adolescent TC program that I had helped to construct in the context of a traditional mental hospital setting. At the time of her entry into the program, she was suffering from depression, and had been addicted to cocaine and alcohol and had used a variety of psychoactive pills for several years.

During the six-month period that I knew her in the hospital, her treatment included individual psychiatric counseling and group therapy with professional therapists. I worked directly with her in a drug-addict encounter group and a psychodrama group I directed. In addition to gathering information from the many psychodrama and group therapy sessions I ran with her, I interviewed her several times on an individual basis.

Jill, an only child, began smoking marijuana at 13, around the time her parents had split up. She lived with her mother, whom she found cold and unfeeling. According to Jill: "My mother just bored me to death. She never talked to me. When I learned some psychiatric jargon, I would say she was catatonic. It was like living with a stone. I missed my father terribly—and saw him rarely—because he was always traveling on business and out making money. He really didn't have to work, since my grandmother had left him and me a small fortune.

"Around the time I was 14, I met Jim. You could say, for me, he was an older man. He was 20. I realize now it was all bullshit but he had this intellectual line that got to me. He was always talking against war and how people rip each other off and how bad that was. In the meantime he was really fucking me over. I really thought I was in love with him and he was my one and only. But I found out later I was only one of his girlfriends. He was just a terrible liar. About a year after my parents had split, my father remarried and I got to live with him. His new wife seemed O.K. at first, but turned into a total bitch. I had fooled around with some coke with Jim, but my stepmother really turned me on to it. My father didn't know how heavy she was using. All he cared about was that she fucked him whenever he wanted to. She would get stoned and tell me that's how she held on to him.

"After my dad went off to work, I would have a nice breakfast with my stepmom. She would put out a good spread. It consisted of scrambled eggs, coffee, and several lines of coke. This would get me up and off to school for the day. For lunch I would smoke a joint; and on other days when it was available, I would do some more coke or have a few ludes. This routine went on for a couple of years until I was 16.

"I might add that Jim and I did lots of drugs and sex. In my drug haze, I fell madly in love with Jim, and almost worshiped him.

"I knew my stepmom was partying and fucking lots of other guys when my dad was away on his business trips. The bitch was into younger guys, and she often flirted openly with Jim. He denied any interest in her. You guessed it. One day I came home early from school and there they were, fucking in my father's bed. They hardly stopped when they saw me. I got into a big screaming hassle with the two of them. They decided to calm me down. We all had a few lines of coke and they just giggled about what had happened. I was smashed by the incident and felt horrible. But it didn't seem to bother them at all.

"Later, when we were alone, I screamed at Jim how I loved him and asked how he could do this to me. He was totally cold to my feelings. Finally he said, 'If you don't like it, bitch, get lost.'

"That night I went over to his house and found out he wasn't home. I told his parents I would just wait on the lawn for him. They must have gone to sleep. So I'm sitting out there in terrible pain, full of pills, smoking dope, feeling all alone and sorry for myself, and getting more depressed by the minute. The only one I felt I had in the world was Jim, and he had abandoned me.

"When I came down from my coke highs, I had thought a lot about suicide around that time. I carried some razor blades in my purse. (They were also good for cutting up hash and lining up coke.) So there I was, all alone, depressed, and I decided to do it. I cut my wrists and they were bleeding lightly. I was stoned and actually feeling mellow watching blood ooze out of my wrists. That'll show them all, I thought. Then I got this crazy idea. In my insanity I thought it was logical for me to write Jim a letter in my own blood. I had a pen in my purse and would dip it in my blood. The writing was red and blue from the pen. I talked about my grief, depression, loneliness, what a dick he was, and on and on and on.

"His parents must have seen what I was doing through the window. They called the police and my father. They scooped me up and rushed me to the emergency ward. I really hadn't lost that much blood—but I was obviously nuts.

"In a way my suicide attempt worked. My father, for the first time in ages, began to talk to me. I told him about his bitch wife and how she had lines of coke waiting for me at breakfast time and how she fucked Jim. Well that blew it, for her anyway. He knew he had to get me some therapy. For me it was the start of around six drug programs. They were all 60–90-day detoxification programs with a little bullshit group therapy. None of them worked, and as soon as I was out the door, I would use again.

"Along the way, over this year or so when I was in these programs, my dad divorced the bitch. Then he got himself another one, who was just as bad.

"My father became distant again, as I moved in and out of these different places. In a few of them, I was able to have friends of mine smuggle in drugs. Jim and I were on again, off again. I still felt that I loved him in spite of the fact that he continued to use me. He was always off with other girls, and besides, I never forgave him for fucking my stepmom.

"So that's how my life was between 13 and 16 until I entered this program, which seems to be working for me. I've been almost totally drug-free for over a year, thanks to the program. I have had a few slips, but mainly I'm learning to live drug-free, go to school, and unload some of the people who have been destructive in my life. This includes my unavailable father and that dick Jim."

The program worked for her because it was not *only* a detox-ification or a psychological problem-solving program. The program had TC elements that had an enormous positive therapeutic impact on Jill.

Before analyzing the combination psychiatric hospital/TC forces that worked for Jill, it is of value to comment on the types of programs that did *not* work for Jill.

She had become involved for about two years during her adolescence (14–16) in the turnstile type of 60–90-day detox programs that claimed more than they delivered. She would be drug-free for a period of time in these short-term programs. In these programs her basic impulse-control mechanisms and problem-solving faculties were untouched by the treatment. Also, the negative impacts of her family system were not dealt with in any depth. These pseudoprograms enabled her parents to keep Jill as the "identified patient" while they maintained the illusion that they were healthy people who happened to have a problem daughter.

All of this changed when they placed Jill in the program that had the best aspects of a psychiatric hospital combined with the built-in elements of a TC program. The psychiatric hospital where I worked with Jill incorporated many principles of a therapeutic community. Consequently it effectively treated the range of her problems, and presents what might be a model for work with adolescents.

Basically her therapy was supervised by a psychiatrist, who was open to a multifaceted treatment program. He worked in a one-on-one traditional counseling fashion with her; however, he incorporated data into her therapy that emerged in other situations, such as psychodrama and encounter groups, and that he could read about in the continuing reports provided by other members of her therapeutic team. Of considerable importance in Jill's therapy was the fact that she received total family therapy. Her father and mother participated with her, in a variety of confrontive group therapy sessions. Her overall therapy involved the family as a pathological system that required change. Some of the heat was taken off Jill as the "identified-patient," or the only sick one in her family.

Jill, during this period, as indicated, participated in a psychodrama group I directed, plus a special drug encounter group for adolescents that I codirected with several ex-addicts from a standard TC in the area. In psychodrama she confronted some of the basic underlying issues that she was working on with her psychiatrist. These included her problems with her basic social atom, her father, her mother, and Jim.

The several psychodrama sessions I had with her related to her father and the basic theme of feeling emotionally alienated from him and her sense of his lack of real caring for her. They involved a psychiatric aide who, as a psychodramatic auxiliary ego, played the role of her father. In these dramatic, tearful sessions, she would implore this stand-in for her father to "please love her, spend some time with her, and make her feel special." She had felt especially abandoned by him when she reached puberty.

I recall her sobbing, concluding commentary in one session where she said: "Dad, I was always your special little girl and you adored me. You used to hug me and hold me on your lap and tell me how pretty I was. Then, when I was 13, you pushed me off your lap like I was some 'thing.' Our family broke up and you left me with Mom. I love Mom—but she's like a dead person. She never talks or feels anything. You were the important one in my life."

In this session several 14- and 15-year-old girls shared similar feelings of being abandoned by their fathers at puberty. In the group discussion that followed the role playing, several psychological points were made that fit many teenage girls who become substance abusers to deal with their emotional pain. When they make the transition from childhood to adolescence, many teenage girls feel abandoned by their fathers. This is often because their fathers, especially if they are insecure men, as Jill's father was, handle some of the normal sexual feeling they might have for them by coldly rejecting their daughters. Of course, this is superior to the problems that ensue from some fathers who act out their feelings either flirtatiously or directly in sexual abuse. What is more appropriate is an honest awareness of some sexual feelings that are handled without overreacting and rejecting their daughters. These issues were discussed by the group after Jill's psychodrama, and some insights were acknowledged by her and several others.

Jill learned from many psychodrama sessions and discussions with her psychiatrist on this theme that she had limited control over "getting her father back"; however, she had total control over her response to her intense pain and feeling that her father had abandoned and rejected her. She further concluded that the onset of her drug problems was related to her feelings of low self-esteem from being rejected by her father, and that her self-destructive drug abuse was connected to her conflict and alienation from her father. She said, "I learned from my therapy that I'm not alone with these feelings of being abandoned by my dad. I felt something was wrong with me. Now I can see it's partly his problem, too." Her insight that it was a family problem rather than that she was a "bad, sick girl" relieved some of the pressure on her negative self-esteem that had propelled her into becoming a drug addict. The foregoing is only a brief sketch of some of the psychodynamics that were related to Jill's drug-abuse-symptom syndrome that were considerably relieved and resolved during her therapy in the TC-structured hospital.

A difficult aspect of her problem that required resolution was that she had been using drugs for several years to alleviate her feelings of pain about her family situation and a sense of low self-esteem. In her first drug encounter group, she commented, "When I became depressed, drugs were my therapy. I could always count on a lude, getting drunk, or some coke to get rid of my pain. Also, I saw how Jim and lots and lots of sex with him wasn't love but mainly getting away from my bad feelings."

Jill's prior automatic response to any emotional pain was drugs, alcohol or sex. These compulsive acts had been built into her lifestyle for four years, and had to be changed.

In her counseling sessions, she explored, and to a large extent resolved, her difficulties with her parents. In the drug encounter-group sessions, she was confronted by me, the ex-addicts, and others in the group with the necessity of eliminating her self-destructive drug abuse symptom. Here she was intensely verbally encountered about her substance abuse, and no psychological excuses were accepted for what was pointed out to her as self-destructive behavior.

In the adolescent encounter drug group she regularly attended, several ex-addicts from an outside total drug-addict TC who I had hired to work with me, were valuable adjuncts to Jill's overall therapy. They were masters at encounter therapy, based on their experience in the outside TC. Of particular importance was an ex-addict counselor named Renee from the outside TC. Renee, then 21, had a life experience that was very similar to Jill's. At that time, she had been drug-free in her TC for two years. Renee became, for Jill, a friend, a role model, and a kind of AA/TC sponsor. In fact, she took Jill to support group sessions at her TC. In group Renee had many comments, such as, "Jill, I remember when I was your age I had the exact feelings you're talking about and I handled them..." She would then delineate for Jill exactly how she handled her problems after she became drug-free.

In the conceptual scheme of the adolescent drug encounter group was the idea that when addict A helps addict B, addict A is helped. In brief, it was not a one-way therapeutic contract between Renee and Jill; Renee's helping Jill in group and in many personal conversations was helpful to Renee in terms of reviewing the path she had traveled out of her own addiction. (Later on, Jill served as a role model for other young people in the program.)

Two other teenagers who helped Jill immediately as role models for staying drug-free were Bill and Jane. They were both adolescent ex-addicts who had been in the hospital therapeutic community but were now living in the outside community. They had successfully traveled the track Jill was on and were able to help Jill through some difficult times in her social growth.

They were particularly helpful to Jill in a slip situation she revealed in the encounter group. When Jill went on pass, she went out with a young man on a date, she had a few drinks and had smoked some "crack" cocaine. She tearfully and fearfully copped out in the encounter group: "I have something to tell the group. I went out with this guy, Jack, and I like him a lot. I had a few drinks, and when Jack offered me some coke, I felt I couldn't say no. I mean I could say no—but I felt if I did, he would think I was a jerk, and I'd never see him again. Anyway, I did use coke and I feel horrible. I thought I was cured."

Coming from a self-righteous position, Bill blasted Jill. "I'm really fuckin' pissed-off at you. You've been sitting in this group for four months and you haven't learned yet that this dick who offered you coke was not your friend. 'Friends' don't offer recovering addicts poison."

After some other verbal blasts from members of the group, including Jill's sponsor, Renee, telling some stories about her slips, the group became very supportive of Jill's plight and talked about their own slips. It was very valuable to hear from her peers about this. In fact, the group had become for Jill both a support and a control group. It was a "control group" in terms of her comment, "When I did the coke, I really didn't enjoy it like I used to. My first thought was, shit, I'm going to have to cop out to the group and I felt terrible." In a way the group had disabled her from going too far wrong because it had inculcated her with an antidrug attitude.

Another part of the program that was of great significance in Jill's recovery involved the program directors and the adolescent-ward psychiatric aides. Here, on a daily basis on the ward, when she was in the custodial setting, a form of continuing therapy was taking place in discussions and informal conferences. For example, after a visit with her parents, Jill would often be extremely angry about their lack of understanding of her problems or their callousness and distance. On a nonschedule basis, either the adolescent-ward director or a psychiatric aide with whom she had built a relationship would have a therapeutic session on the spot, at a time when it was often most vital for Jill to have someone to talk to. The aides, some of whom were recovered addicts themselves, and several residents in the program functioned as Jill's caring circle of positive friends.

The total process of the traditional psychiatric counseling Jill received, and the special TC elements and groups in the hospital program, helped Jill to become drug-free. This kind of program, with these varied elements, should be integrated into more traditional hospital programs. Ex-addicts and TC approaches can be effectively combined with traditional psychiatric problem-solving theories and techniques with positive results. My viewpoint is that this combination of therapeutic approaches portends the wave of the future in the effective treatment of substance abusers of all types and ages.

Frankie

Frankie's family was a violent gang, until king heroin took over his life. He had some proclivity in his early years in elementary school to become an artist, but nothing in his environment permitted him to pursue this career. Violence and drugs pervaded his life when he was growing up on the Upper West Side of Manhattan.

After a violent-gang youth, Frank turned to a criminal career of using and dealing drugs, especially heroin. This life resulted in his "doing time" in a federal prison (Danbury), New York City's Riker's Island Penitentiary (five times), Bellevue Hospital in New York City, and the federal hospital for drug addicts in Lexington, KY.

In addition to a pattern of drug addiction, pimping, and theft, Frank had a violent streak. "Frankie would never use a knife, unless he had to. Mostly with his fists he would beat a guy down and try to kill him right there. They pulled him off this big guy one time—he wouldn't stop punching him in the face." This was a casual observation by Frankie's ex-crime partner, the girl turned prostitute with whom he had lived for five years in New York City.

When Frankie was 26, a New York judge, who was tired of seeing him go through the city's revolving-door prison system, gave him a choice: a long prison sentence at Sing Sing or a last-chance effort in a TC. Frankie chose a TC alternative in California.

Frankie's first reaction to the TC was confusion: "The first thing they hit me with flipped me. This tough-looking cat says to me, 'There are two things you absolutely can't do here, shoot drugs or fight.'" Frankie said, scratching his head, "I was all mixed up—these were the only two things I knew how to do."

Despite his confusion he found the environment interesting and exciting and quite different from prison where he had "done time." There were, for him, "lots of hip people." Among this group was Jimmy, who at 48 had been an addict, a criminal, and a con man for more than 30 years; and was clean at the time for over five years in the TC. He was assigned as Frankie's sponsor. Jimmy ran the kitchen at that time. Frankie got his first job, scouring pots and pans and mopping floors. According to Frankie, Jimmy could not be "conned" or manipulated out of position like the guards and therapists that Frankie had encountered on Riker's Island and at various federal hospitals. Jimmy, of course, knew the score; to him Frankie, with all his exploits, was a "young punk" who could give him no trouble. "I've met kids like this all my life—in and out of the joint." he said.

According to Frankie, "At first, I hated this bastard. I used to sometimes sit and plan ways to kill him." When Frankie wanted to fight Jimmy over a disagreement about work, Jimmy laughed and told him that if he wanted to fight, he would be thrown out of the place, and get sent back to New York and a long prison term.

The usual prison situation was reversed, and this confused Frankie. In prison, if Frankie got into trouble, confinement became increasingly severe, with the "hole" (solitary confinement) an end point. In the Bellevue Hospital psychiatric ward, where Frankie had also spent time, it was a straitjacket. What made Frankie behave in order to stay in the TC? It was not only the potential threat of prison. In another setting his low impulse control would have propelled him out the door.

What was important for Frankie was that there were others who understood him, had made the same "scenes," and intuitively knew his problems and how to handle him. Although he would only grudgingly admit it, he respected people he could not "con." He belonged, and was now part of a "family" he could accept.

Frankie could also make a "rep" in the TC without getting punished or locked up. In prison the highest he could achieve in terms of the values of other prisoners was to become "king" of the inmate world, acquire a "stash" of cigarettes, obtain some unsatisfactory homosexual favors, and land in the hole. In the TC he felt he could acquire any role he was "big enough or man enough to achieve," and "growing up" carried the highest approval of his fellows. He could actually move up the status ladder, and become a director in this organization. For the first time in his life, Frankie was receiving status—in his gang terms, a "rep"—for being clean and nondelinquent.

Of course, when he first arrived, Frankie attempted to gain a rep by conniving and making deals, in accord with his old mode of relating. When he did, he was laughed at, ridiculed, and given severe "haircuts" by other old-time con men in group sessions. They were, he learned, ferociously loyal to the organization, which had literally saved their lives and given them a new life status. He too began to develop an *esprit de corps* in the TC. As he once put it, "I never would give three cheers for Riker's Island prison. But I'm part of this place. It's a home to me."

Frankie found that rep was acquired in this social system (unlike the ones he had known) by truth, honesty, and industry. The value of his other life required reversal if he were to gain a rep in the TC. These values were not goals per se that someone moralized about in a meaningless vacuum, but were means to the end of acquiring prestige in this tough social system with which he increasingly identified.

In the groups, three nights a week, Frankie participated in a new kind of group psychotherapy, unlike the kind he had "fooled around with" in prison. Here the truth was viciously demanded. Any rationalizations about past or current deviant behavior were brutally demolished by the group.There was an intensive search for self-identity. He found that, in the process, which he began to trust, he learned something of what went on beneath the surface of his thoughts. Frankie admitted that, for the first time in his life, he had found other people who had some idea of his underlying thoughts. He had had individual and group therapy in prison, but there he could con the therapist and, most important, "I said what I thought they wanted to hear so I could get out sooner."

Frankie, who at first had followed his usual pattern of self-centered manipulation of others, now began to care about what happened to others, who were real friends to him. He began to identify with the organization and learned on a "gut level" that if any other member failed, in some measure he, too, failed.

Frankie began to comprehend what others thought in a social situation. The concept of empathy, or identifying with the thoughts and feelings of others, became a significant reality.

In the status system, Frankie's rise in the hierarchy was neither quick nor easy. He first moved from the "dishpan" to serving food at the kitchen counter. After several months he began to work outside on a pickup truck that acquired food and other donations.

Here he had his first slip, no doubt, in part, to test the waters. With two other individuals who worked with him on the truck, a group decision was made one day that "smoking a joint might be fun." They acquired some grass from a dealer known to one of the group.

When they arrived back from work, their slightly "loaded" appearance immediately became apparent to the group. ("They spotted us right away.") They were hauled into the main office and viciously (verbally) attacked and ordered to cop out (tell) or "get lost." A general meeting was called, and they were forced to reveal all before the entire group, in a fireplace scene. That night Frankie was back washing dishes.

Frankie learned the hard way that the norms of the TC were the reverse of the criminal code he knew. In another slip situation, Frankie, with two other members, went for a walk into town. One of them suggested buying a bottle of wine. (Of course, no drinking was permitted in the TC.) Frankie and the other member rejected the proposal. However, no one revealed the incident until two days later, when it came up in group. The group jumped hardest on Frankie and the other individual who had vetoed the idea, rather than on the one who had suggested buying the wine.

Frankie and the other "witnesses" were expected to report such slips immediately, since the group's life depended on keeping one another straight. For the first time in his life, Frankie was censured for *not* being a "snitch." The maxim that "thou shalt not squeal," basic to the existence of the usual underworld criminal culture, was reversed and ferociously upheld.

In another area for the criminal addict, the no-physical-violence rule was at first difficult for Frank to grasp and believe, since his usual response to a difficult situation was to leap, fists first, past verbal means of communication, into assault. As a result of the group's and other new patterns of interaction, Frankie's increasing ability to communicate began to minimize his assaultive impulses. Although at first he was kept from committing violence by the fear of ostracism, he later had no need to use violence, since he then had some ability to interact effectively. He learned to express himself, in what was for him a new form of communication, on a nonviolent, verbal level. On occasion Frankie would regress and have the motivation for assault, but the system had taken hold. In one session I heard him say, "I was so fucking mad yesterday, I wished I was back at Riker's [prison]. I really wanted to hit that bastard Jimmy in the mouth."

Unlike Bob who had been somewhat successful in the theater, Frankie had a sketchy work record. Since most of his time was taken up with gang fighting, pimping, armed robbery, or pushing heroin, aside from some forced menial labor in prison, he was seldom engaged in anything resembling formal work. His theme had been "work was for squares." He learned how to work in the TC as a side effect of his desire to rise in the status system. He also learned, as a side effect of working, the startling new fact that "talking to someone in the right way made them do more things than threatening them."

As a consequence of living in this new social system, Frankie's social learning and ability continued to increase. His destructive pattern of relating to others withered away. It was no longer functional for him in this new way of life. The TC developed his empathic ability. It produced an attachment to different, more socially acceptable values and reconnected him to the larger society in which the TC functioned as a valid organization.

The TC process unearthed a diamond in the rough. Frankie always had a proclivity for art. As he later described it to me, "When I was a kid, I always liked to draw—but no one paid any attention to my sketches. The only thing I got was that I was teased by the other kids. I did some secret artwork in prison but tore it up. One day in group in a 'status probe,' they asked me what I really liked to do 'when I grew up.' I was scared to say it, but I said, 'I want to be an artist.' It was amazing that for the first time in my life no one laughed. They even encouraged me to go to art school."

The TC truly worked for Frankie and the society. It converted a potential gangkiller into an artist. Frankie to date has been drug-free, works now as a lithographer, and has created many interesting works of art.

CROSS-COMPARING TCs WITH TRADITIONAL TREATMENT SYSTEMS

The following analysis will attempt to delineate why the TC system works for substance abusers and why more traditional treatment approaches are not as effective.

In a traditional institution, the assumption is that if the inmates or patients follow the rules of the institution, and properly interact with their professional trained therapist, they will change and become better citizens who can function more effectively in the larger society. This model does not have as effective a success rate as the TC.

Most offenders have a close familiarity with traditional "correctional" systems. For example, Frankie and Bob learned how to do their time in reformatories, prisons, jails, mental hospitals, and addict hospitals which did not help them. They were programmed with a set of attitudes for handling encounters with society's traditional treatment facilities. They had learned the proper set of attitudes and responses and these were reinforced in the institution.

Most members of hospital and prison officialdom are stereotyped by the inmate code as authority figures. For most inmates, the officials are perceived as objects to be manipulated for quick release, or they are tricks to beat for small scores to relieve the boredom and monotony of custody.

In contrast, offenders entering a TC are usually baffled by what they encounter in this very different treatment system. Frankie learned in the TC that everyone was a "right guy," including the administrators, most of whom had been in his position at one time. When he tried to play his usual institutional games, he was laughed at. He could not hate the officials in the TC, because they were people like himself, or people who had experienced his position in life. (This same baffled response is found in adolescent substance abusers when they hear a teenager telling them, usually for the first time in their lives, that drug use is bad.)

If Frankie wanted to "break out" or go AWOL (a common subject of conversation in most institutions), he was invited to get lost by the TC staff. At every turn he discovered new responses to old situations and, most important, other people who knew how he felt and understood him. Instead of receiving a callous reaction, he was told, "I remember how I felt when I first got here," and this was often followed by a detailed description of the precise feeling he was experiencing at the time.

TCs are often disconcerting for a TC newcomer with an institutional past because it is a new and strange situation. Yet, at the same time, the sight of others like themselves who "made it" gives them confidence. They have role-models, people they can emulate. In a TC they find a new society. They encounter understanding and affection from people who have had life experiences similar to their own. They find a community with which they can identify, people toward whom they can express their best human emotions, rather than their worst. They find understanding friends who will assist them when they begin to deviate or fall short of what they have set out to do: to develop and mature. In the new society of the TC they find a vehicle for expressing their best human qualities and potentialities.

The concepts of *caste* and *stratification* are two sociological categories that help delineate the differences between a TC and most traditional treatment institutions. The differences are as follows: An inmate or patient subculture develops within most custodial institutions, producing a "we–they" attitude between the professional administration and the residents or inmates. The underground inmate society has norms, patterns of behavior, and goals different from and often in conflict with those of the overall institution. This is partly due to the fact that inmates cannot rise in the status system and become staff members.

Inmates and officialdom are usually divided into two segregated strata. The inmates may, in one context, be viewed as a caste of "untouchables." They are restricted to an inferior power position in the hierarchy, and in their "prison," there is no possibility of their moving up. It is conceded by most administrators that this inmate–administration conflict situation contradicts and impedes therapeutic progress for the inmate. This is especially true in a correctional institution or prison.

The inmate subsystem helps the patients or inmates cope with the new set of problems that they find in most institutions. They feel rejected by the larger society and try to compensate for this rejection. One way they do this is to reject and rebel against the *administrators* of society's rejection—the institutional staff. A true TC does not have a "we–they" caste system. It provides an open-ended stratification situation. Upward mobility is distinctly possible in the organization, and, in fact, status-seeking movement in the system is encouraged.

TC members are not usually identified as inmates, wards, prisoners, or patients, and this also makes a big difference in their self-identities and outlook. The person can identify with the constructive goals of the organization for which he or she works. He or she automatically becomes an employee in the TC organization, at first on a menial level, and later on, is encouraged to take part in the TC's management and development.

In traditional institutions most inmates or patients tend to feel helpless, dependent, and hopeless about their destinies. They have limited power in the institution, since it is run by administrators who are usually indifferent to the inmates' or patients' opinions about its management. Moreover, as I have noted, the institution's administrators are seen as representatives of society's rejection of the inmates, and this sets up additional blockades to their progression in the institution. Inmates have a clear authority object for their frustrations and hatreds—the staff. In a TC there is no such split, since the administration consists of co-workers and colleagues. There is no "they" to rebel against within the organization.

Involvement in a TC helps to foster empathy in a person whose basic problem is alienation from society. Identification with the TC involves feelings of caring and concern for the other members, and for the destiny of the totality of the organization. The development of these empathic qualities reverses the person's past, often sociopathic lack of social concern, and has a real impact on positive personality change. Vital to this personality change are various group processes, such as the encounter group, and the resident's sponsor and caring circle of friends.

Group sessions in the TC are more closely related to the real-life interpersonal and work problems that confront the members. Given the lack of caste division, lines of communication are open

throughout the organization. This, plus a gold-fish-bowl atmosphere, is conducive to a more extensive examination of a resident's deeper underlying problems. TC group sessions make
intense efforts to surface all possible data about a member since this
is vital to the protection and growth of both the person and the TC
organization. Since all TC members work for the organization,
many real on-the-job problems are funneled into the TC's group
psychotherapy. All of these factors give a TC's group process a
reality not found in the closed-off social systems of most traditional
institutions.

There have been attempts at self-government in prisons and
mental hospitals. In these settings, however, the inmates recognize that final decisions on important policy matters remain with
the administration. In a TC perhaps for the first time in an individual's life, the member assumes a significant role in controlling his
or her future, and they have, often for the first time in their lives, a
degree of power in their new "family" and community.Leadership
in a constructive situation is a new experience, and it appears to
develop personal responsibility and a sense of independence in the
TC resident.

Because there is a generally held belief by the residents that
"the TC saved our lives," the esprit de corps in the organization is
quite powerful. Few inmates would give three cheers for a hospital
or a prison, but residents in a TC enjoy praising the organization
that saved their lives. The various Bobs, and Frankies who are the
residents of a TC, unlike patients and inmates, are involved with
the growth and development of *their* organization.

In summary, the following elements reflect the signifiant difference between the social structure and organization of effective TCs
and traditional correctional institutions:

1. There is a qualitative difference between indoctrination in TC
and in other settings. The contractual arrangements for therapy
and the prospect's expectations of success are different. The indoctrination of the prospect by people who have themselves been in
the newcomer's shoes and have succeeded appears to be a significant element, providing the newcomer with a role model. Also, the
"indoctrinator" sees where he or she was upon looking at the
newcomer, and this is valuable for reinforcing personal growth.

2. TCs provide the possibility of upward mobility, whereas
most institutions are caste systems. Becoming a TC member pro-

vides incentive for changing one's negative attitudes to antidrug, anticriminal motivation. The TC resident can, with the proper attitude and behavior, achieve any role in the organization. In contrast, in the custodial institution, inmates or patients are locked in to their dependent positions.

3. There is a qualitative difference between the TC and the form of group therapy carried on in prisons and hospitals. This is partly a function of the described differences in the overall social-system context. The TC resident, as a voluntary participant, has little to gain by faking progress, whereas in other institutions, the appearance of being "rehabilitated" may be rewarded by an earlier release from custody. The TC person is encouraged to reveal and deal with problems honestly by others who have traveled the established TC route to recovery and independence.

4. The work assigned in a TC is real work, unlike the often contrived jobs in prisons and mental hospitals. All work serves the real needs of the organization. This includes the functions of the procuring of food, and of the office staff, maintenance and service crews, automotive crews, and the coordinating staff. Everyone in a TC is employed in meaningful work, which gives them a greater sense of belonging to the TC, and that they are, perhaps for the first time in their lives, self-supporting.

5. The TC subculture is integrated into the larger societal structure in a way that traditional institutions seldom are. The flow of members of the community through a TC and the participation of TC members in the larger society place it closer to the real-life situations of the outer world than do the artificial communities of the traditional institutions that attempt personality and behavioral change in an unreal social system.

THE MAIN SOCIAL–PSYCHOLOGICAL FORCES AT WORK IN A TC

The foregoing elements make up the essential social–psychological forces at work in an ideal TC, and have the following impact on the personality and behavior of the recovering alcoholic-addict.

Involvement

Initially the TC society is able to involve and control the new-comer by providing an interesting social setting comprised of un-derstanding associates who will not be outmaneuvered by manipulative behavior. The indoctrinators understand the new-comer because they were once in his or her position.

Achievable Success Goals

Within the context of this system, the newcomer can (perhaps for the first time) see a realistic possibility for legitimate achieve-ment, independence, and prestige. A TC provides a rational op-portunity structure for the newcomer. He or she is not restricted to inmate or patient status, since there is no inmate–staff division and all residents are immediately *staff members*.

New Social Role

Being a "TC professional" person is a new social role. It can be temporarily or indefinitely occupied in the process of social growth and development of new projects. TC—trained staff people are increasingly in demand. (Therapeutic Communities of America now provide TC professionals who qualify as "addict counselor certificated".)

Social Growth

In the process of acquiring legitimate social status in a TC, the resident necessarily, as a side effect, develops the ability to relate, communicate, and work with others. The values of truth, honesty, and industry become necessary means to this goal of status achievement. With enough practice and time, the individual social-ized in this way reacts according to these values—naturally. This is a most effective system for people who, upon entrance into a TC, had an egocentric-sociopathic posture toward life.

Empathy and Self-Identity

The constant self-assessment required in daily TC life and in the group sessions fosters the consolidation of self-identity and empathy. The individual's self-estimation is under constant assessment by relevant others, who become sensitive to and concerned about that individual. The process provides the opportunity for a person almost literally to see himself or herself as others do. He or she is also compelled, as part of this process, to develop the ability to identify with and understand others, if only to acquire higher status in the system. The side effects are personal growth, greater social awareness, an improved ability to communicate, and a greater facility for being empathic about the needs of others.

Social Control

The control of the addict-alcoholic's deviance is a by-product of the individual's status seeking. Conformity to the norms is necessary for achievement in a TC. Anomie, the dislocation of social goals and the means for acquiring them, is minimalized. The norms are valid and adhered to within the social system, since the means are available for legitimate goal attainment in the TC.

Another form of control is embodied in the threat of ostracism. This, too, becomes a binding force. The relative newcomer in a TC usually does not feel adequate to participate in the larger society. But after a sufficient period of TC social living, the resident no longer fears banishment and is adequately prepared for life outside (if this is his or her choice). However, residents may remain voluntarily because they feel a TC is a valid way of life. In a TC they have learned and acquired gratifying new social roles that enable them to help others who can benefit from the approach that saved their lives.

Yet another form of social control is the group process. Here people are required to tell the truth, which helps to regulate their behavior. Transgressions are often prevented by the knowledge that any deviance will rapidly and necessarily be brought to the attention of their pals in a group session. Residents are living in a community where others know about and, perhaps more important care about, their behavior. This process enhances the resident's motivation to learn about and follow the rules of his or her community. This learning process enhances the possibility that the resident will have a greater respect for the rules and laws of the larger society.

THE SOCIAL VACCINE CONCEPT

The combined impact of these various forces produces a person with a new identity who is insulated from the need to return to using drugs or alcohol. The former addict-alcoholic develops an antidrug attitude and personal identity that enables the person to lead a happier, more productive drug-free life.

In addition to their personal success, TC graduates can be valuable assets in society's overall war against substance abuse. In a sense they are antibodies in the overall social system who have been immunized against substance abuse—and they can be a vital force in preventing, and helping others to resist, "the disease".

The social vaccine concept may be summarized as follows: The individual who has had the substance-abuse disease, has gone through the process of recovery, and is now functioning effectively drug-free in society, provides a kind of antibody or social vaccine for the overall social system. In terms of a dictionary definition, "a vaccine is a living attenuated organism that is administered to produce or increase immunity to a particular disease."

This immunization process was first introduced to the West by an English physician, Edward Jenner. Jenner demonstrated that inserting a low level of virus into a person's physiological system stimulated antibodies that would defend and prevent an immunized person from having a more virulent form of the disease.

Loosely transposing this concept from a physiological to a social system, I would speculate that antidrug, former-addict paraprofessionals properly employed in TCs create antibodies to the disease in the larger society.

In this context I would suggest that paraprofessional former addicts are individuals who, once their problem has been arrested, can, in time, and in sufficient numbers, serve as antibodies to the disease of substance abuse in the overall society. To some degree the force of anti-alcoholic AA members has produced this kind of antibody on an international level for helping to prevent and control alcoholism.

The explosive development and proliferation of therapeutic communities around the world has produced a social vaccine that can increasingly, if properly applied, significantly reduce the international substance-abuse problem.

In brief, I perceive the TC development as a vital therapeutic system for immunizing people who have passed through the fire—and have recovered from their disease. These people can provide valuable experimental data and an antidrug posture that is useful to help prevent others—especially young, vulnerable people—from falling into the morass of a substance-abuse problem. As the TC movement develops, therefore, in quality and numbers, the TC system and its graduates, in the role of paraprofessionals or as active concerned citizens, can significantly contribute to the prevention, the control, and potentially the eradication of the virulent disease of substance abuse in the world.

8

Afterword: Practical Questions and Answers About TCs

Now that you have a reasonable comprehension of the history, methodology, and dynamics of TCs, there may be some practical questions that occur to you related to your personal need or professional involvement in a TC organization. The following questions and answers are derived from my 25 years of answering questions about TCs in a variety of group settings. Because every TC has a slightly different approach to these issues, and the TC worldwide movement is in a state of enormous growth and development, I will attempt to provide general answers to these basic questions. The questions and answers should be of interest to you, if you are a substance abuser, a relative or friend of a substance abuser, a professional in the field, a student of the problem, or a concerned civic-minded citizen.

Q. I am a substance abuser and I need help. What do I do?

A. Check out the section in the telephone book entitled "Drug Abuse and Addiction Information and Treatment Centers," choose one, and make an appointment. In the appendix of this book, you will find a list of selected TCs. Find one in your community, or in the geographic area where you would like to go for treatment. Many people prefer going to an area for treatment that is removed from their current area of residence.

Q. I am the friend (or relative) of a person who is destroying his (or her) life with drugs or alcohol; however, the substance abuser won't listen to me. How can I get the substance abuser into a TC?

A. First of all, you should know that this is a common problem. Most substance abusers practice denial with a variety of false platitudes, such as, "I don't have a problem, and besides I can quit anytime I want to." The best way to handle this type of situation is to call a TC, make an appointment, and consult with the experts about *your* problem with getting this person the help he or she needs.

Q. What does it cost to get TC treatment?

A. There is no uniform answer to this question. Almost every TC has a different payment approach. To a great extent, the amount charged for treatment is related to the financial ability of the applicant and his or her family. Many TCs have a waiting list; however, there is usually a flexibility factor related to the immediate needs of the applicant. The best answer to this question will be supplied to you at your entrance appointment.

Q. How long does TC treatment take?

A. Depending on the severity of the substance abuser's problem, treatment may be as short as three months or require two years. The length of time required for treatment is dependent on a variety of variables, including: severity of addiction; social and emotional status and condition of the person; and the degree of sincere motivation of the substance abuser. Most bona-fide TCs require a residency of from six to 18 months for treatment. In my opinion, any program that is less than 90 days is simply a detoxification situation: At least six months to a year is required for any program to effectively resocialize a substance abuser. Moreover, all substance abusers need to participate in some after-care program, either in their TC, or in support groups like AA, NA, or Cocaine Anonymous (CA).

Q. What do I do about my job and family when I enter a TC for treatment?

A. In general, in most TC programs, you will have limited contact with all former associates for the first 30–60 days. This is for the purpose of integrating yourself into the program. After this time-out from your past life (which included self-destructive substance abuse), friends and relatives who are *clean* can visit. In most TCs, provision is made for some necessary family group sessions.

With regard to your job, that aspect of your life will need to be put on hold during this time when you are going through intense emotional changes. You will work in the context of the TC organization in a job that is compatible with your emotional needs and ability. In some TCs, after about six months, if it is indicated, you may be able to live in and work out.

Q. What is the TC success rate?

A. The data on success rates for TCs are complex. A basic problem in determining this issue is related to how you define "cure" or "success." The AA position that "once an alcoholic, always an alcoholic" is compatible with my viewpoint on substance abusers. Relapse seems to go with the substance abuse territory. People who quit using drugs or alcohol need to be totally abstinent, and follow the AA admonition to stay clean "one day at a time." Consequently I see success as involving the achievement of "clean-person-days" on a daily basis. If a substance abuse stays clean for two years after having gone through a program, I see the person as being a success. Beyond this, substance abusers have to be eternally vigiliant about the continuing existence of their lifelong need to stay clean.

My collation of various research findings on the "success" issue for TCs inicates that for those people who stay in residence for at least 90 days, there is a 50 percent success rate. In this context, my criterion for success is that the substance abuser remain clean for at least two years after leaving the program. Obviously, different TCs have varied criteria for calculating what constitutes "success."

Q. How are TCs funded?

A. TCs are funded in a variety of ways. Most depend on a combination of government funds, private donations, revenue from businesses they run (e.g., novelty sales, moving businesses, gas stations, etc.), and income from charges to most residents. All residents in a TC work in some capacity for the organization, and this tends to provide revenue.

Q. I understand that the treatment personnel in a TC comprise a combination of recovering or ex-substance abusers and a number of traditional professional therapists (e.g., psychiatrists, psychologists, social workers, marriage and family counselors). What is the relative status of these various therapists in a TC and how are they paid?

A. Every TC I have studied has a different emphasis on the relative status of different professional categories. Some rely almost exclusively on the treatment ability of the recovering or ex-substance abuser, and use professional therapists in a secondary role. In other organizations the traditional professionals are in charge, and they utilize the treatment powers of the recovering substance abuser in the context of the organization. Some people who have recovered from their problem in a TC, make a decision to pursue a career in the TC field. In this regard, they can pursue traditional scholarly degrees, or, in some cases, they can be accredited as "drug counselors" by the Therapeutic Communities of America organization. In brief, many former substance abusers continue to work on a salaried basis in the TC they grew up in, or in another TC. In general, as in any field, salary pay scales vary depending on the therapist's ability and the demand for drug counselors at any given time.

Q. What kind of people will I find in a TC?

A. Most contemporary TCs comprise people from all socioeconomic classes. There is an emphasis on character building; consequently, in most TC organizations, the focus is on a life-style of high integrity, personal responsibility, and honesty. These combined factors provide a pleasant atmosphere that tends to parallel the learning environment of an intellectually vibrant college campus.

Q. I have heard that some TCs are cultlike and autocratic. How true is this information?

A. There are often problems in the development of any social movement. It is true that there have been several TCs where the personal problems or "power trips" of specific leaders or leadership have resulted in severe organizational problems. However, I consider these glitzes of no major significance when viewed in the context of the overall sweep of the positive development and growth of the international TC movement. At various World Federation of Therapeutic Community meetings, these power and personal leadership problems have come under close scrutiny and analysis. As a result of these intense discussions of these issues, the leaders in TCs are aware of these possible pitfalls, and of their responsibility to the proper ethical utilization of the TC treatment approach.

Q. Is participation in an encounter group in a TC a difficult experience?

A. Many people are apprehensive about participation in an encounter group. I have been personally and professionally in thousands of such groups around the world over the years, and have found the experience to be educational, emotionally enlightening, and, in most cases, pleasurable and intellectually stimulating.

Q. There is a great need in our community for a TC. How do we start and develop one?

A. I would first suggest that you convene a group of people, certainly including some local concerned political leaders and professionals involved in the treatment of substance abusers. This book can serve as a guide for the organizing group. After some preliminary discussions related to community needs, it would be advisable to contact some TC leaders for consultation and development procedures. I direct a consultant organization for the development of TC organizations and am available for consultation and planning.

Appendix: Directory of Selected Therapeutic Communities

The following list of therapeutic communities was mainly supplied by David Mactas, president of The Therapeutic Communities of America. These TCs, for the most part, fit the model, organization, and utilize the methods described in this book.

An excellent summary of the general TC approach is provided in the brochure of the Marathon House TC in Providence, Rhode Island. The following statement, in their brochure, is prototypical of the services offered to a substance abuser who enters a TC:

"The primary goal of Marathon House is to foster personal growth. Growth is accomplished by changing an individual's lifestyle through the impact of a community of concerned people working together to help themselves individually and collectively. The range of services offered is comprehensive individual treatment planning; assessment and referral; individual and group counseling; vocational assessment and family counseling; licensed and approved educational program; organized recreation and other group activities; aftercare and follow-up programs; and emergency shelter.

"The 'Therapeutic Community' represents a highly structured setting with definite social and ethical boundaries. Each house sets its own rules for privileges and 'earned' advancement. We feel that the process of being part of a house community is an especially important factor in making positive growth possible. For many, it's the first time they have been part of something greater than themselves—a member of a working community who is counted on to help everyone, not just him or herself.

"As in any family setting, people in a Marathon House therapeutic community are residents, not patients in an institution. Each person plays a significant role in managing her-his community, and acts as a positive role model for others in the program. Residents and staff alike act as facilitators, too, emphasizing personal responsibility for one's own life and self-improvement. Residents are both supported and served by staff so that there is a meaningful sharing of labor—a true investment in the whole community—sometimes even for the very purpose of survival.

"Peer pressure is often the catalyst that converts criticism and personal insight into positive change. High expectations and high commitment from both residents and staff support this change. Insights into one's problems are gained through group and individual interaction. Learning through experience, failing, and succeeding, and experiencing the direct consequences of one's actions are considered to be the most potent influences in achieving lasting change."

The foregoing statement is representative of the treatment approach and services of most TCs. Obviously each TC has its own distinctive qualities. The best way to determine if a TC fits your needs is to contact one of the organizations on the following list directly.

TCA Members

Abraxas Foundation, Inc.
The Bank Tower
307 Fourth Avenue, Suite 1400
Pittsburgh, PA 15222
412-562-0105

Akeela House, Inc.
2804 Bering Street
Anchorage, AK 99503
907-561-5266

Alpha House
1325 S.W. Gibbs Street
Portland, OR 97201
503-241-0266

Amity
P.O. Box 60520
Tucson, AZ 85751-6520
602-749-3797

Apple, Inc.
P.O. Box 402, 220 Veterans Highway
Hauppauge, NY 11788
516-979-7300

Aurora Concept, Inc.
78-31 Parsons Boulevard
Flushing, NY ll366
718-969-7000

A-Way Out, Inc.
41-14 27th Street
Long Island City, NY 11101
718-784-0220

Behavioral Health Agency
120 West Main Street
Casa Grande, AZ 85222
602-836-1675

Brass Foundation, Inc.
7100 South Shore Drive
Chicago, IL 60649

Dr. Thomas Bratter
Adolescent Program
88 Spier Road
Scarsdale, NY 10583

The Bridge
8400 Pine Road
Philadelphia, PA 19111

CARE, Inc.
80 East Chestnut Street
Washington, PA 15301
412-228-2200

Center Point Program
812 "D" Street
San Rafael, CA 94901
415-454-7777

Combined Addicts and Professional Services
480 North First Street, Suite 108
San Jose, CA 95112
408-286-1090

Concept House
162 N.E. 49th Street
Miami, FL 33137
305-751-6501

Crash, Inc.
P.O. Box 8057, 2410 "E" Street
San Diego, CA 92102
619-297-5131

Creative Health Systems, Inc.
1314 High Street
Pottstown, PA 19464
215-326-9250

Crossroads Community
5801 North Kings Highway
Alexandria, VA 22303
703-960-9554

CURA, Inc.
61 Lincoln Park
Newark, NJ 07102
201-622-3570

Damon House, Inc.
P.O. Box 76
20 Joyce Kilmer Avenue
New Brunswick, NJ 08901
201-828-3988

Daytop Village, Inc.
54 West 40th Street
New York, NY 10018
212-354-6000

Delancey Street Foundation
2563 Divisadero Street
San Francisco, CA

Delancey Street Foundation
1344 16th Street
Santa Monica, CA 90401

Disc Village, Inc.
P.O. Box 568
Woodville, FL 32362
904-878-1196

Discovery House
P.O. Box 177, Route 520
Marlboro, NJ 07746
201-946-9444

Dynamite Youth Center Foundation, Inc.
1830 Coney Island Avenue
Brooklyn, NY 11230
718-376-7923

Eagleville Hospital
P.O. Box 45, Eagleville Road
Eagleville, PA 19408
215-539-6000

Earl E. Morris, Jr. Treatment Ctr.
610 Faison Drive
Columbia, SC 29203
803-758-4474

Eastern Nevada Council on Alcohol & Drug Abuse
3740 East Idaho, P.O. Box 2580
Elko, NV 89801
702-738-8004

Eden House
1025 Portland Avenue South
Minneapolis, MN 55404
612-338-0723

Educational Alliance Pride Site
371 East 10th Street
New York, NY 10009
212-533-2470

Free Men, Inc./Tarzana Treatment Center
18646 Oxnard Street
Tarzana, CA 91356
818-996-1051

Gateway Foundation, Inc.
624 South Michigan Avenue
Chicago, IL 60605
312-663-1130

Gaudenzia, Inc.
39 East School House Lane
Philadelphia, PA 19144
215-849-7200

Genesis II, Inc.
1214 North Broad Street
Philadelphia, PA 19121
215-763-2650

Greenwich House, Inc.
27 Barrow Street
New York, NY 10014
212-242-4140

GROUP, Inc.
2342 Telegraph Avenue
Oakland, CA 94612
415-272-9103

HAPEC House, Inc.
208 Dundas Street East
Belleville, Ont. K8N 1E3, Canada
613-962-4296

Horizon House Rehabilitation Services, Inc.
120 South 30th Street
Philadelphia, PA 19104

Hospitality House TC, Inc.
271 Central Avenue
Albany, NY 12206
518-434-6468

House of Metamorphosis
2970 Martin Luther King Way
San Diego, CA 92102
612-236-9492

House of the Crossroads
P.O. Box 3312, 2012 Centre Avenue
Pittsburgh, PA 15230
412-281-5080

Impact Drug and Alcohol Treatment Center
P.O. Box 93607
1680 North Fair Oaks
Pasadena, CA 01109
213-681-2575

Institute for Human Development
1315 Pacific Avenue
Atlantic City, NJ 08401
609-345-4035

Integrity, Inc.
P.O. Box 1806
Newark, NJ 07101
201-623-0600

Interim House
333 West Upsal Street
Philadelphia, PA 19119
215-849-4606

Interventions
1313 South Michigan Avenue
Chicago, IL 60605

Nova Therapeutic Community, Inc.
3473 Larimore Avenue
Omaha, NB 68111
402-455-8303

La Nueva Raza Institute, Inc.
39-21 Crescent Street
Long Island City, NY 11101
718-786-4475

Lower East Side Service Center—Su Casa
46 East Broadway
New York, NY 10002
212-431-4610

Marathon House, Inc.
131 Wayland Avenue
Providence, RI 02906
401-331-4250

Meridan House, Ltd.
6755 14th Avenue
Kenosha, WI 53140
414-654-0638

New Arizona Family, Inc.
1320 North Second Street
Phoenix, AZ 85004
602-258-0707

Newark Renaissance
384 Sussex Avenue/P.O. Box 7057
Newark, NJ 07107
201-483-2884

New Bridge Foundation, Inc.
1820 Scenic Avenue
Berkeley, CA

Odyssey House, Inc.
30 Winnacunnet Road
P.O. Box 474
Hampton, NH 03842
603-926-6702

Odyssey International
817 Fairfield Avenue
Bridgeport, CT 06605

Operation PAR, Inc.
6613 49th Street North
Pinellas Park, FL 33565
813-527-5866

Pacifica House
15519 Crenshaw Boulevard
Gardena, CA 90249
213-679-9031

Pathway Society, Inc.
1659 Scott Boulevard, 30
Santa Clara, CA 95050
408-244-1834

Peer 1
3712 West Princeton Circle
Denver, CO 80236
303-761-2885

Phase
1816 13th Avenue
Belvidere, IL 61008

Phoenix House, Inc.
164 West 74th Street
New York, NY 10023
202-595-5810

Phoenix House Tu Umest
503 Ocean Front Walk
Venice, CA 90291

Pottstown Alcohol and Drug Rehabilitation Program
101-05 King Street
Pottstown, PA 19464
215-326-9770

Project Return Foundation, Inc.
133 West 21st Street, 11th Floor
New York, NY 10011
212-242-4880

Project Rehab
220 Eastern S.E.
Grand Rapids, MI 49503
616-776-0891

PROMESA, Inc.
1776 Clay Avenue
Bronx, NY 10457
212-299-1100

Rubicon Odyssey House
7441 Brush Street
Detroit, MI 48202

Samaritan Village, Inc.
97-77 Queens Boulevard
Rego Park, NY 11374
718-897-4500

Samaritan Village-Highbridge
1381 University Avenue
Bronx, NY 10452

SEADRUNAR
Nan Busby
200 West Comstock
P.O. Box 24344
Seattle, WA 98124
206-767-0277

Second Genesis
4720 Montgomery Lane, Suite 502
Bethesda, MD 20814
301-656-1545

Self Center, Inc.
14000 Roosevelt Road
Philadelphia, PA 19154

SHAR House
1852 West Grand Boulevard
Detroit, MI 48208
313-894-1445

Spectrum House, Inc.
P.O. Box 562
155 Oak Street

Westboro, MA 01581
617-366-1416

Spectrum Programs, Inc.
140 N.W. 59th Street
Miami, FL 33127
305-754-1683

Stay'N Out (New York TCs)
500 Eighth Avenue, Suite 801
New York, NY 10018
212-831-0360

Straight Ahead, Inc.
34185 Coast Highway
Dana Point, CA 92629
714-831-0360

Substance Abuse Services, Inc.
St. Benard Hospital
326 West 64th Street, Room 402
Chicago, IL 60621
312-488-1200

Sunflower House
125 Rigg Street
Santa Cruz, CA 95060
408-423-3890

Synanon Foundation, Inc.
P.O. Box 112
Badger, CA 93603

TASC
755 West North Avenue
Chicago, IL 60610

Tellurian Community, Inc.
300 Femrite Drive
Madison, WI

The Door of Central Florida, Inc.
100 West Columbia Street
Orlando, FL 32806
305-423-6606

The Renaissance Project, Inc.
2 Hamilton Avenue
New Rochelle, NY 10801
914-576-3320

The Third Floor
P.O. Box 12107
Fresno, CA 93776
209-237-6177

The Village South, Inc.
3180 Biscayne Boulevard
Miami, FL 33137
305-573-3784

Today, Inc.
P.O. Box 98
Newtown, PA 18940
215-968-4713

Veritas
68 West 106th Street
New York, NY 10025
212-666-1411

Vitae House, Inc.
P.O. Box 97
Glenmore, PA 19343
215-942-3291

Walden House, Inc.
205 13th Street
San Francisco, CA 94102
415-554-1100

Western Counseling Associates
900 East Karen Street
Las Vegas, NV 89109
702-369-5700

X-Cell, Inc.
c/o Spring Grove State Hospital
Garrette Building
Catonsville, MD 01228
301-788-2145

T.C. REPRESENTATIVES: This list is, no doubt, incomplete, since some TCs do not belong to the Therapeutic Communities of America organization or have not come to the author's attention. If you represent a TC that is not listed here, and would like to be included in the next printing of this book, or if you are listed and desire an address change, please send a letter with pertinent data about your TC to Gardner Press, 19 Union Square West, New York, NY 10003.

Index

ABOUT THE AUTHOR

Lewis Yablonsky, Ph.D., is currently professor of sociology at California State University, Northridge. He has had many years of experience in working with drug addicts and alcoholics. In addition to publishing numerous articles in the field, he is author of fourteen books including *Psychodrama: Resolving Emotional Problems Through Role-Playing* (Gardner Press, 1981).

DATE DUE

MR 30 '90			
JY 20 '90			
AP 15 91			
MY 7 93			

DEMCO 38-297